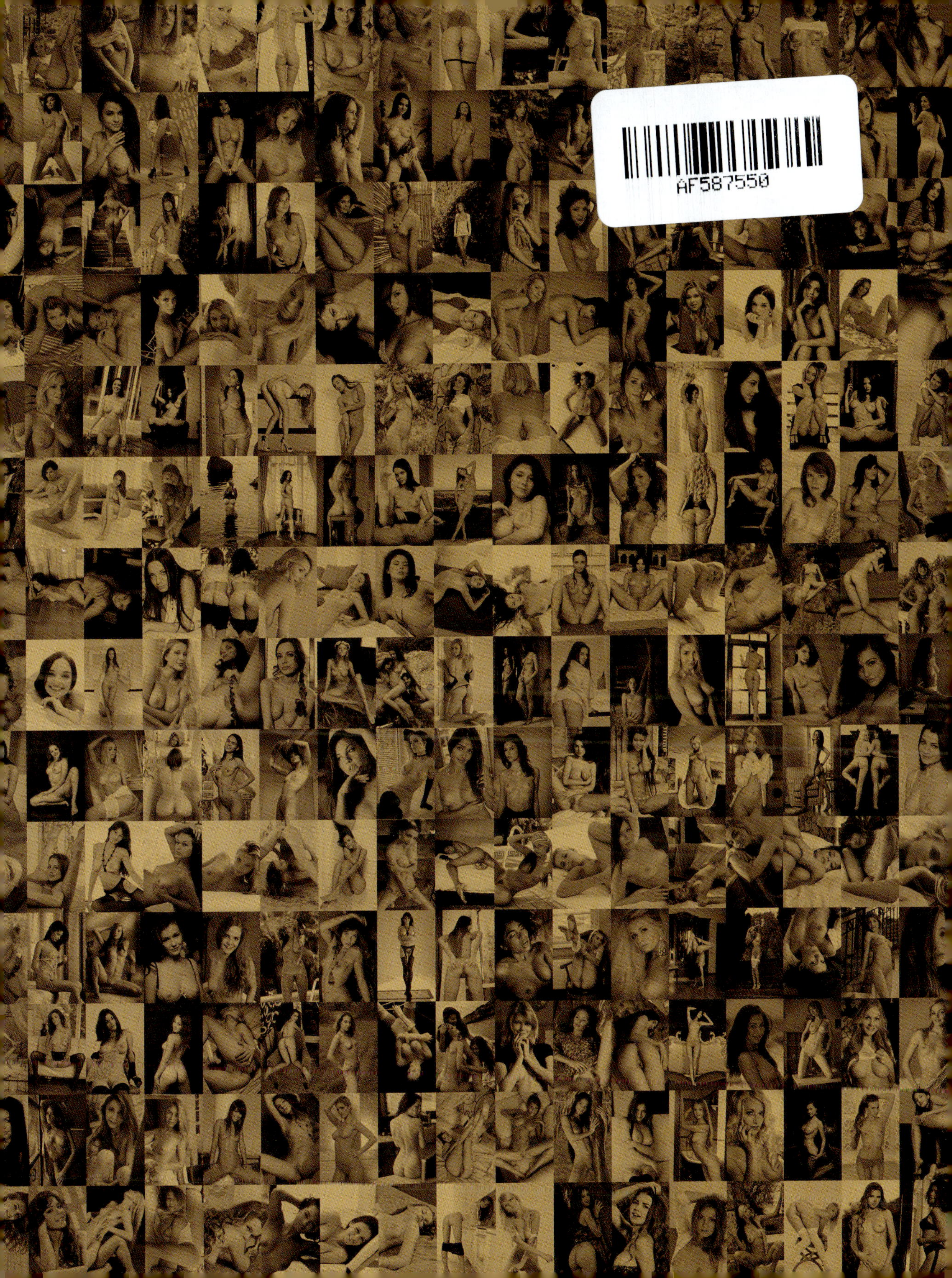
AF587550

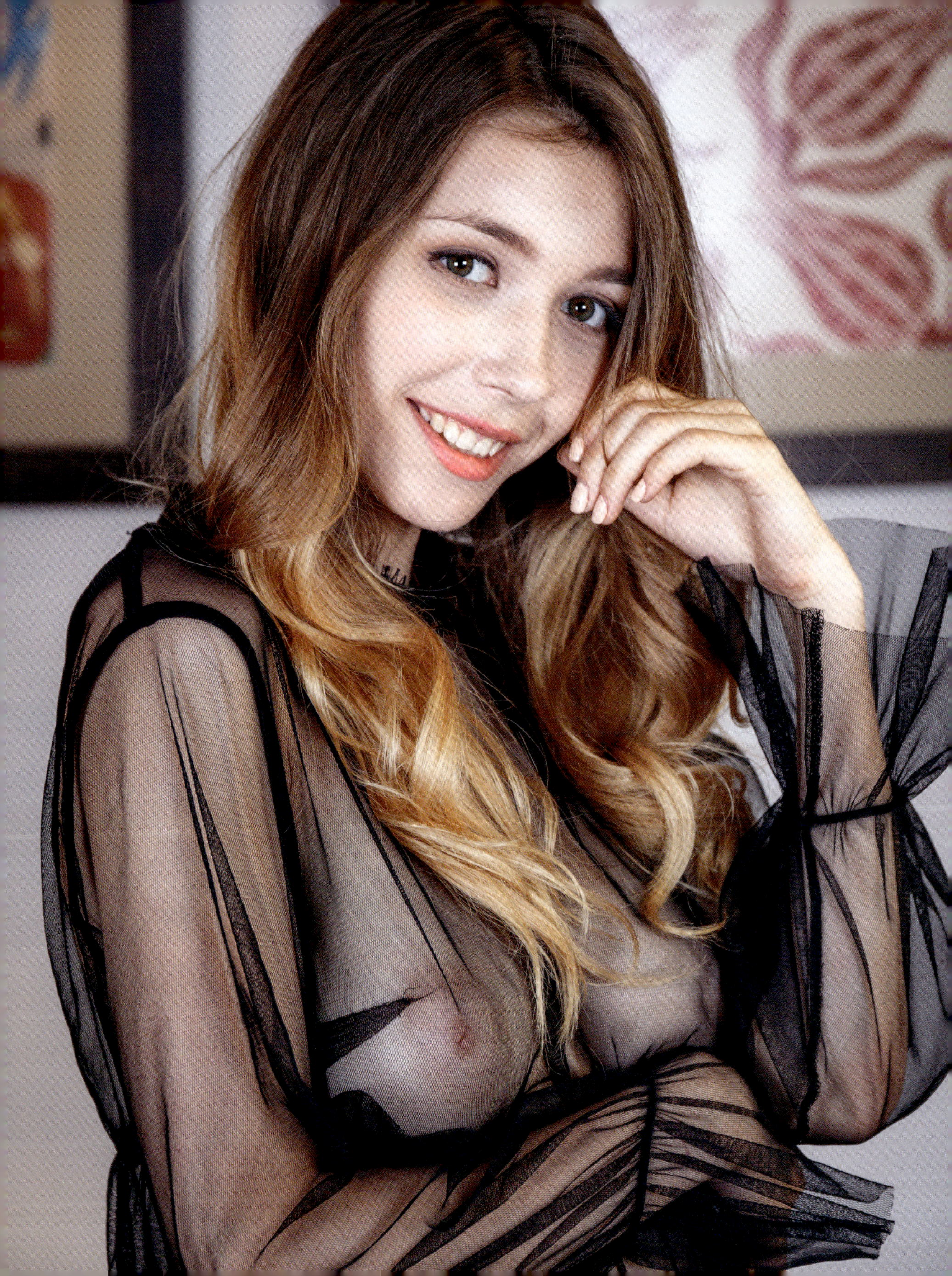

TOP MODELS OF

METART.COM™

WHERE FLAWLESS BEAUTY MEETS ART

MILA AZUL

COLLECTED AND EDITED BY ISABELLA CATALINA

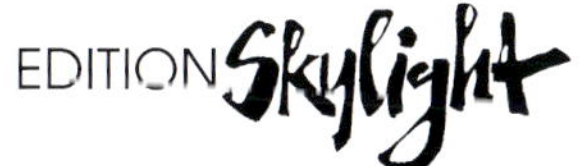

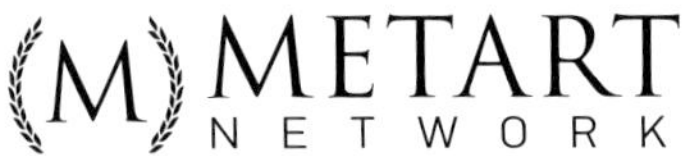

All photos © Copyright 1998–2021
by MetArt TM HLP General Partners Inc.,
Hydentra HLP Int. Limited
9 Karpenisiou Street,
Nicosia 2021, Cyprus
www.metart.com

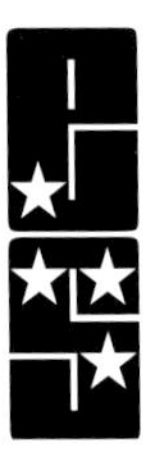

Third edition 2025
Second edition 2022
First edition 2021
Copyright © 2021 by Edition Skylight

EDITION SKYLIGHT
Rosengartenstrasse 13B
CH-8608 Bubikon / Zürich
Switzerland
info@edition-skylight.com
www.edition-skylight.com

ISBN 978-3-03766-680-7

All rights reserved. No part of this book may be reproduced in any form or by any electronic or mechanical means including information storage and retrieval system without the permission in writing form from the copyright owner.

Bibliographic information published by Die Deutsche Bibliothek
Die Deutsche Bibliothek lists this publication in the Deutsche Nationalbibliografie; detailed bibliographic data are available in the Internet at http://dnb.ddb.de.

Printed in Bosnia and Herzegovina

NATURAL WONDER MILA AZUL

Mila Azul is one of MetArt's all-time top models, a vivacious brunette with a sweet face and huge natural breasts. The adorable Ukrainian babe takes such obvious pleasure from sharing her spectacular body, her smile bewitching as she bares her flawless ass and lets her big, beautiful breasts bounce enticingly. Her slender frame and tiny waist make those whopping natural wonders all the more astonishing. Since her first appearance in 2016 at the tender age of 19, Mila has been viewed on MetArt more than three million times, and she is frequently voted the world's number one erotic star by its members. Her innate self-assurance and playful sex appeal are simply irresistible, whether she's dressed up in sexy lingerie, playing the charming girl-next-door, or perfectly nude. And whenever she gets naked, her dark eyes shine with such naughtiness you can't help falling a little bit in love.

MetArt listet Mila Azul als eines der „Allzeit-Top-Models". Die lebhafte Brunette punktet mit süßem Gesicht und ihren natürlichen Brüsten. Die begehrenswerte ukrainische Schönheit genießt es sichtlich, Ihren Körper zu präsentieren und flirtet hemmungslos mit der Kamera. Ihr Lächeln betört uns genauso wie ihr strammer Hintern und ihre prächtigen Brüste, die mehr bieten als die übliche aristokratische Handvoll. Die gertenschlanke Figur und schmale Taille bringen diese zwei hüpfenden Wunderdinger magisch zur Geltung. Seit ihrem Debut mit 19 Jahren haben die MetArt-Freunde den Auftritt dieses antörnenden Springinsfelds mehr als 3 Millionen mal angeschaut. Und sie wird von den MetArt-Abonnenten fortwährend als weltweit bester Erotik-Star ausgezeichnet. Ihr heißer und spielerischer Sexappeal ist einfach unwiderstehlich, egal ob in Lingerie, als Girl von nebenan oder ganz nackt. Und wenn Mila frech mit ihren dunklen leuchtenden Augen schaut, dann kann man als entfernter Voyeur durchaus Regungen einer ersten Liebeswallung empfinden ...

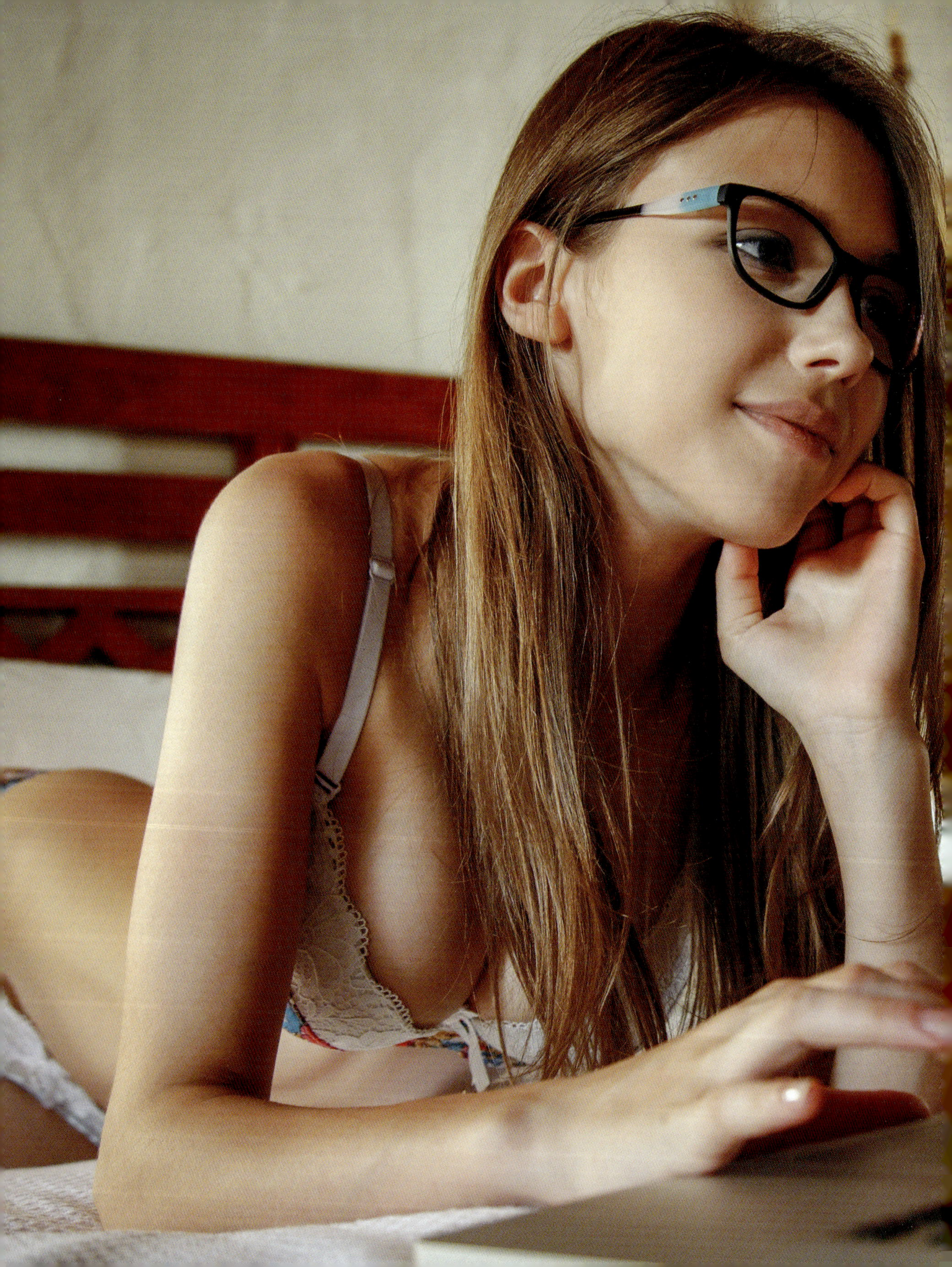

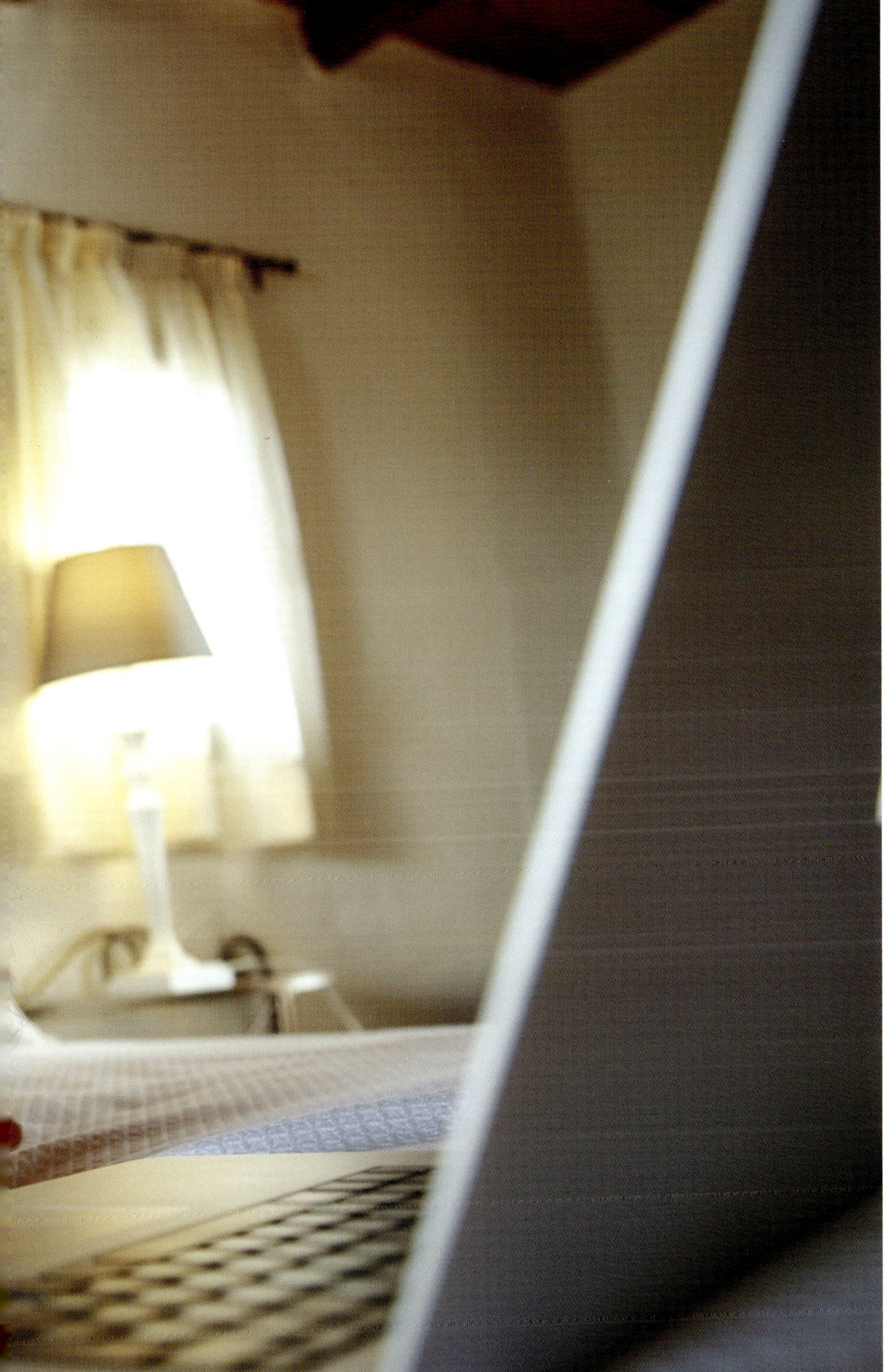

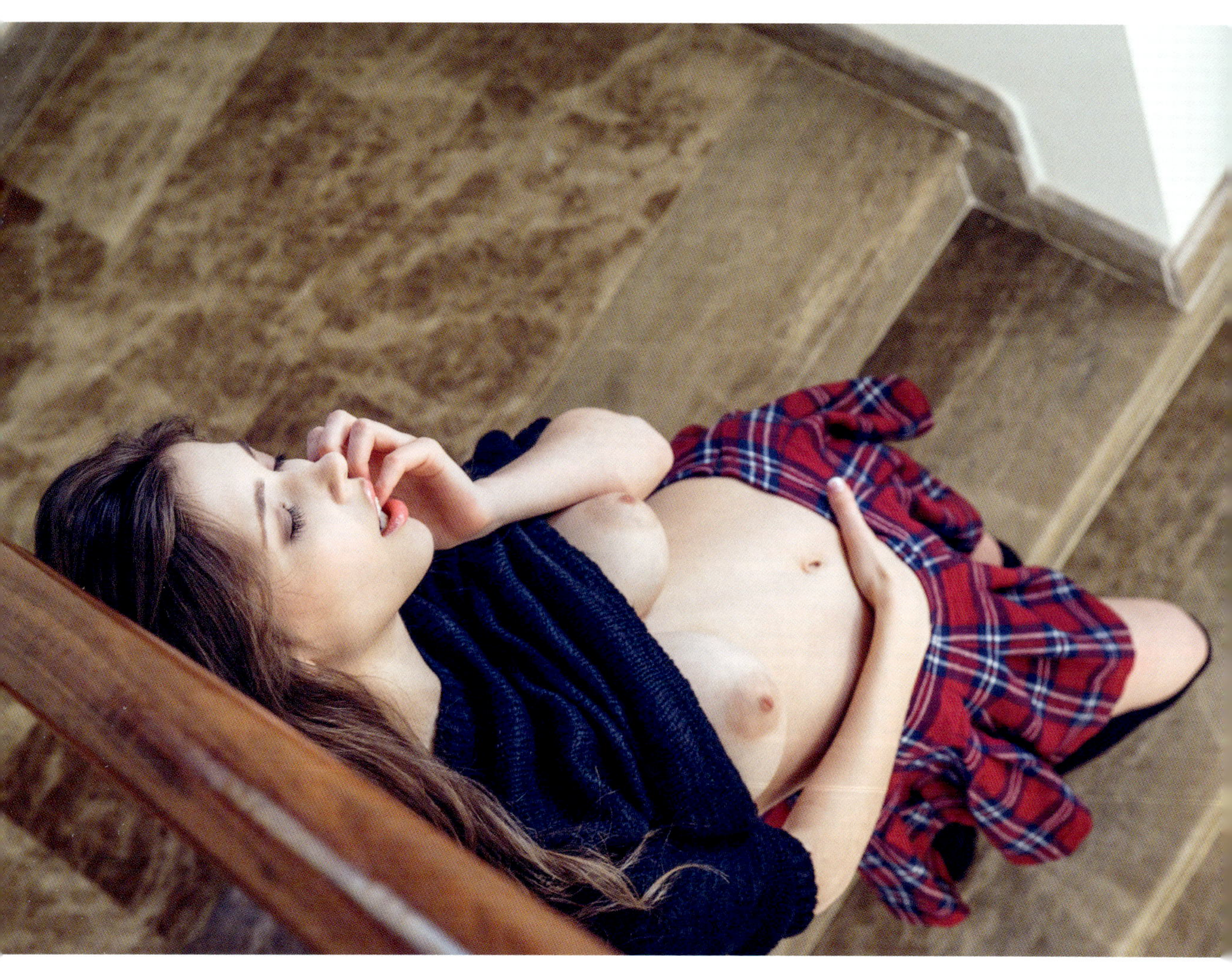

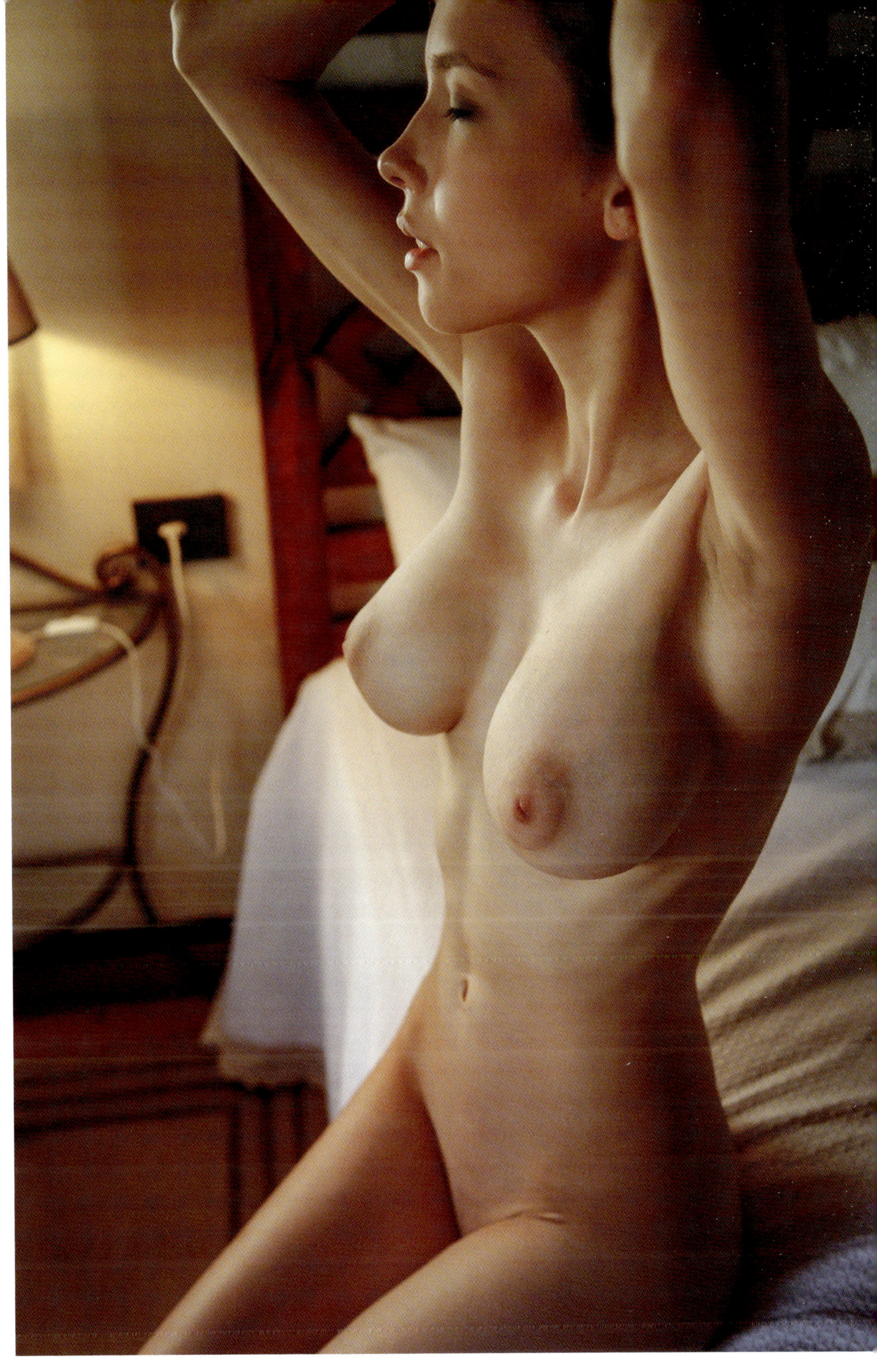

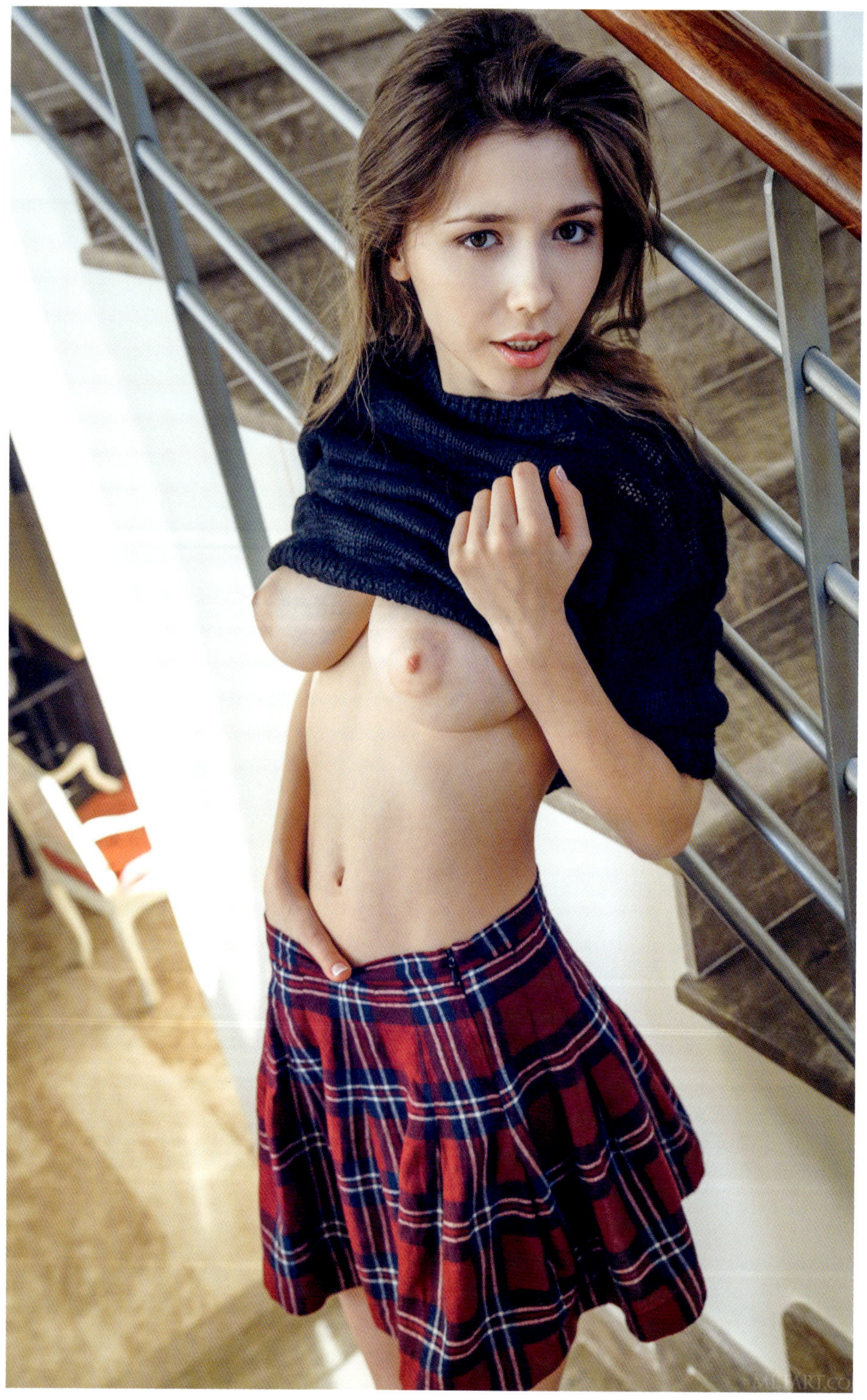

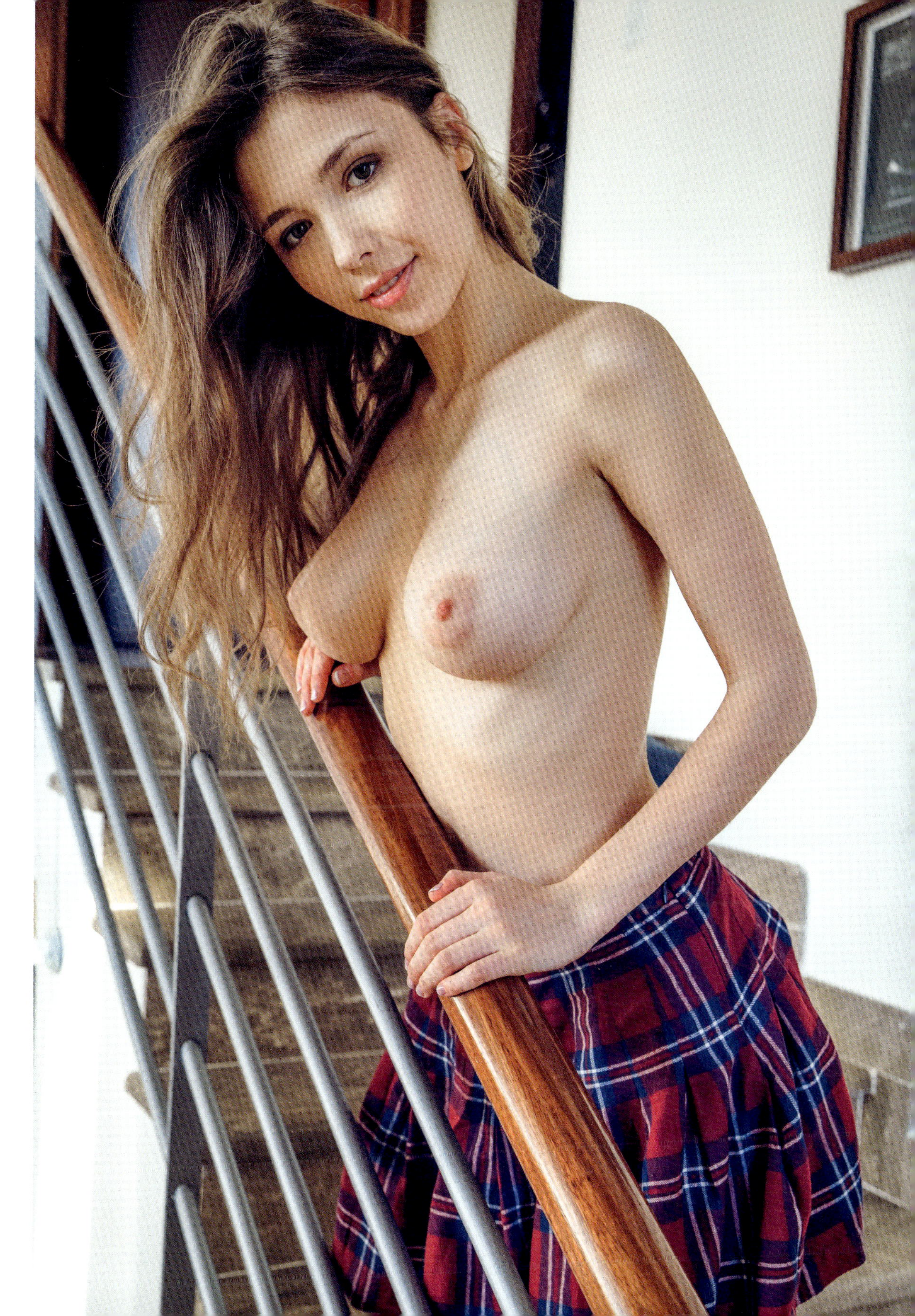

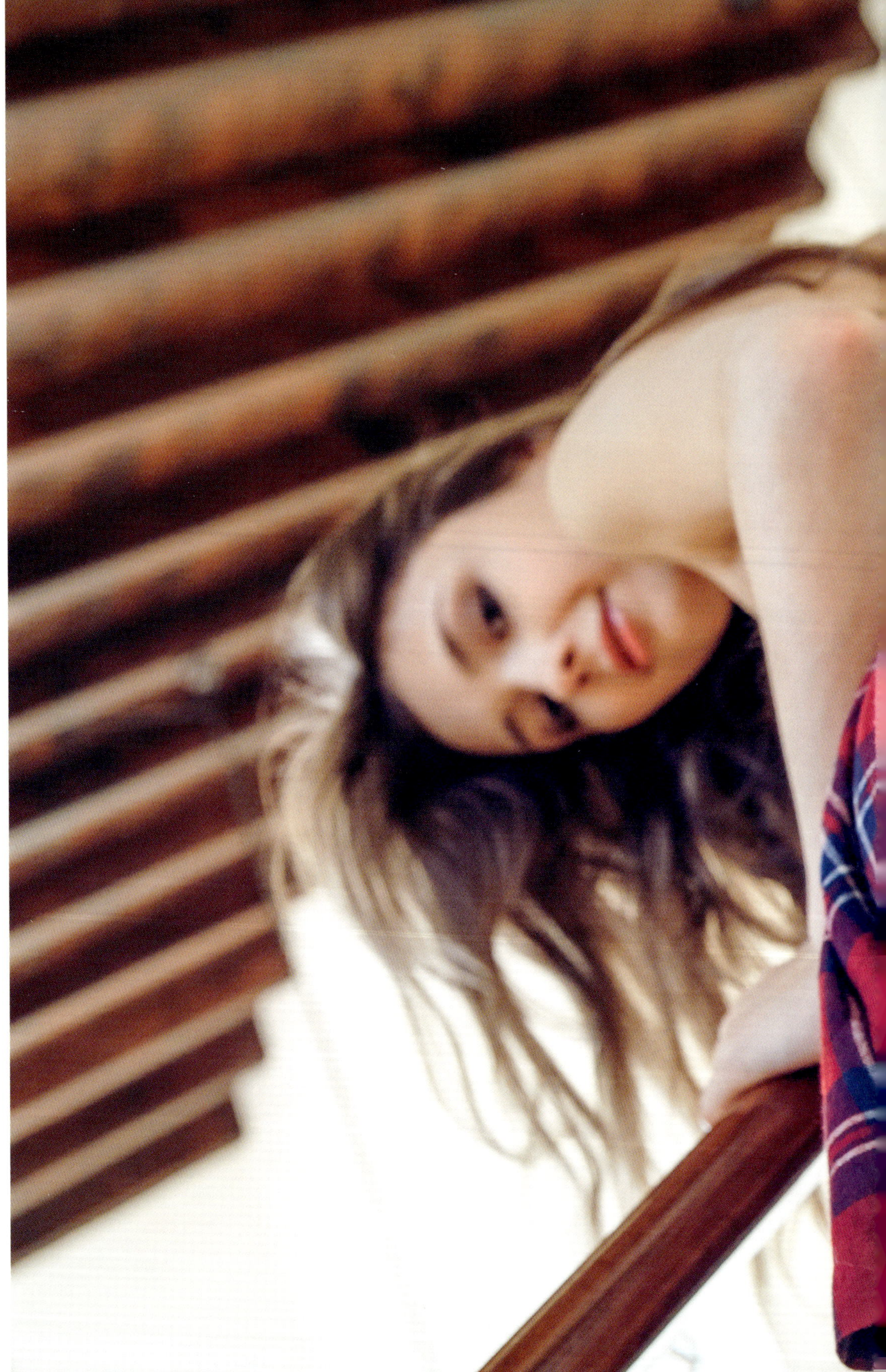

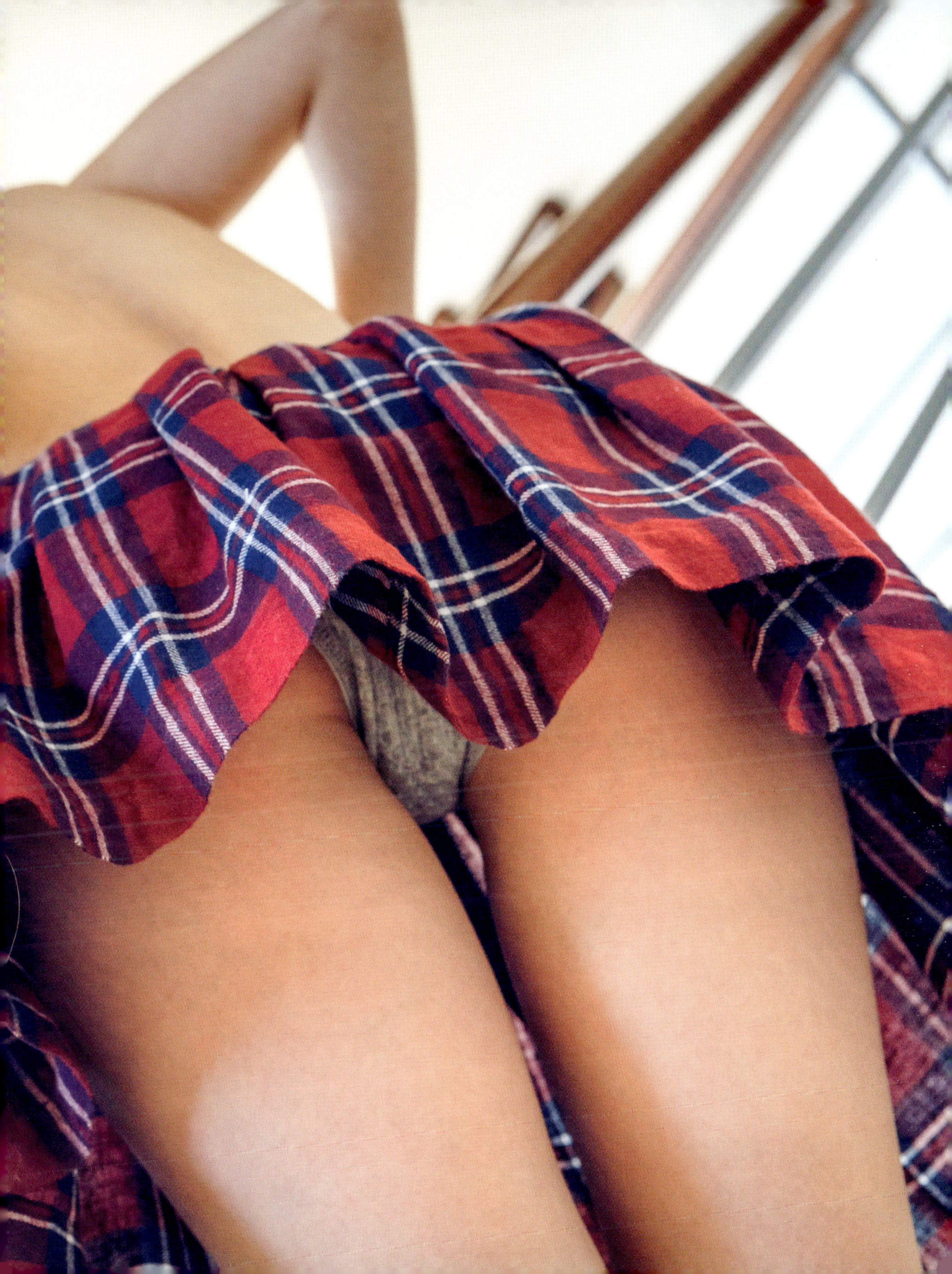

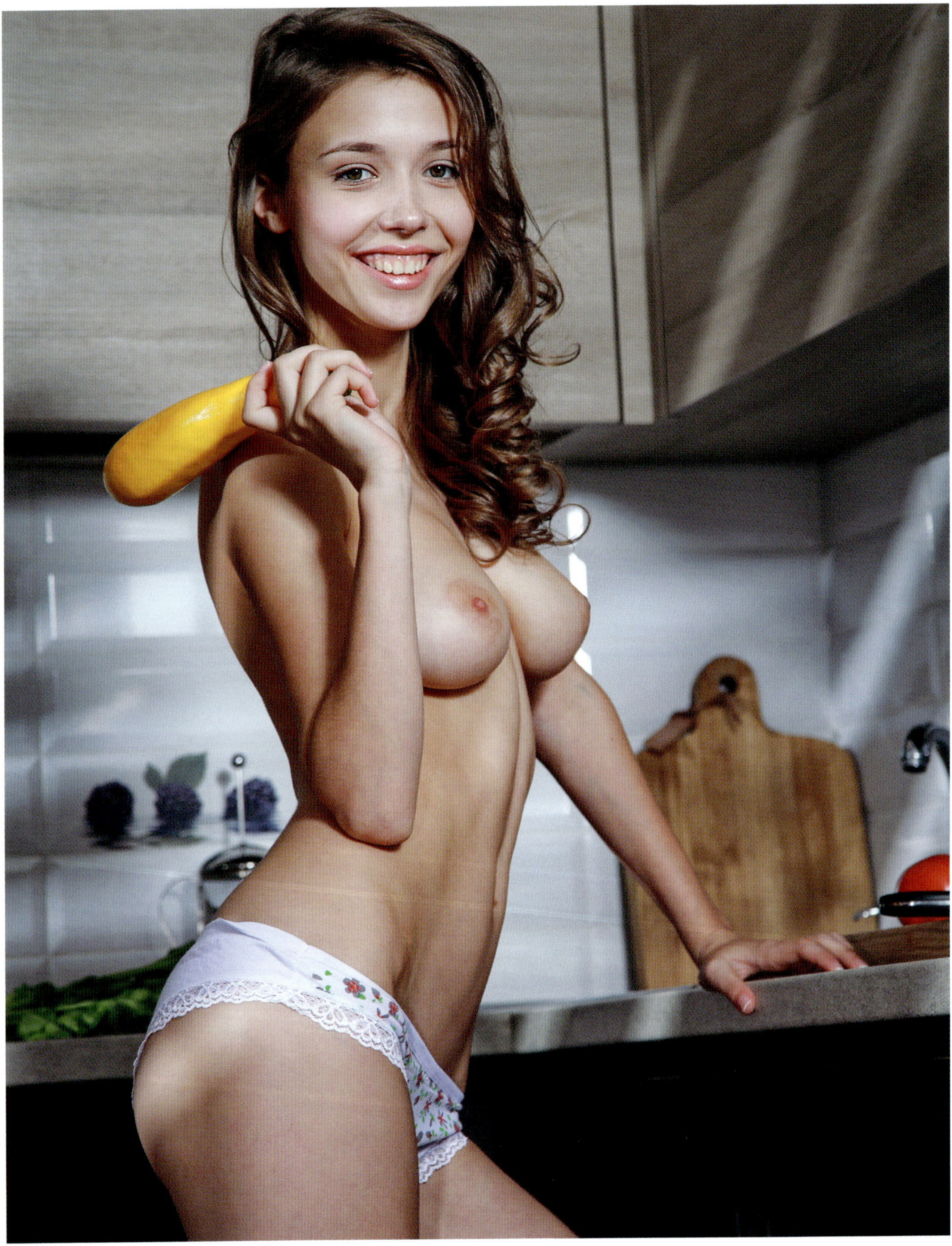

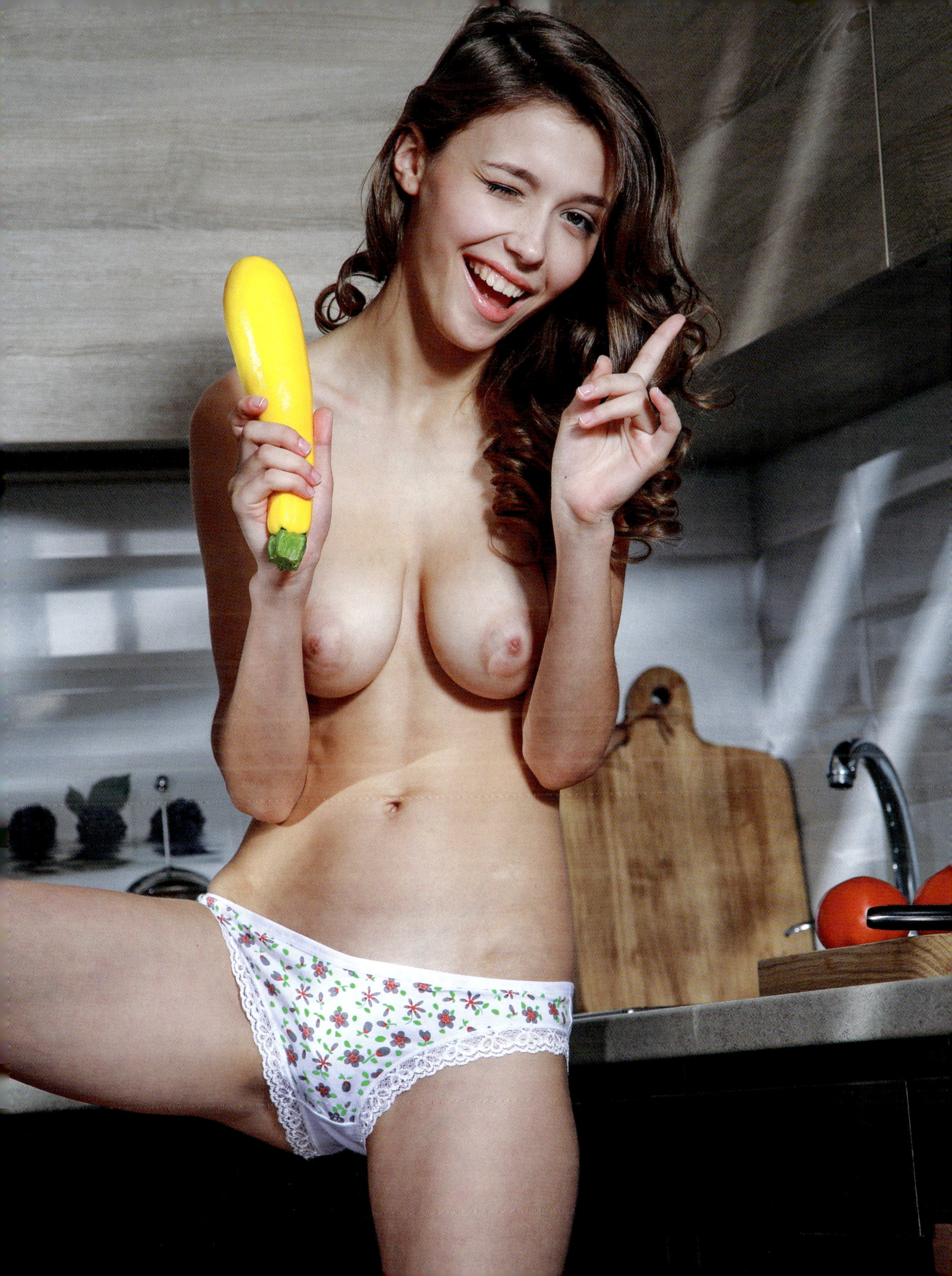

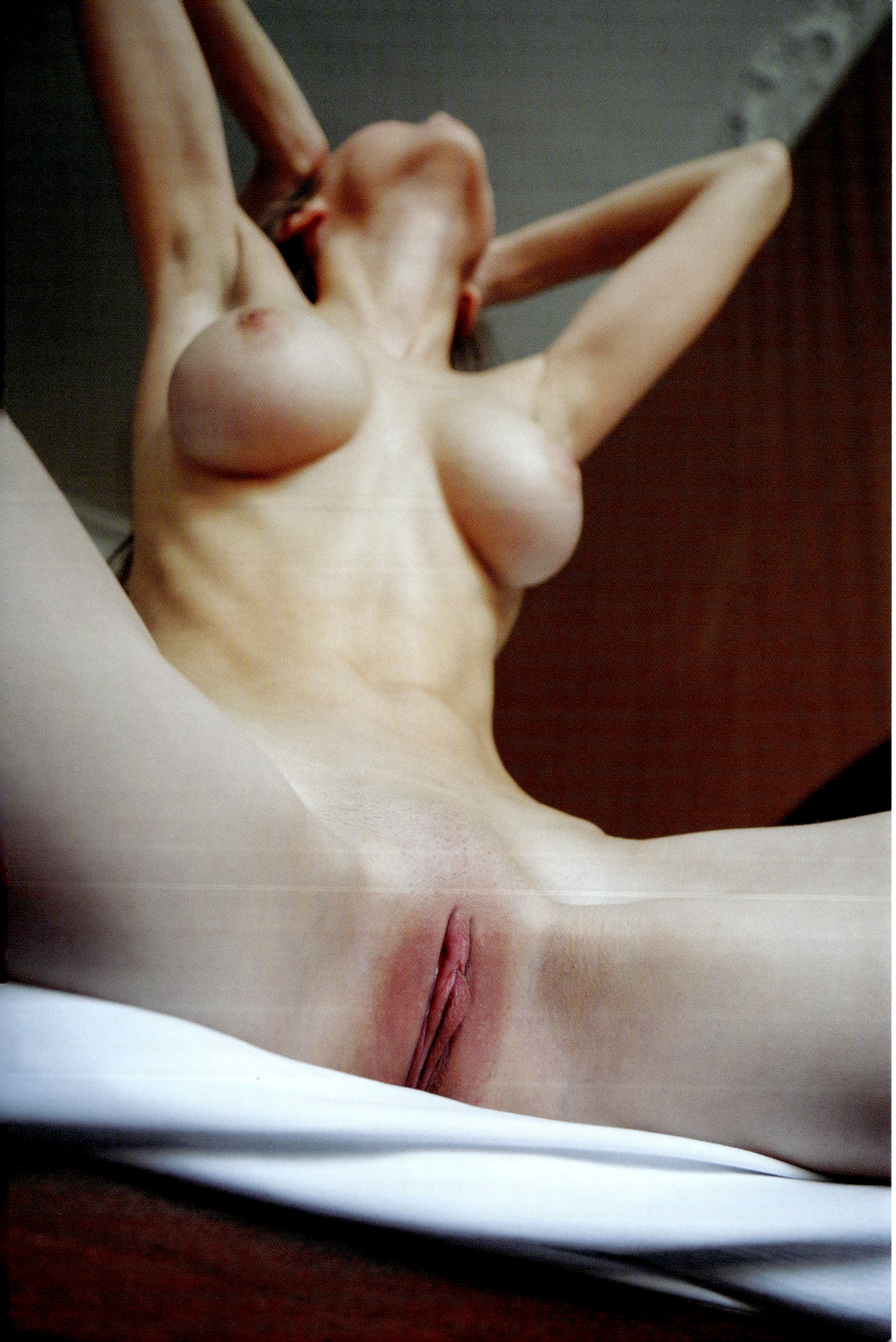

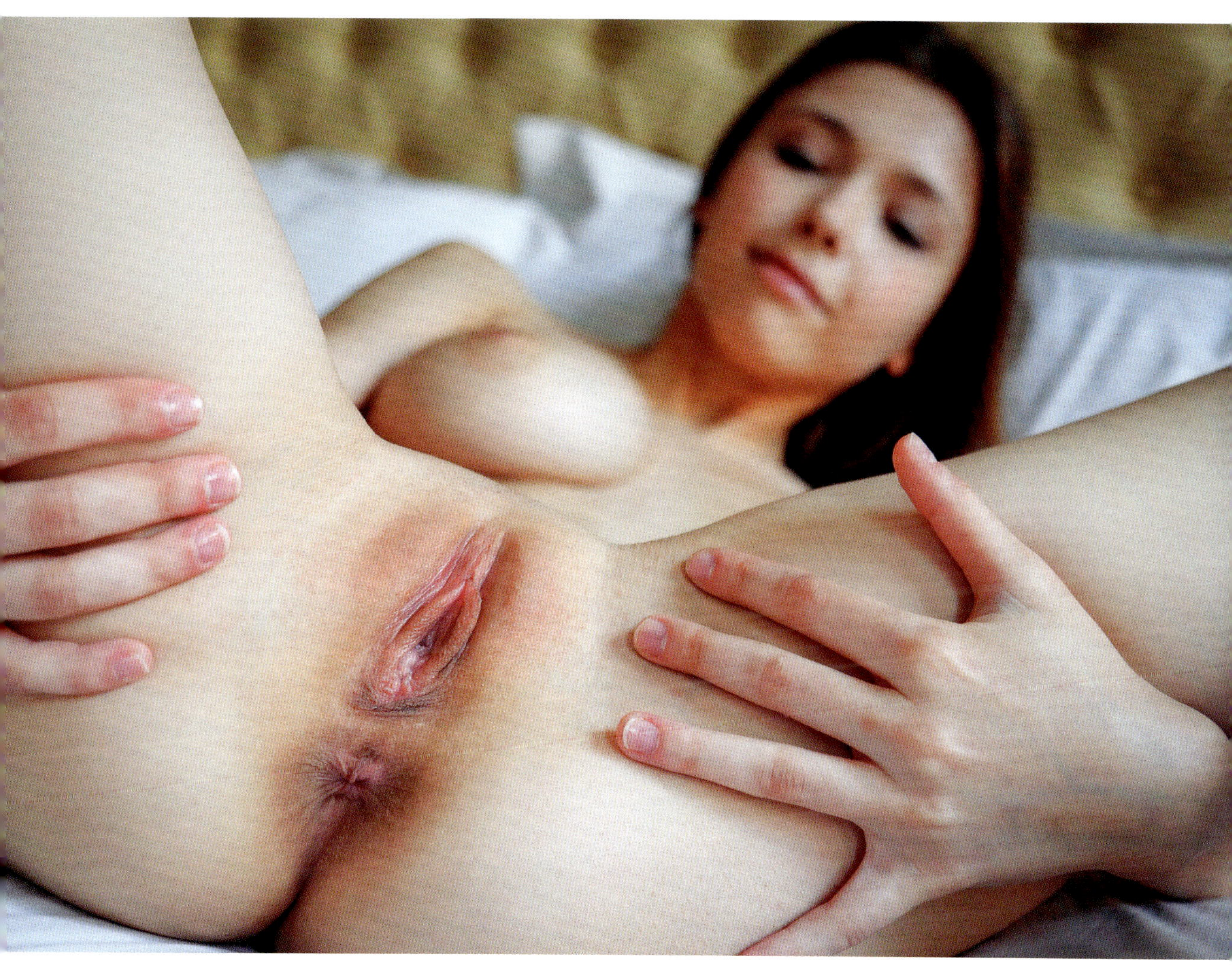

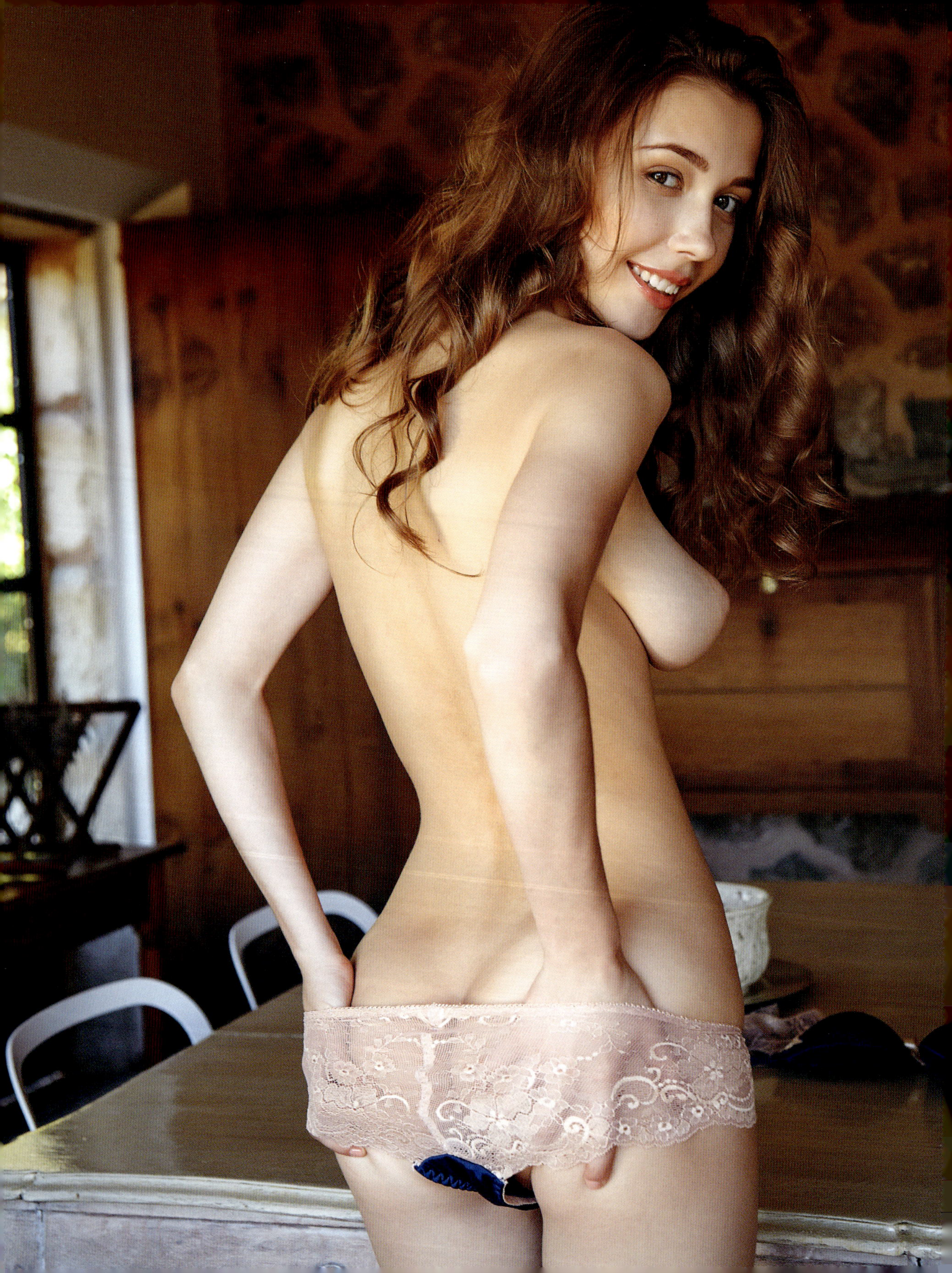

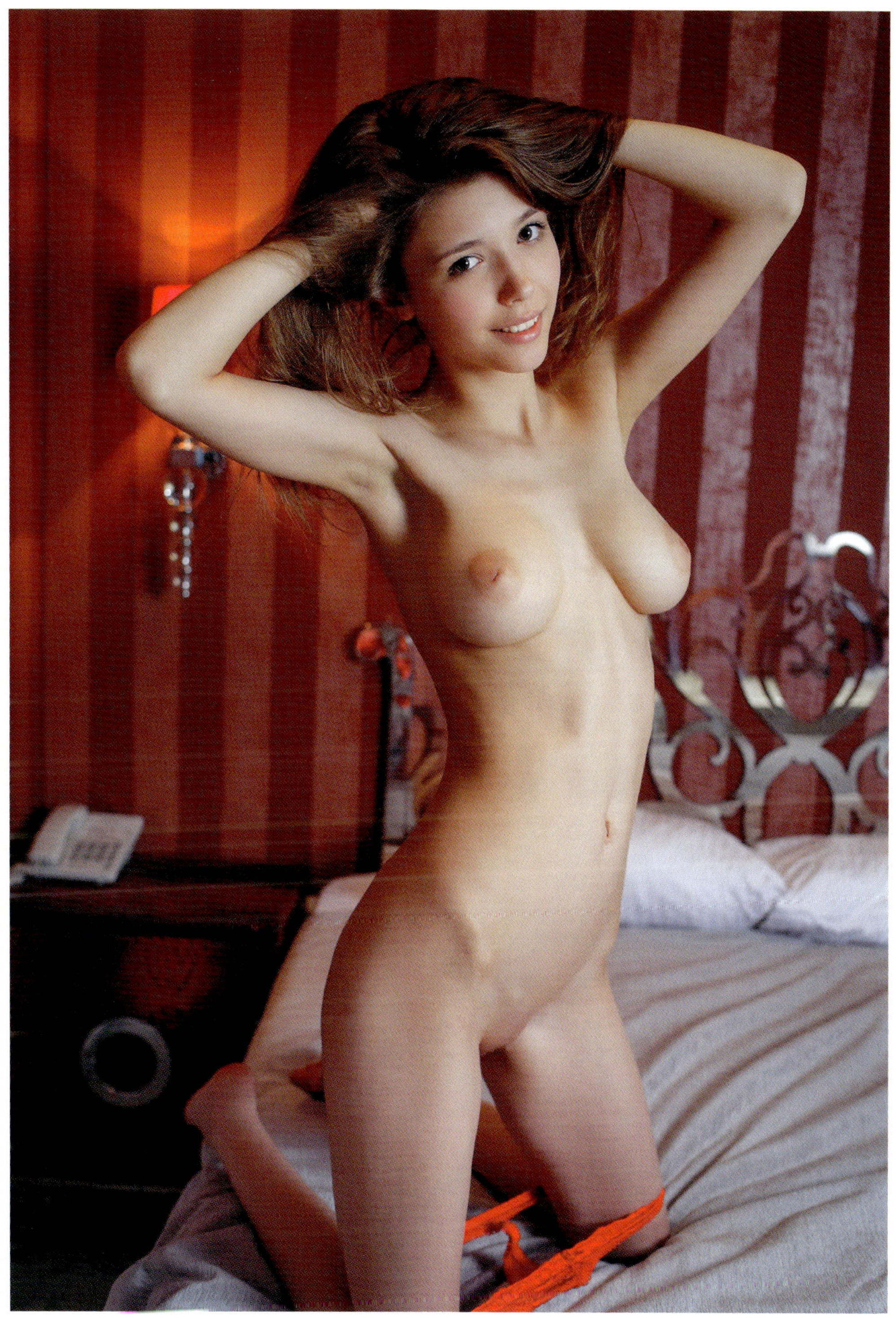

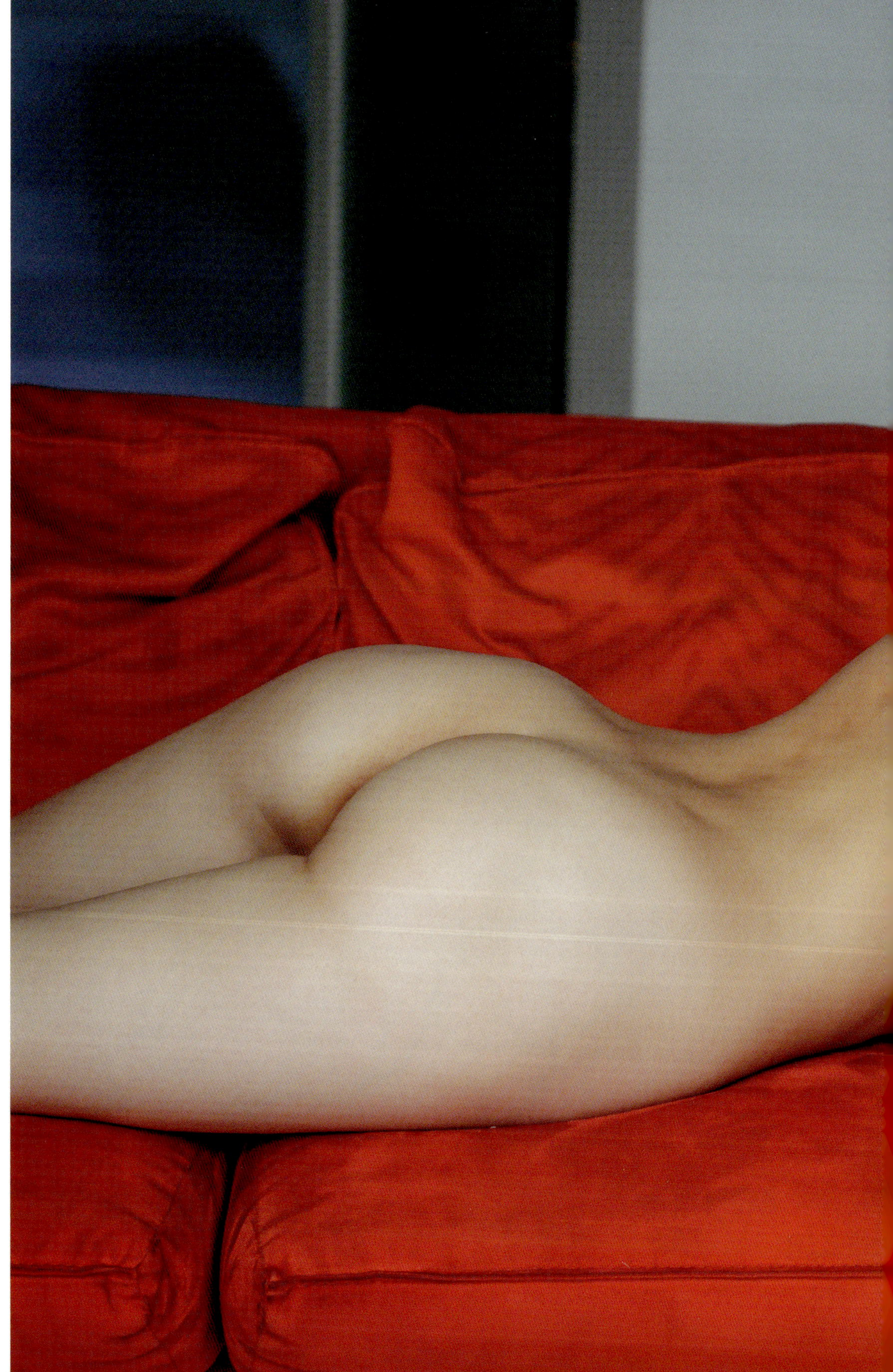

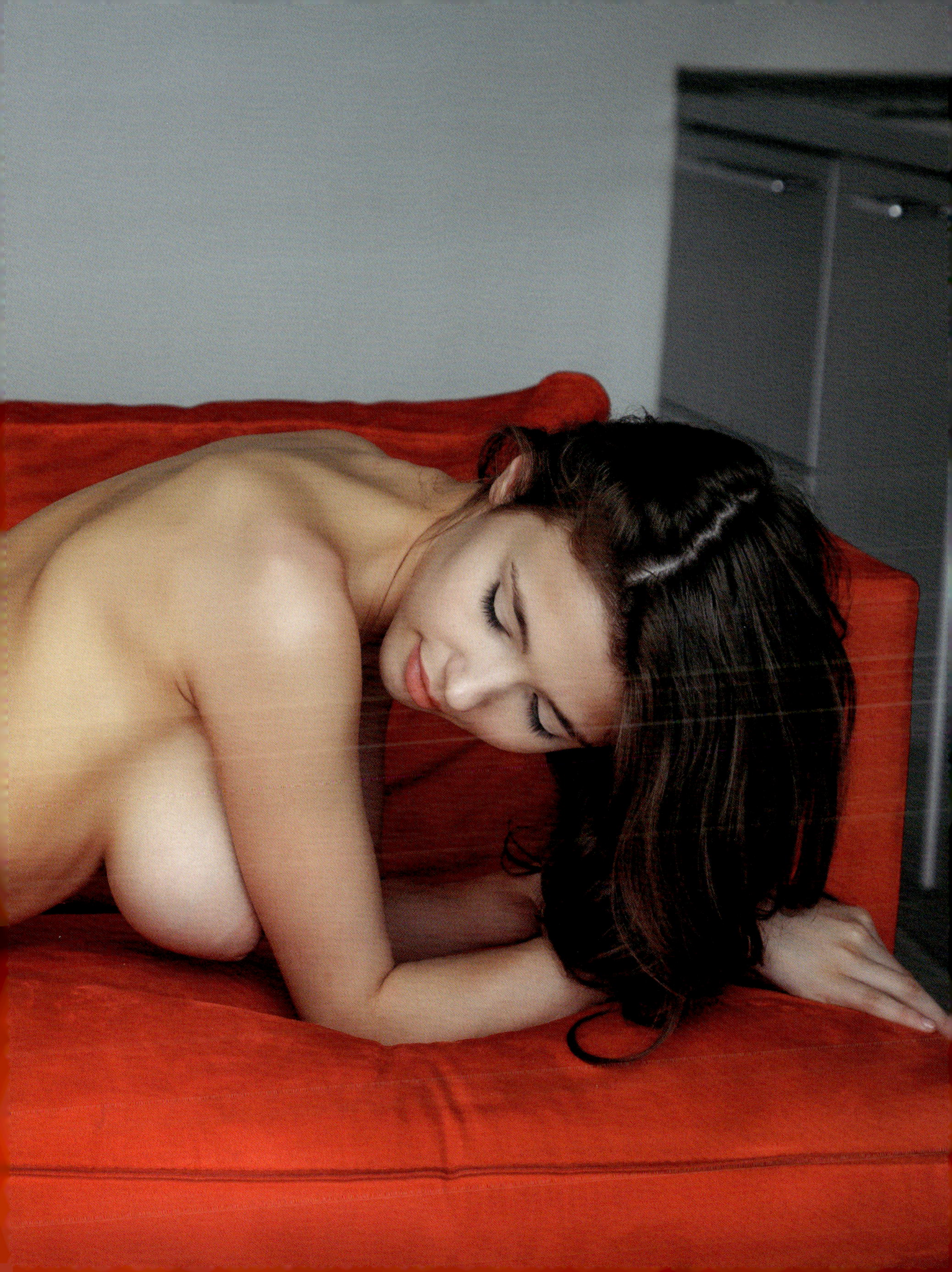

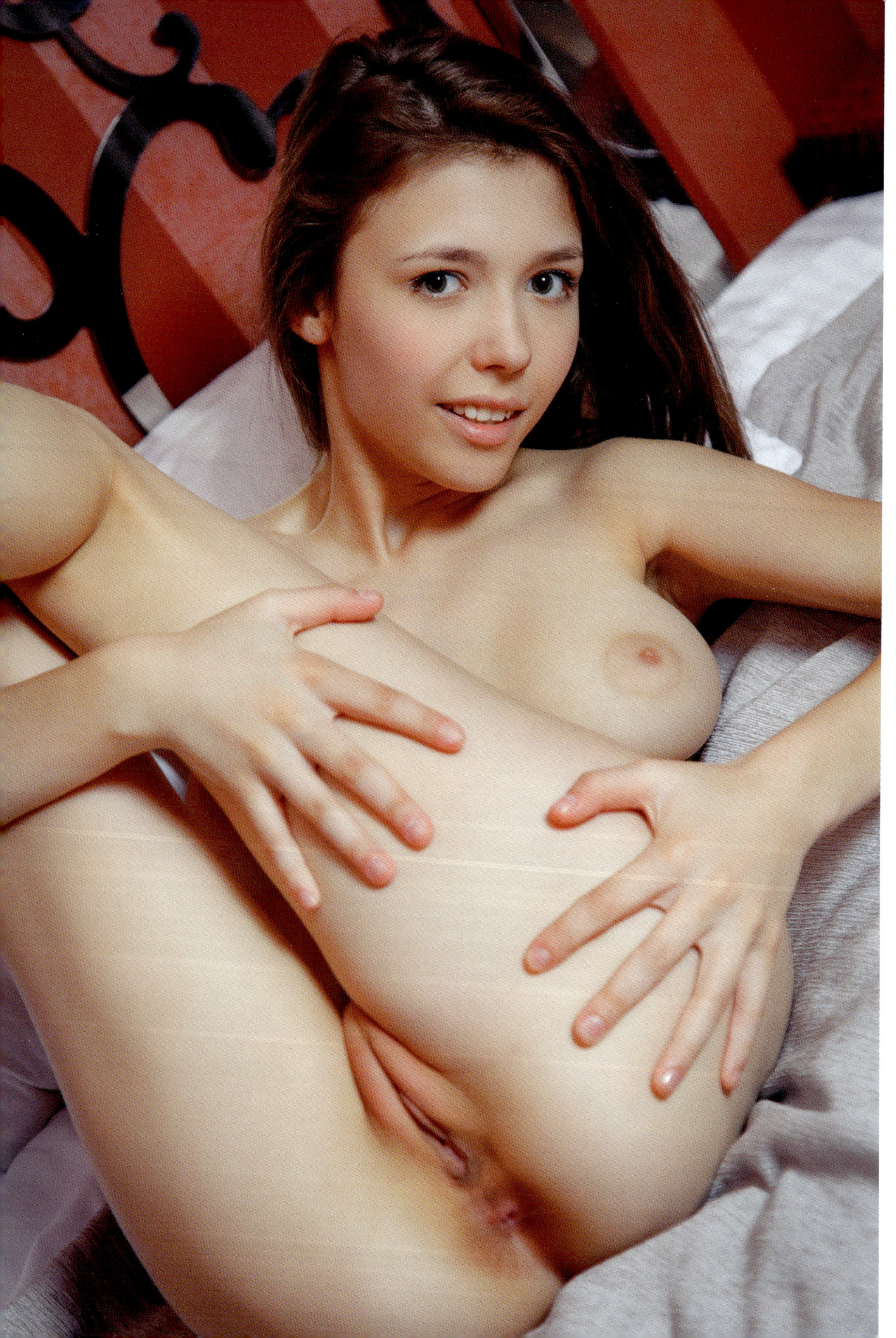

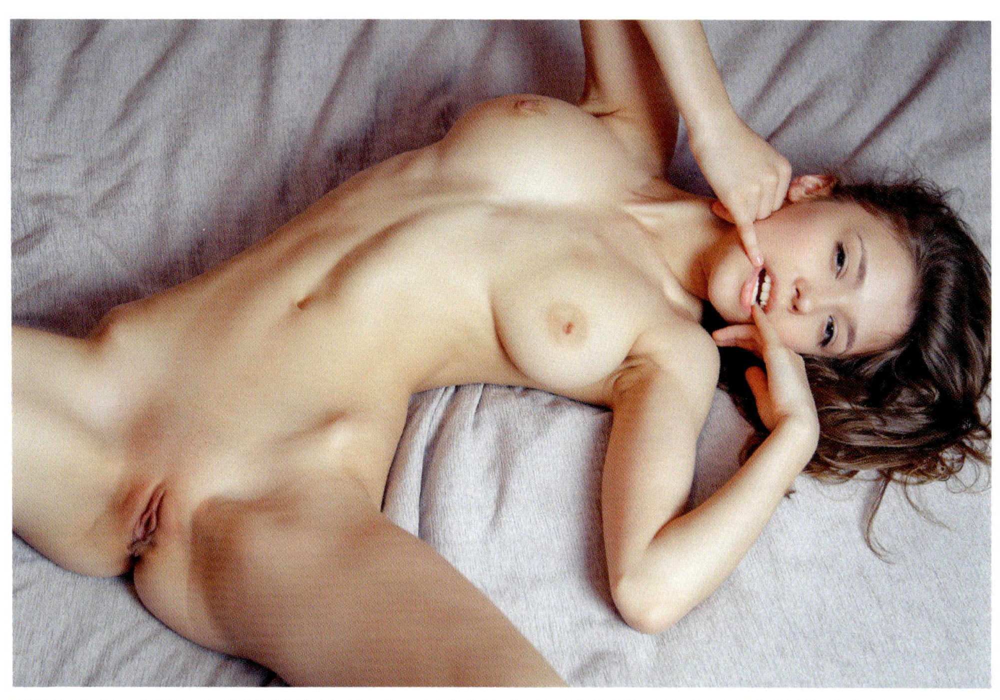

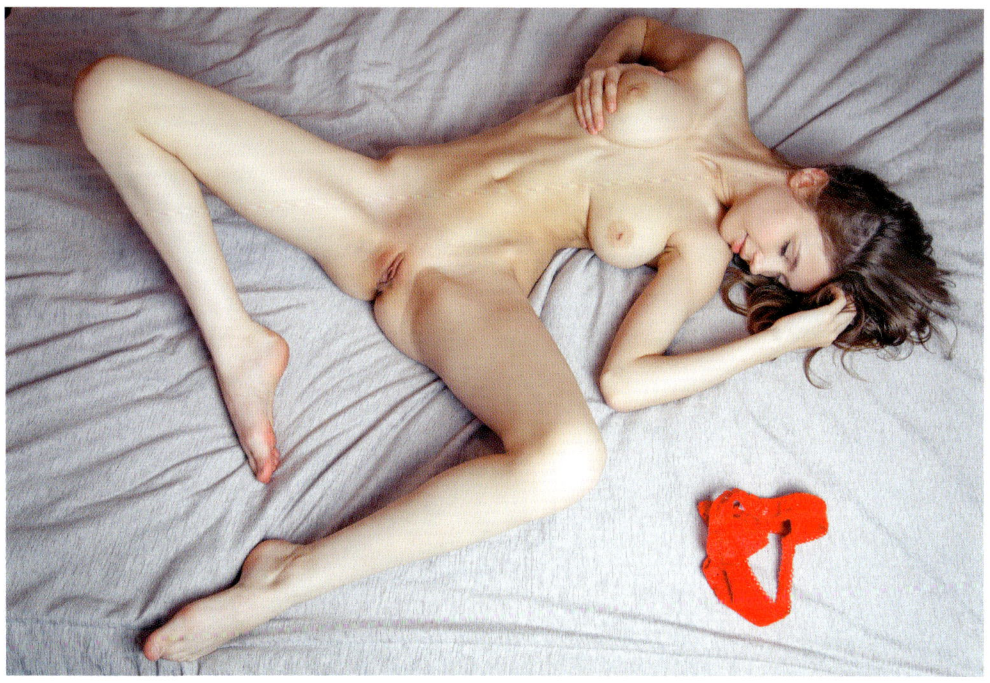

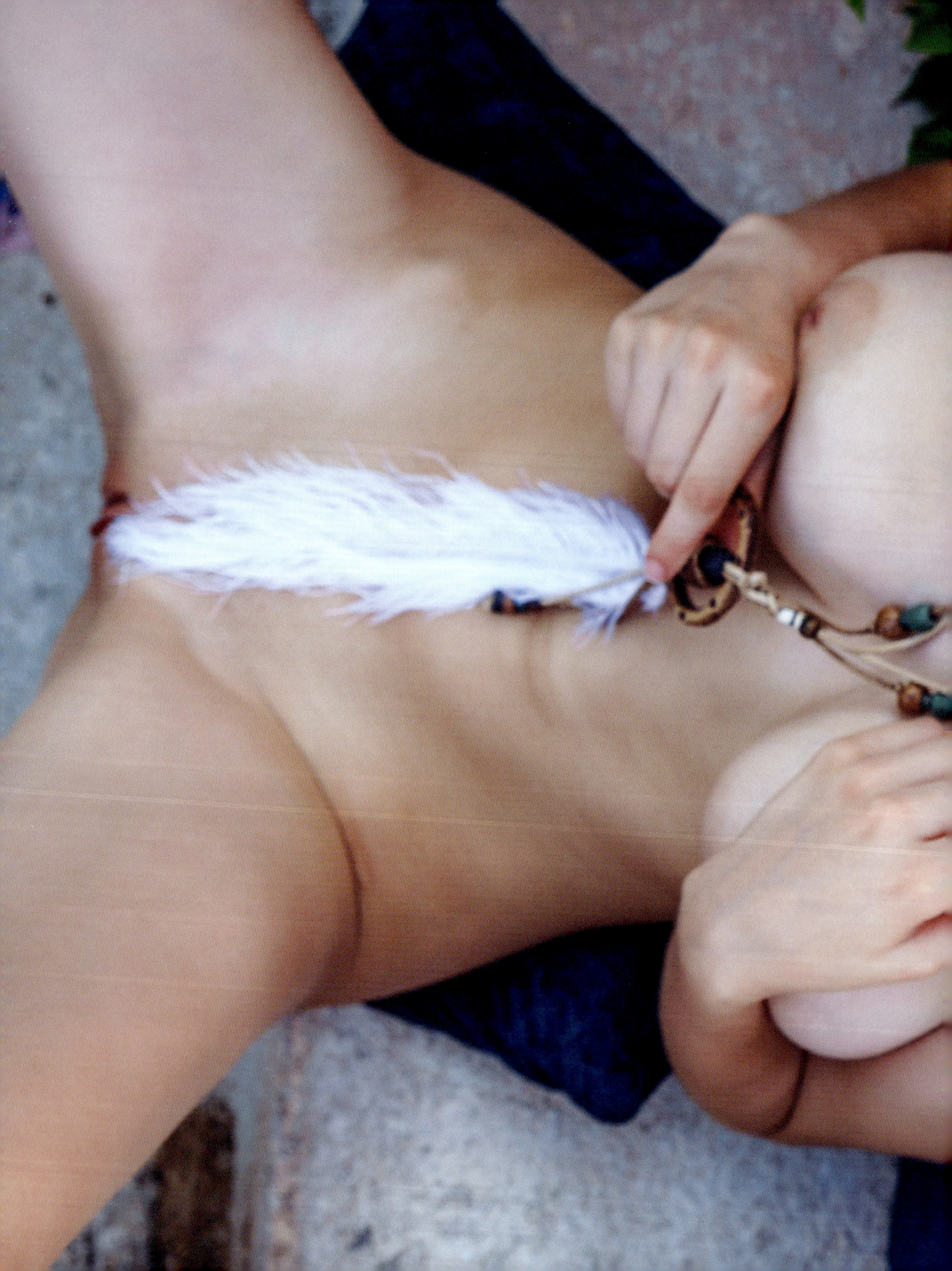

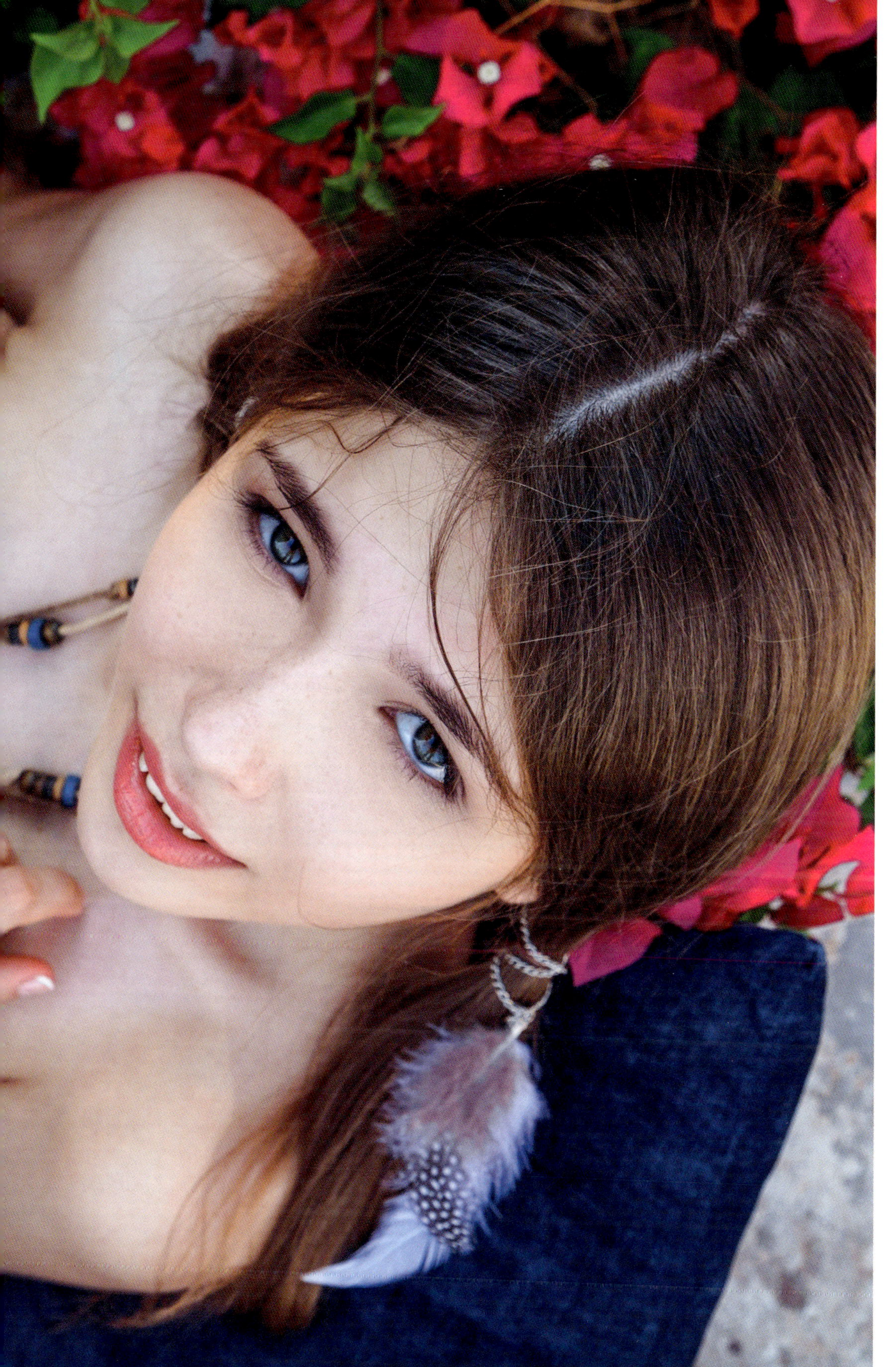

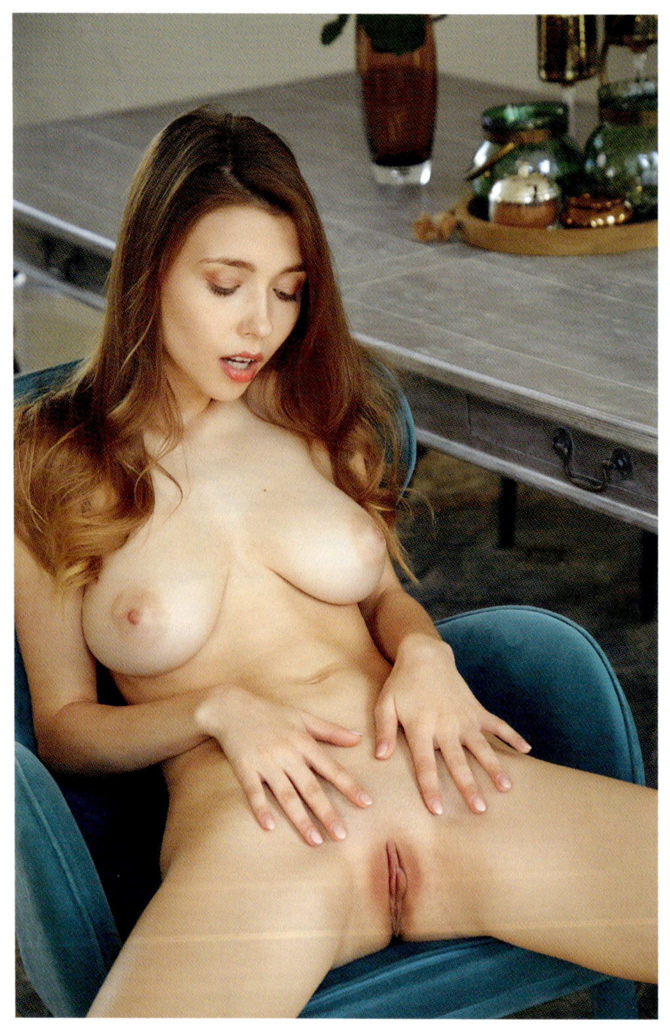

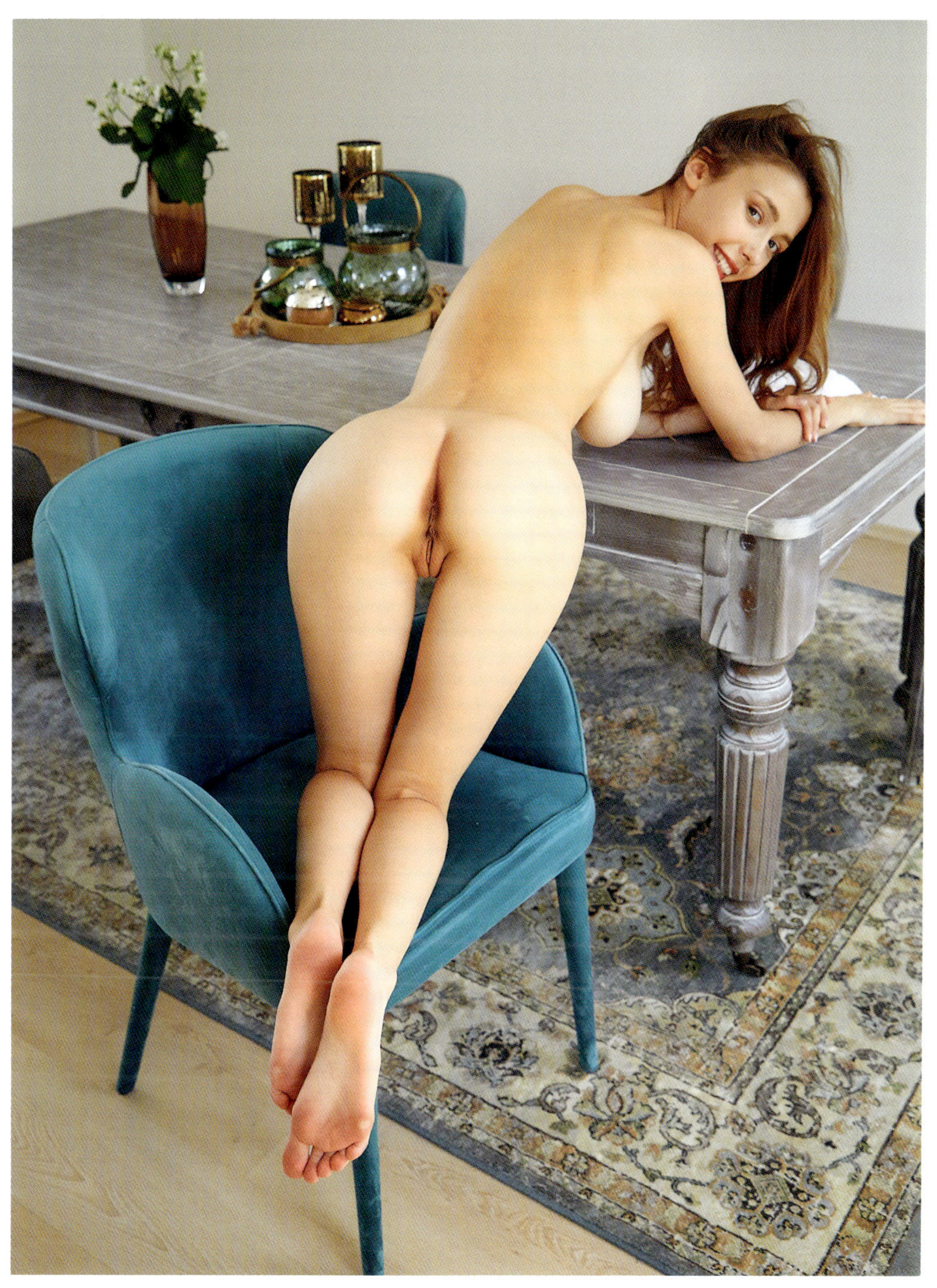

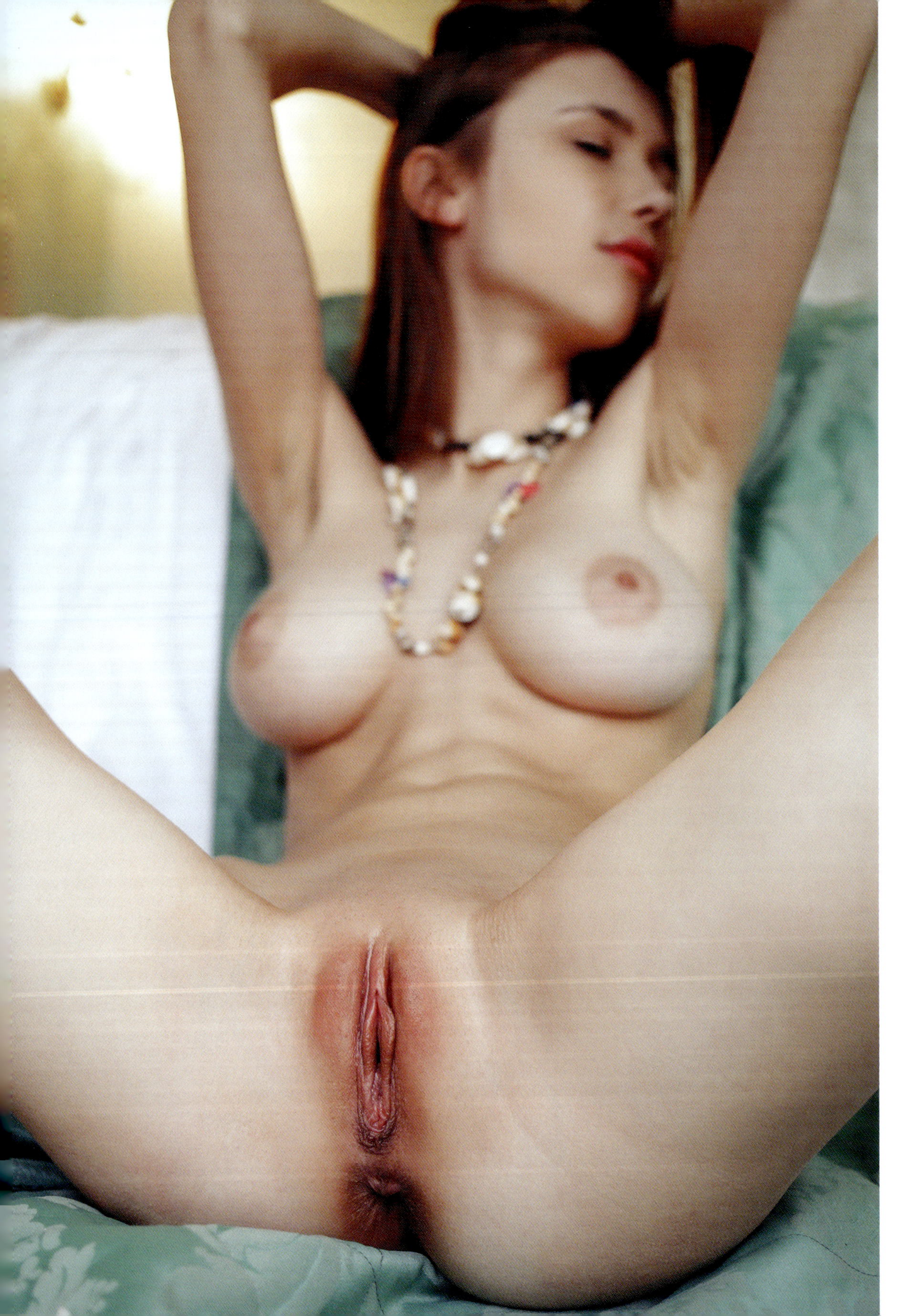

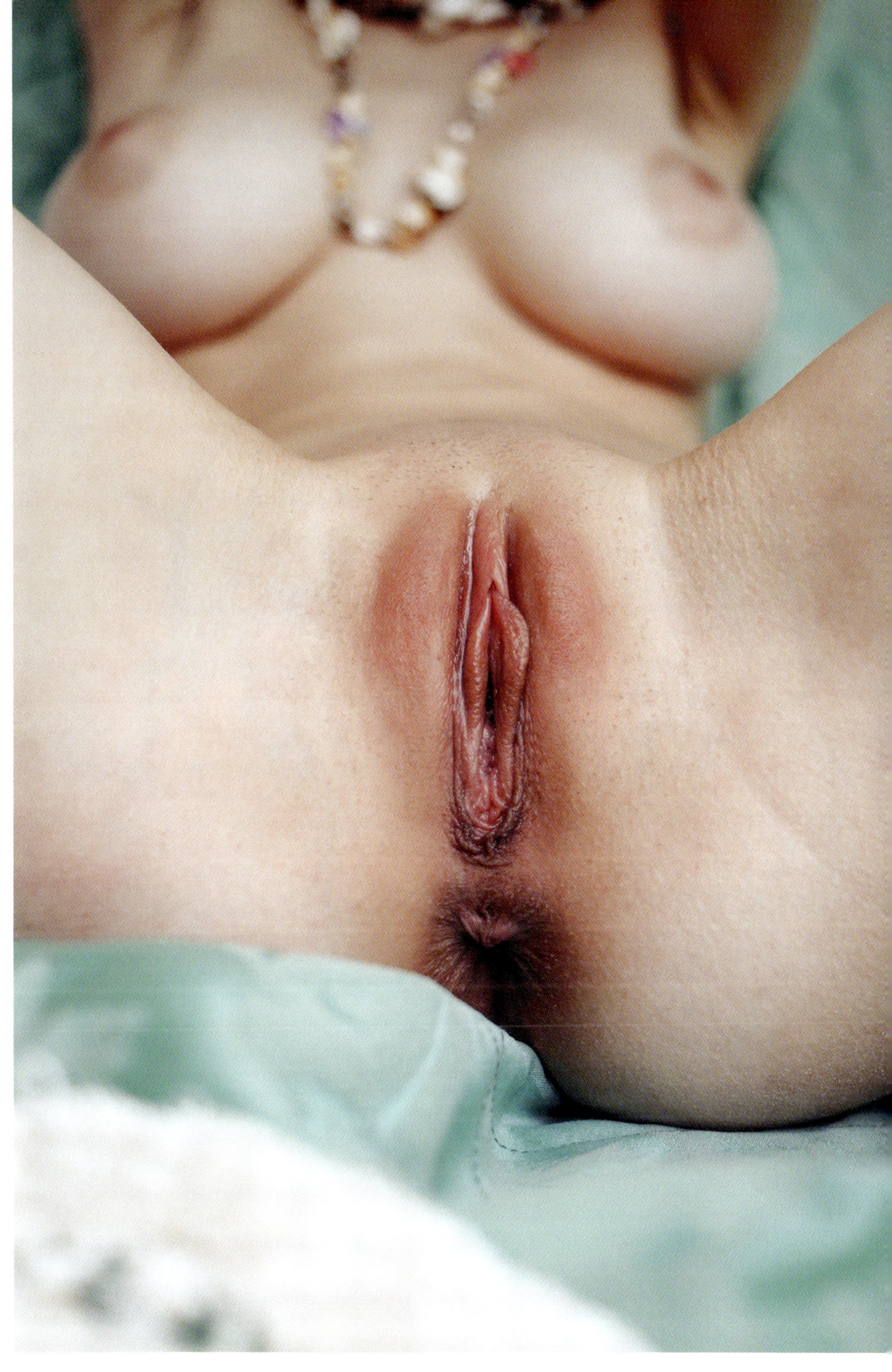

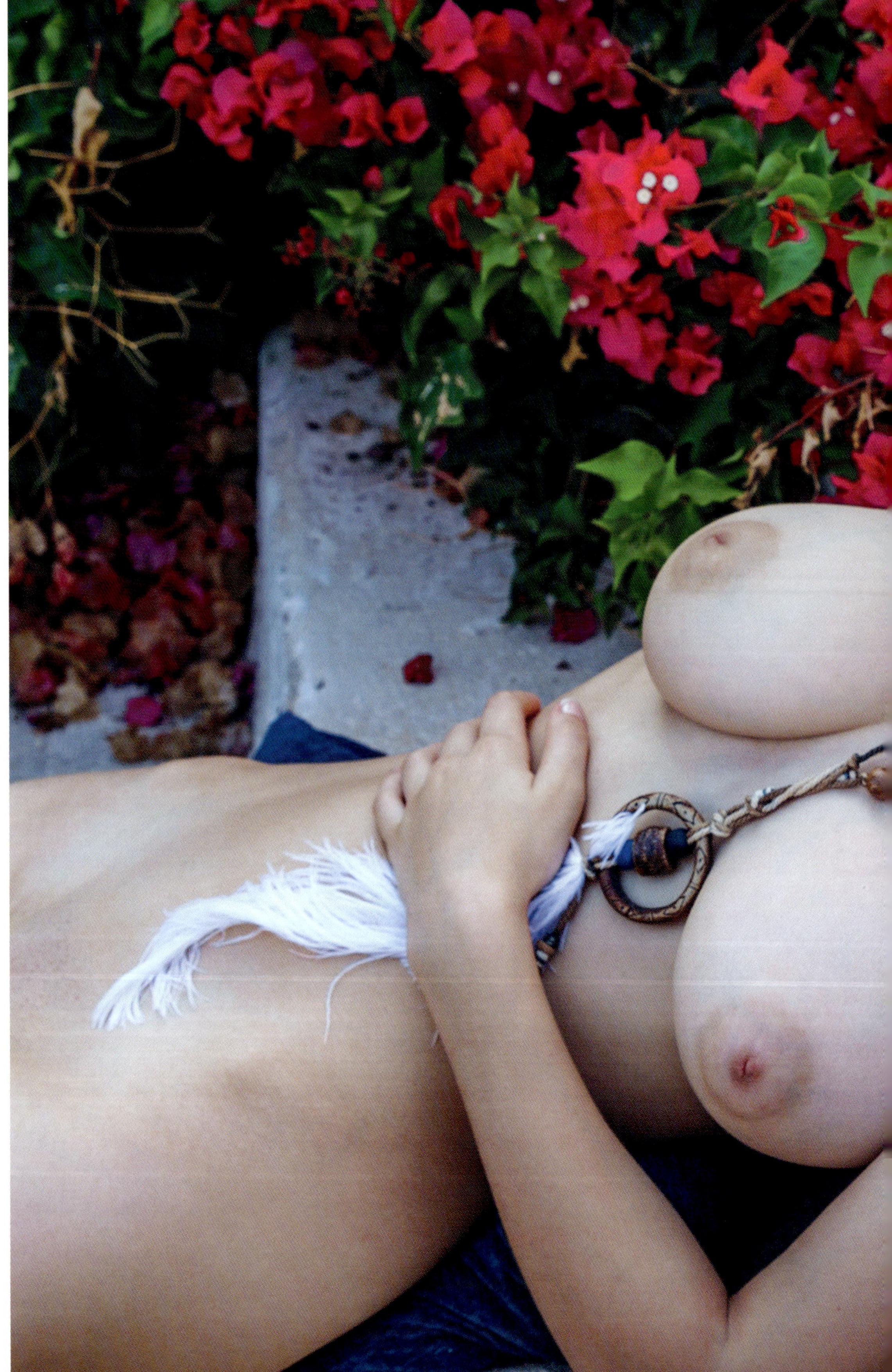

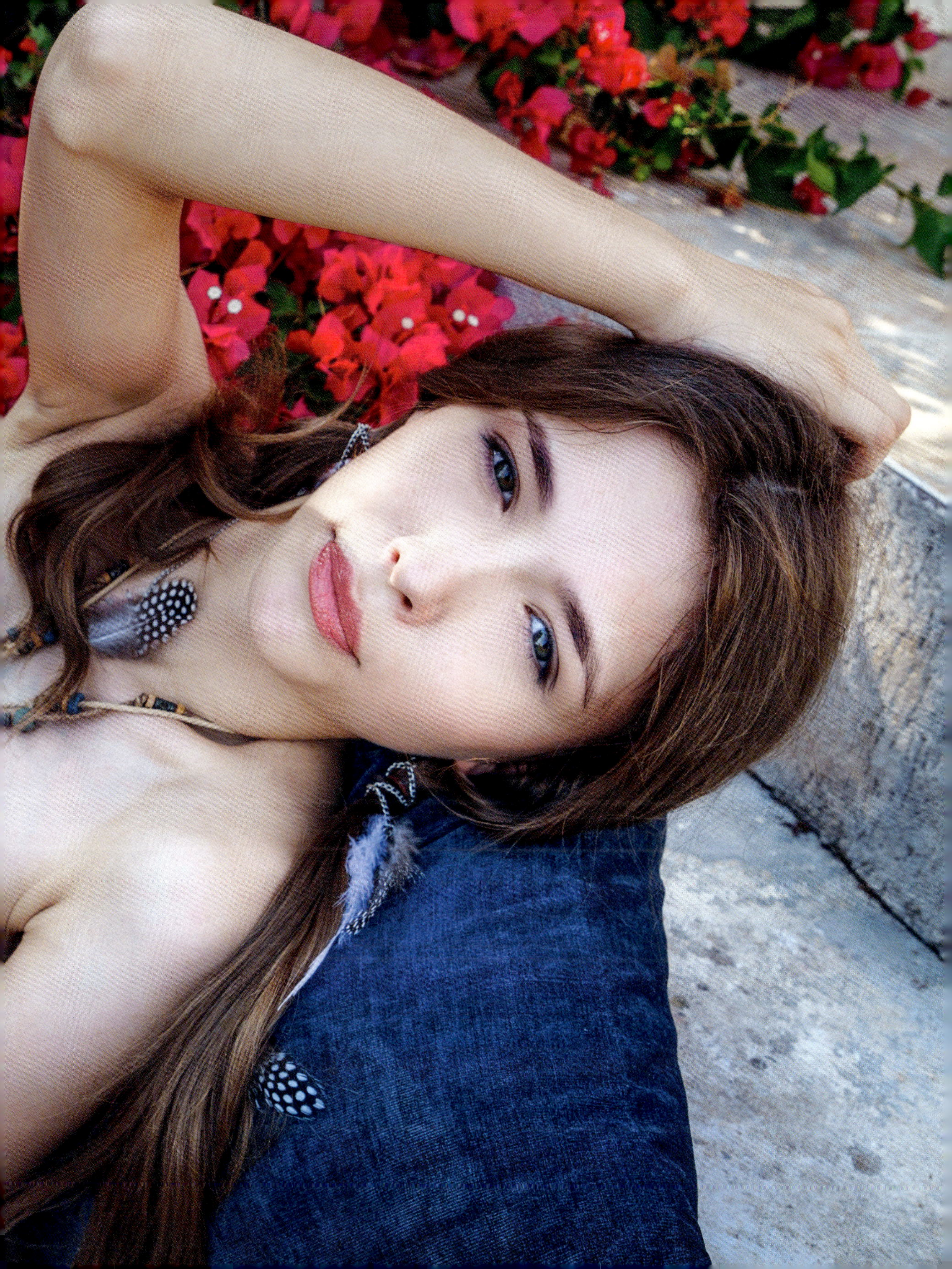

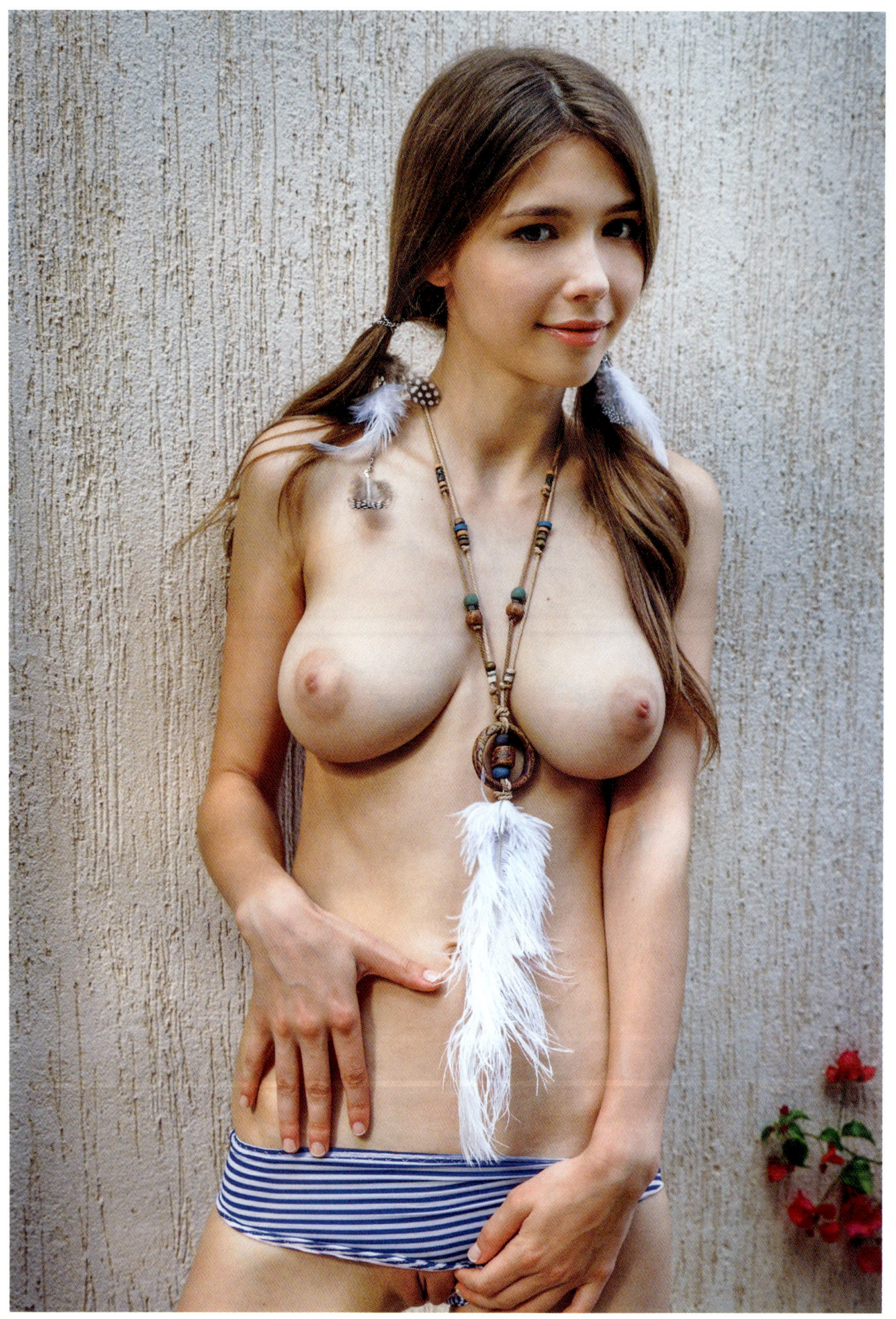

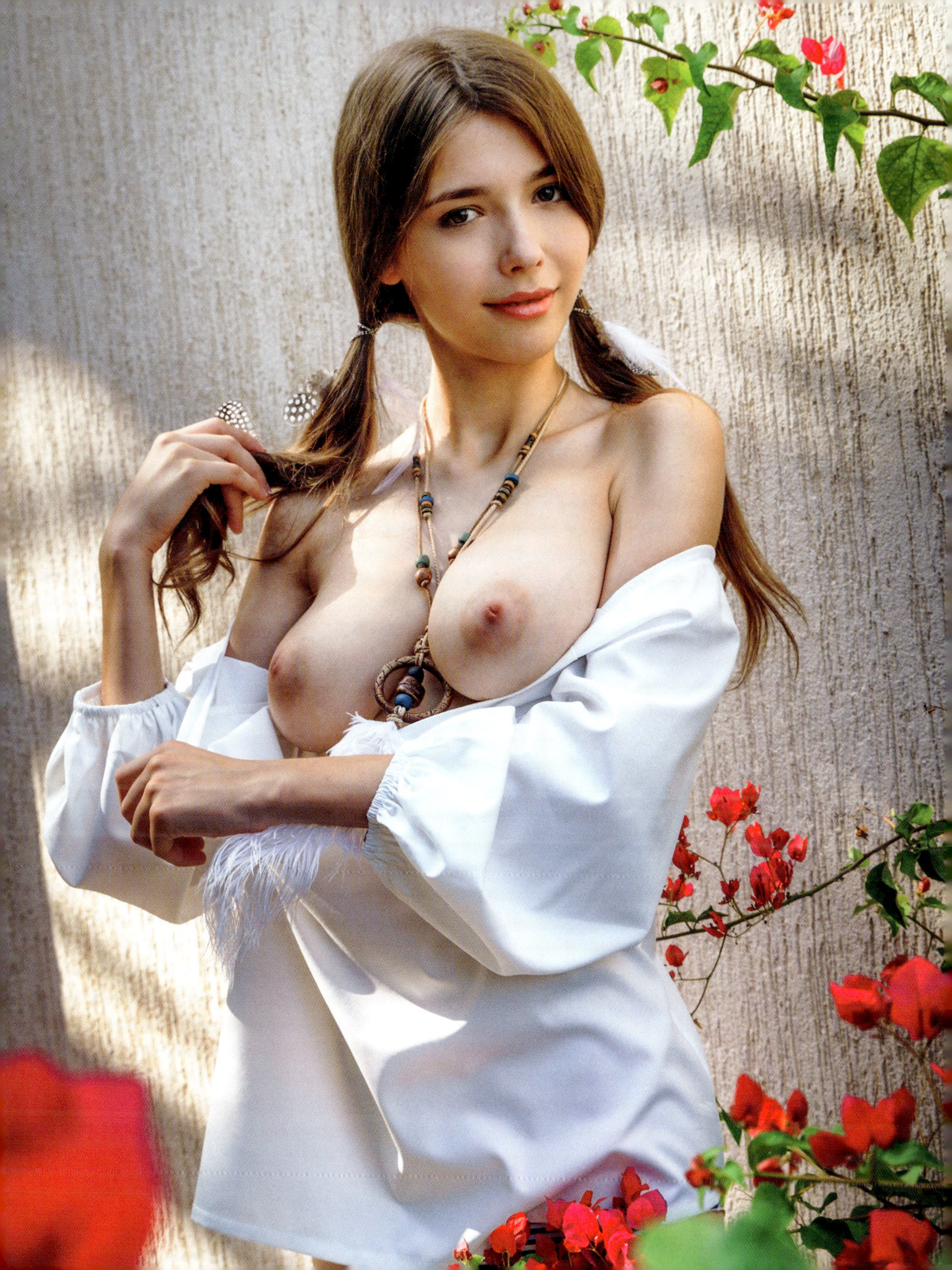

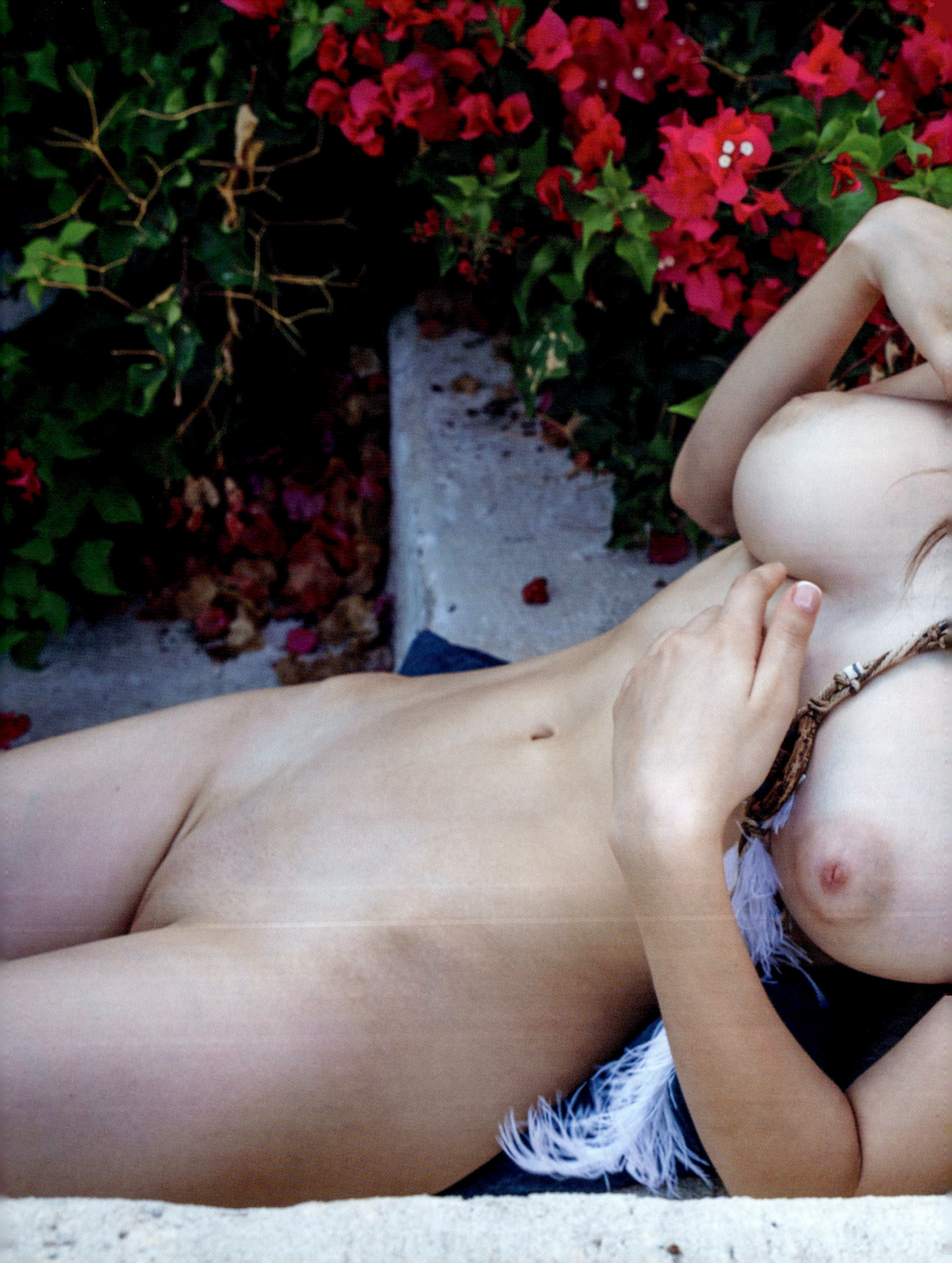

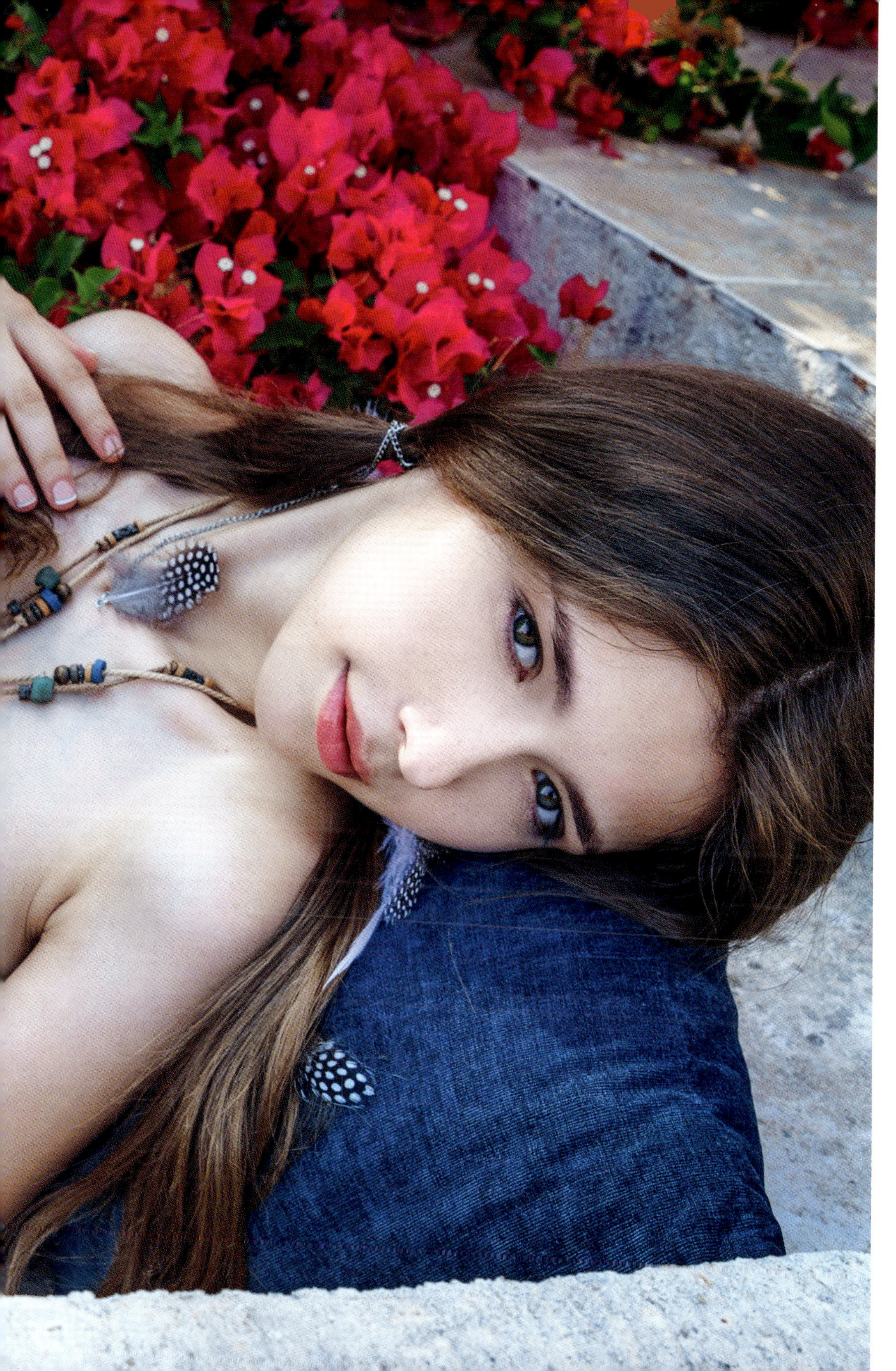

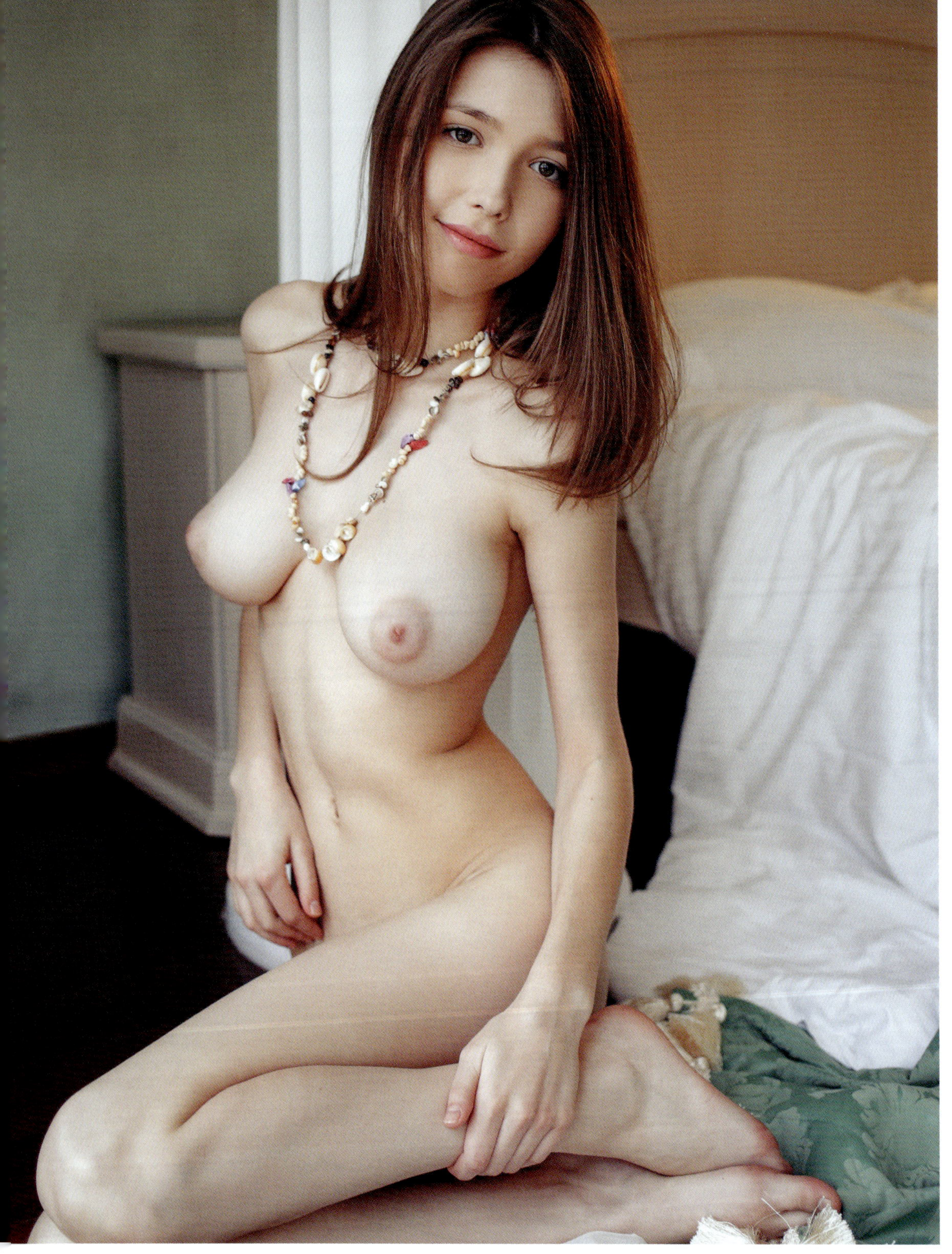

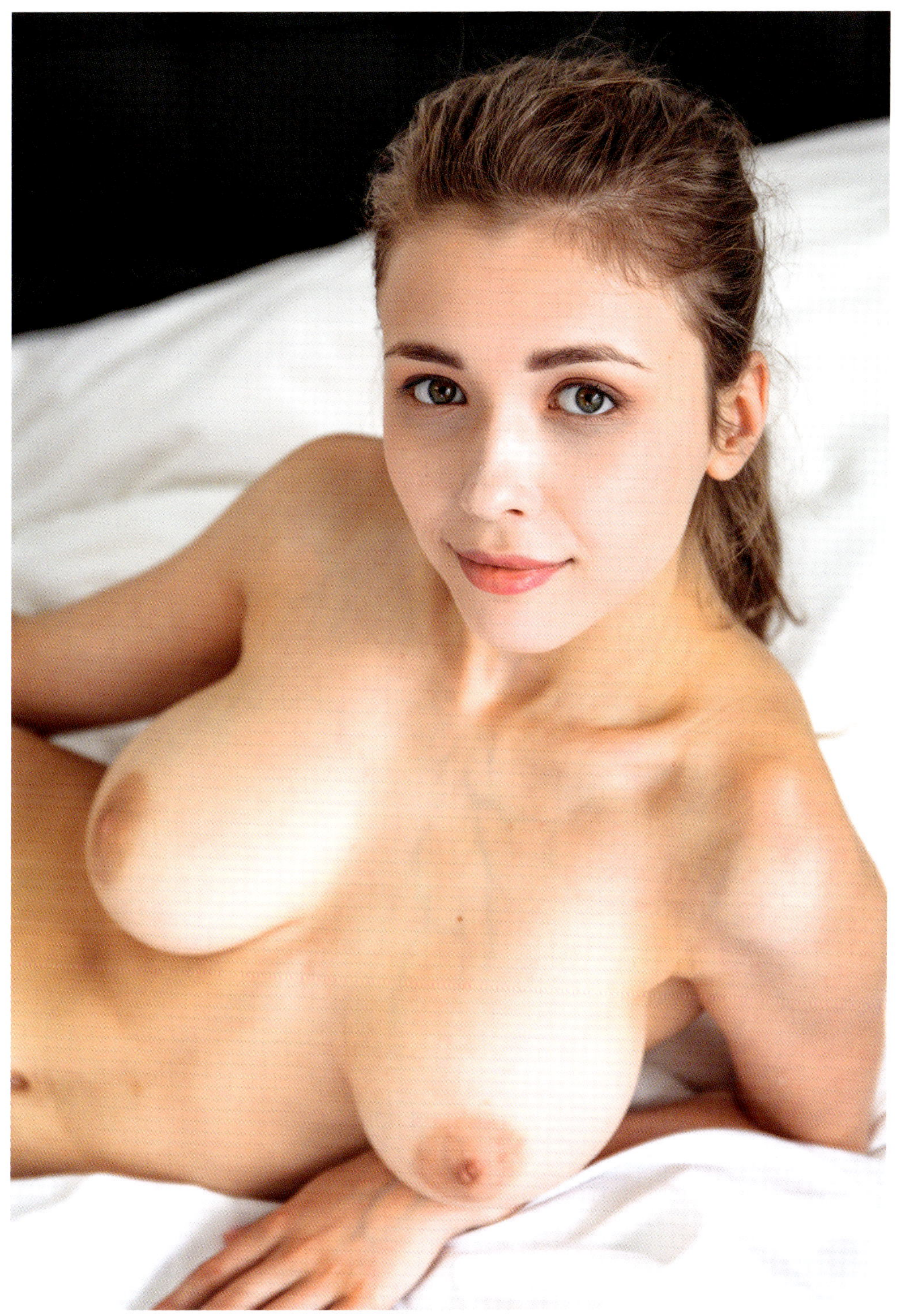

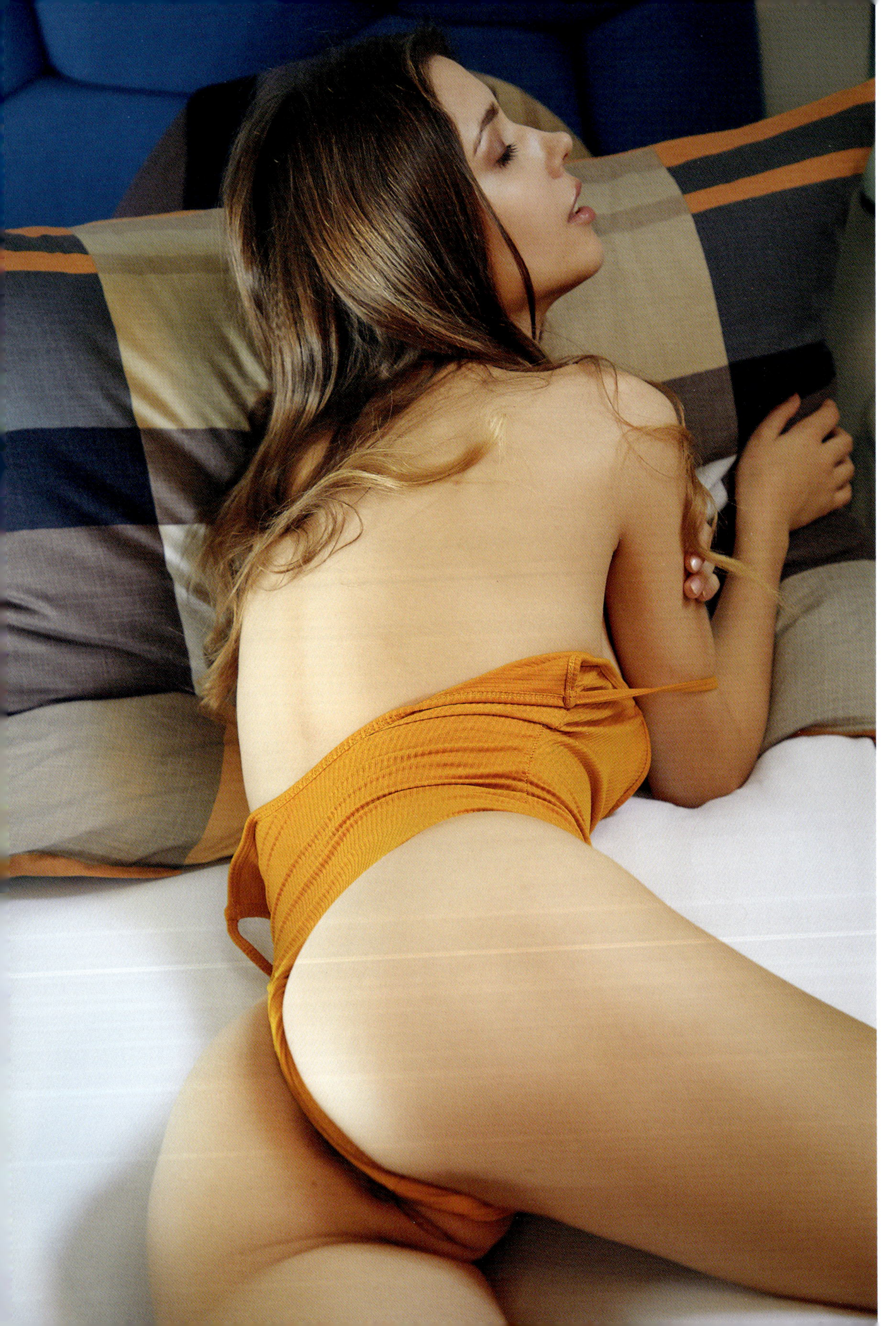

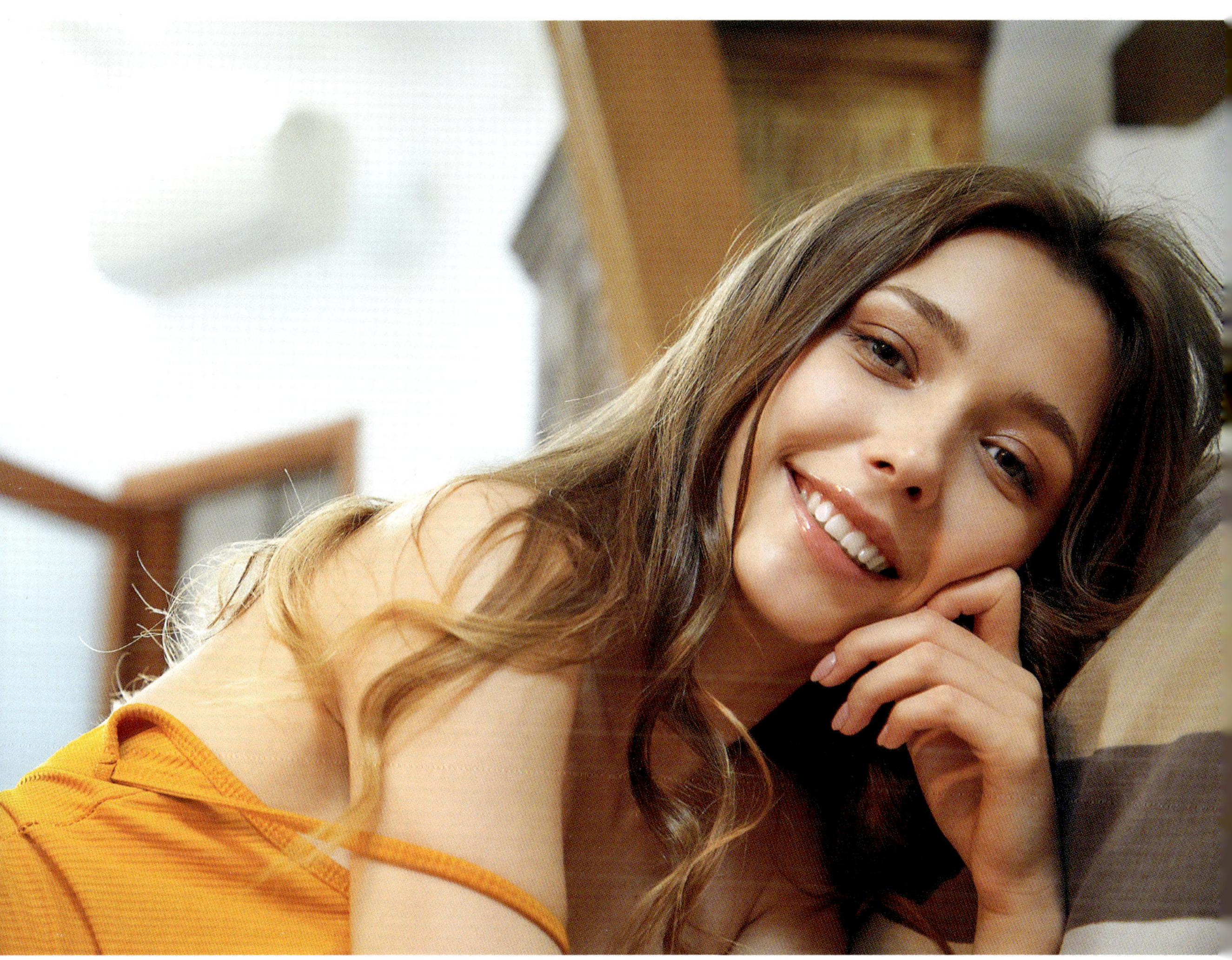

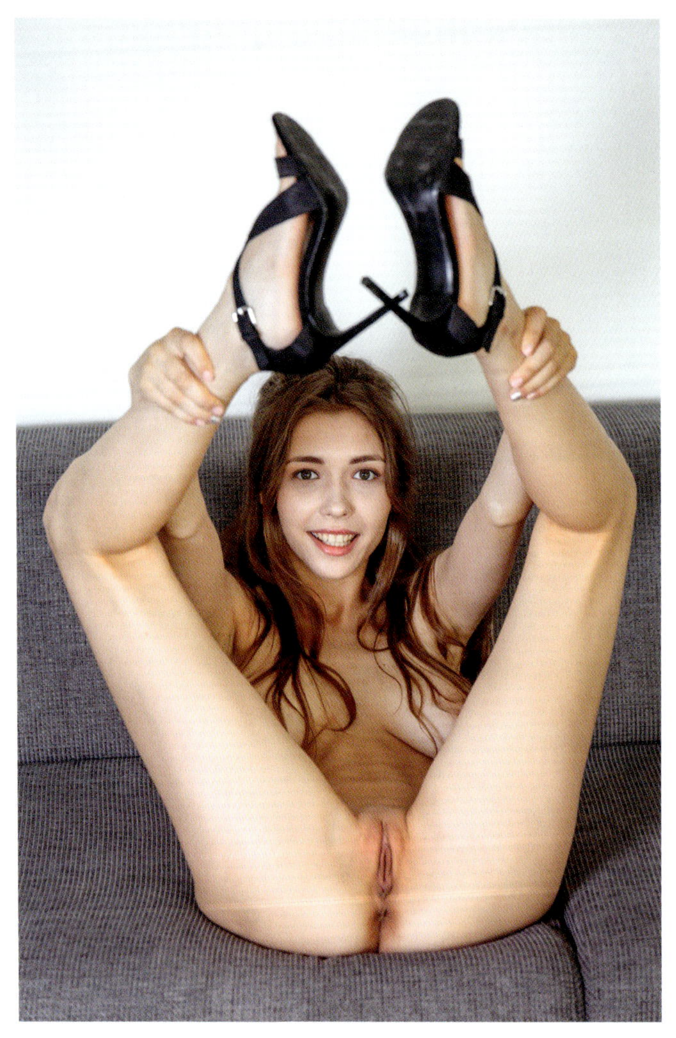

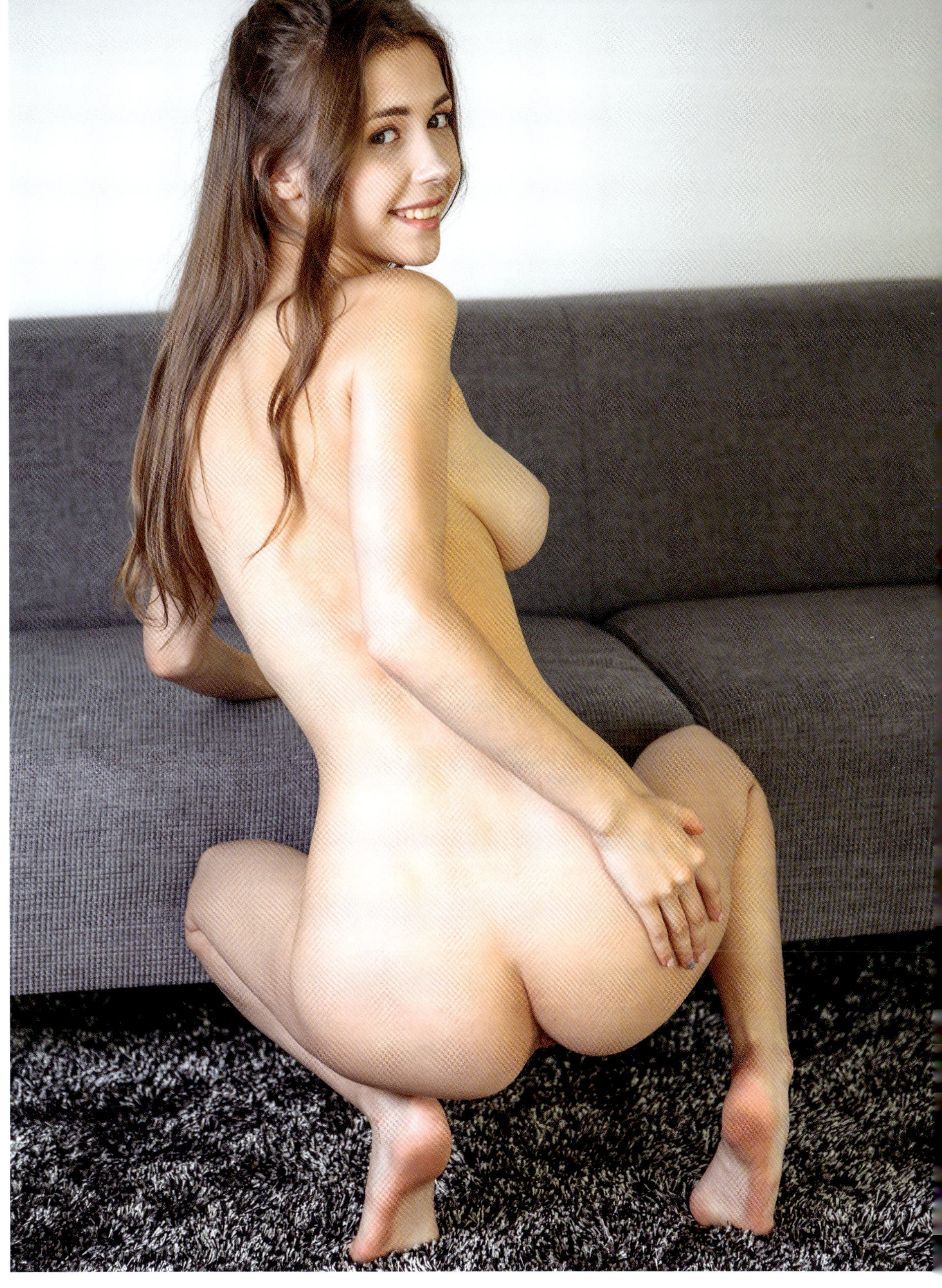

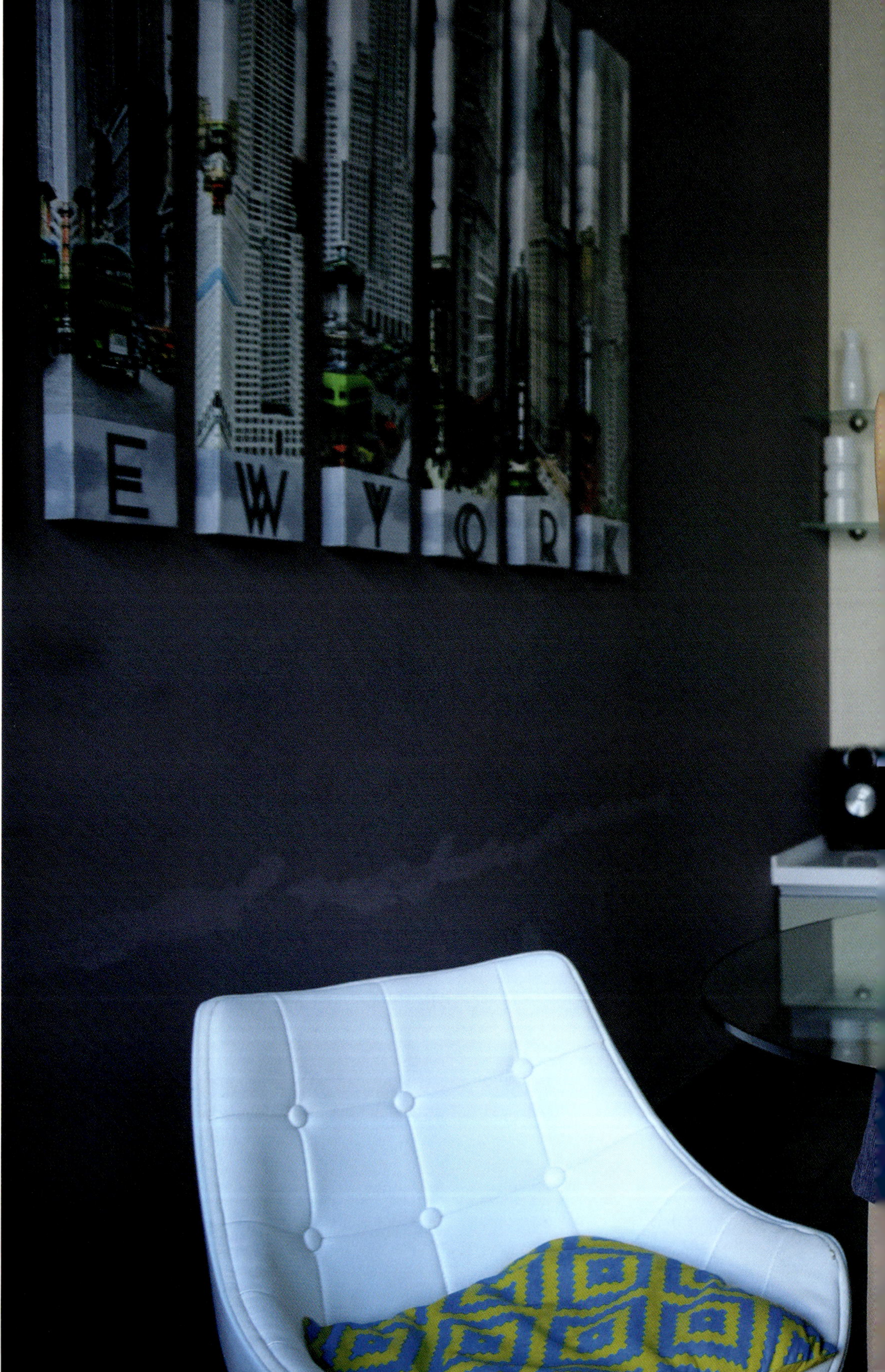
E W Y O R K

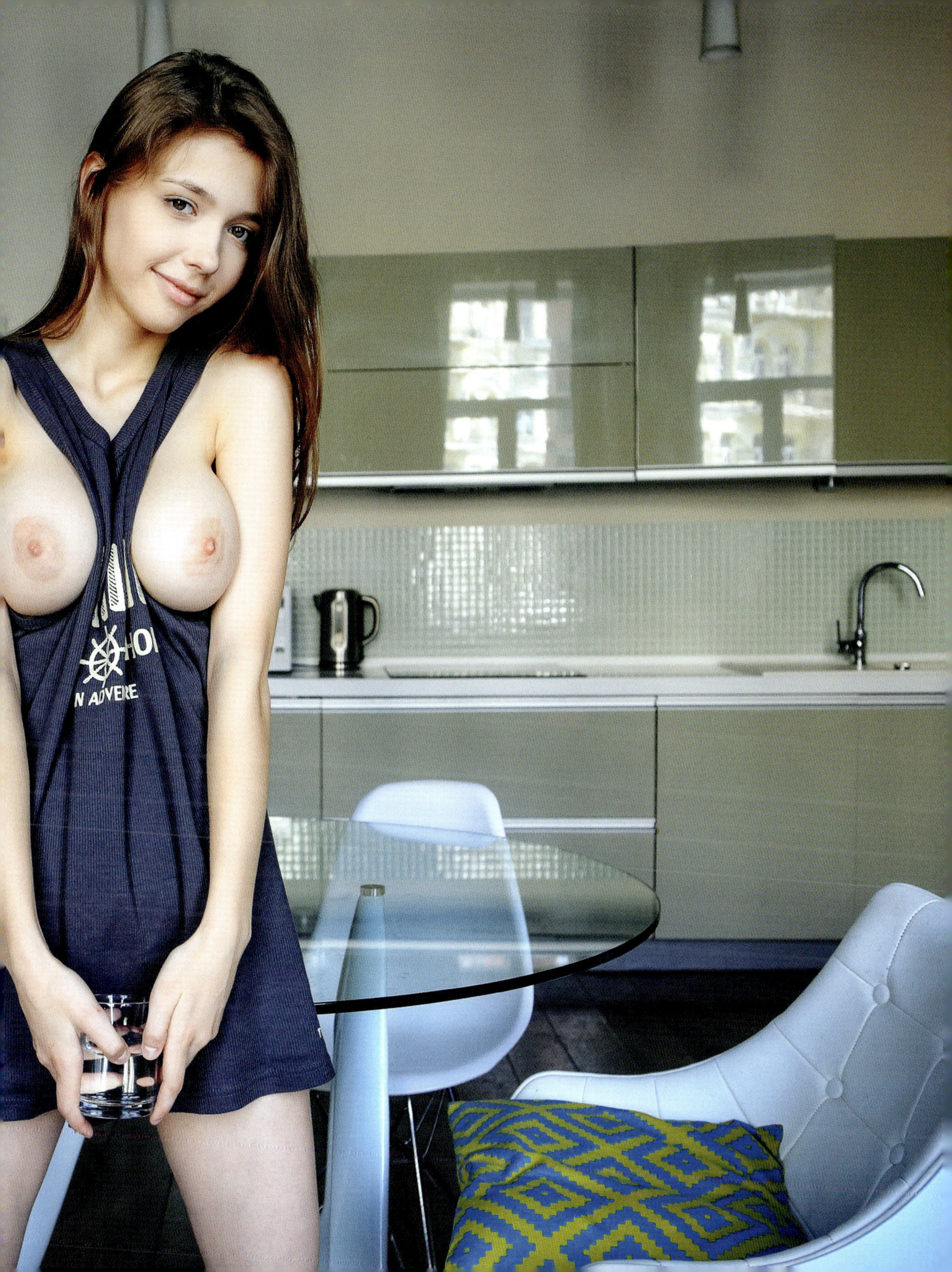

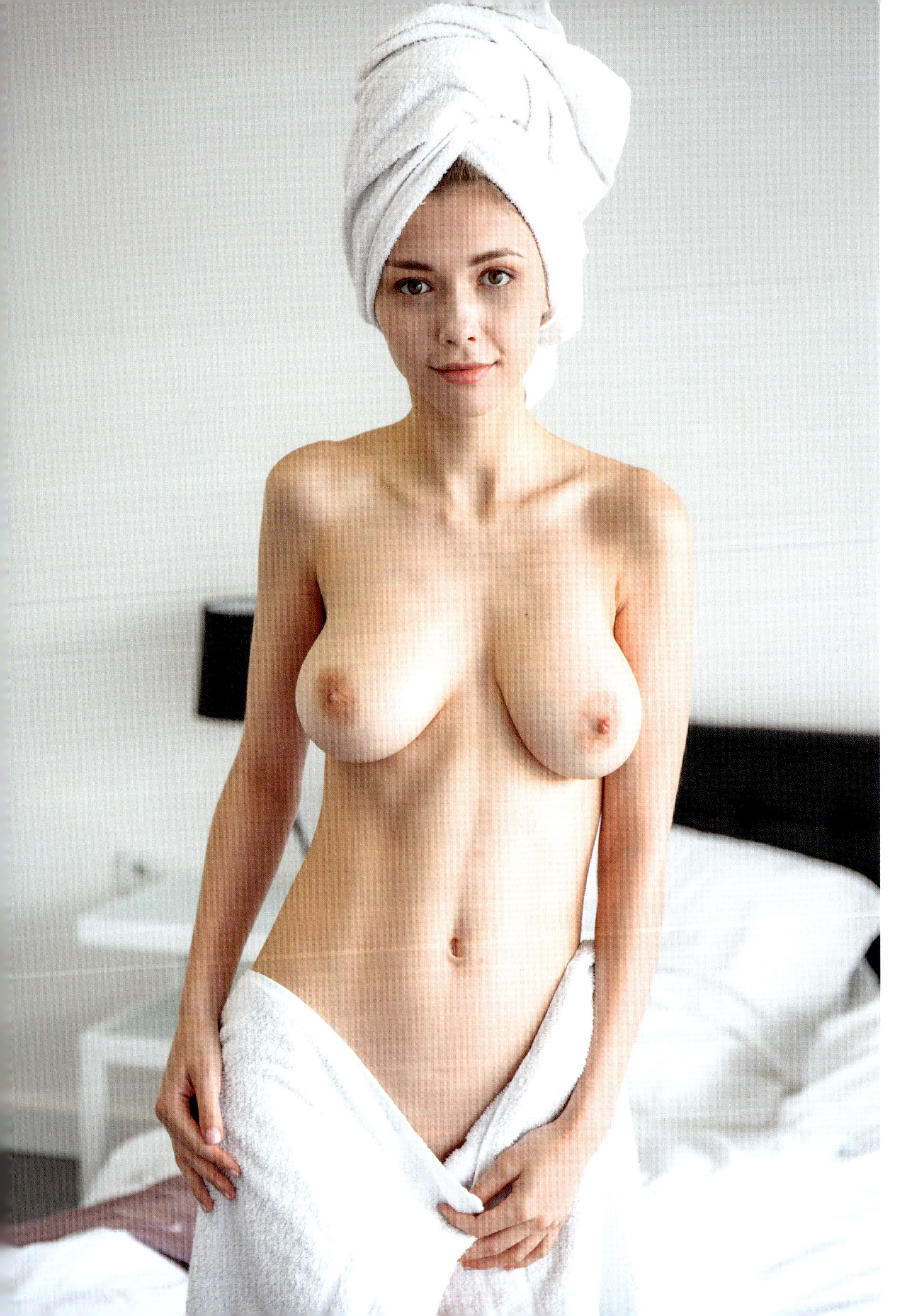

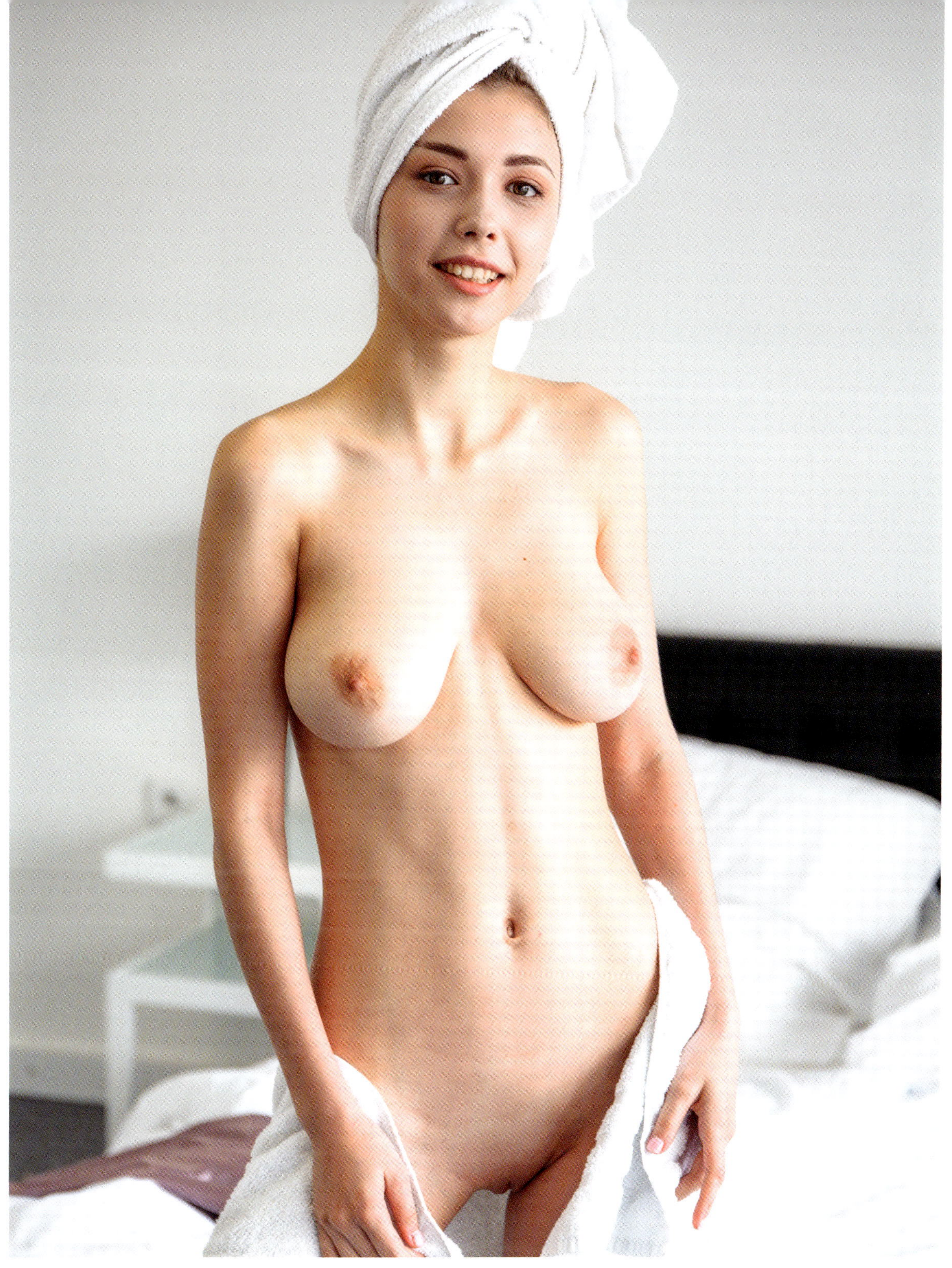

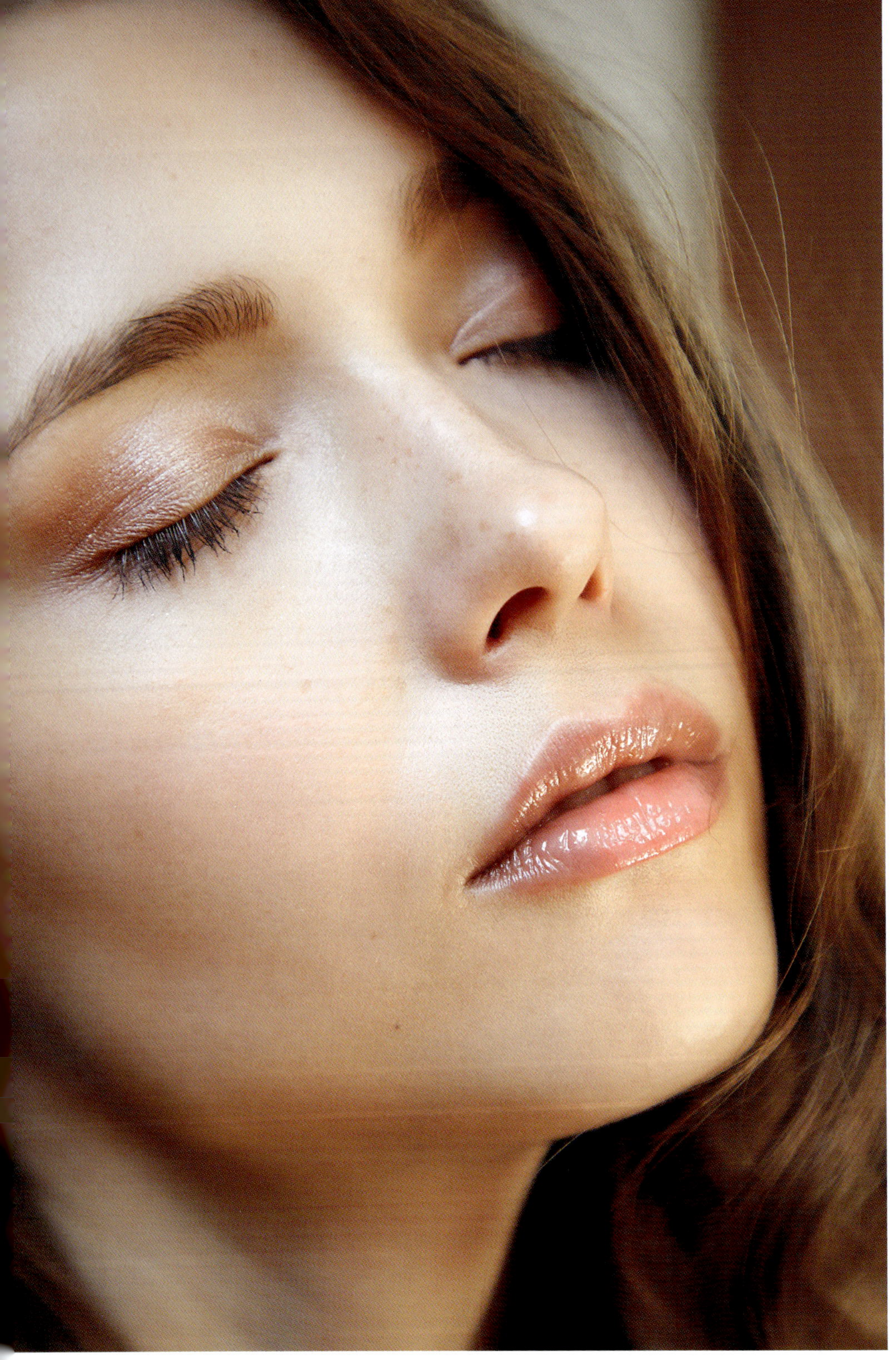

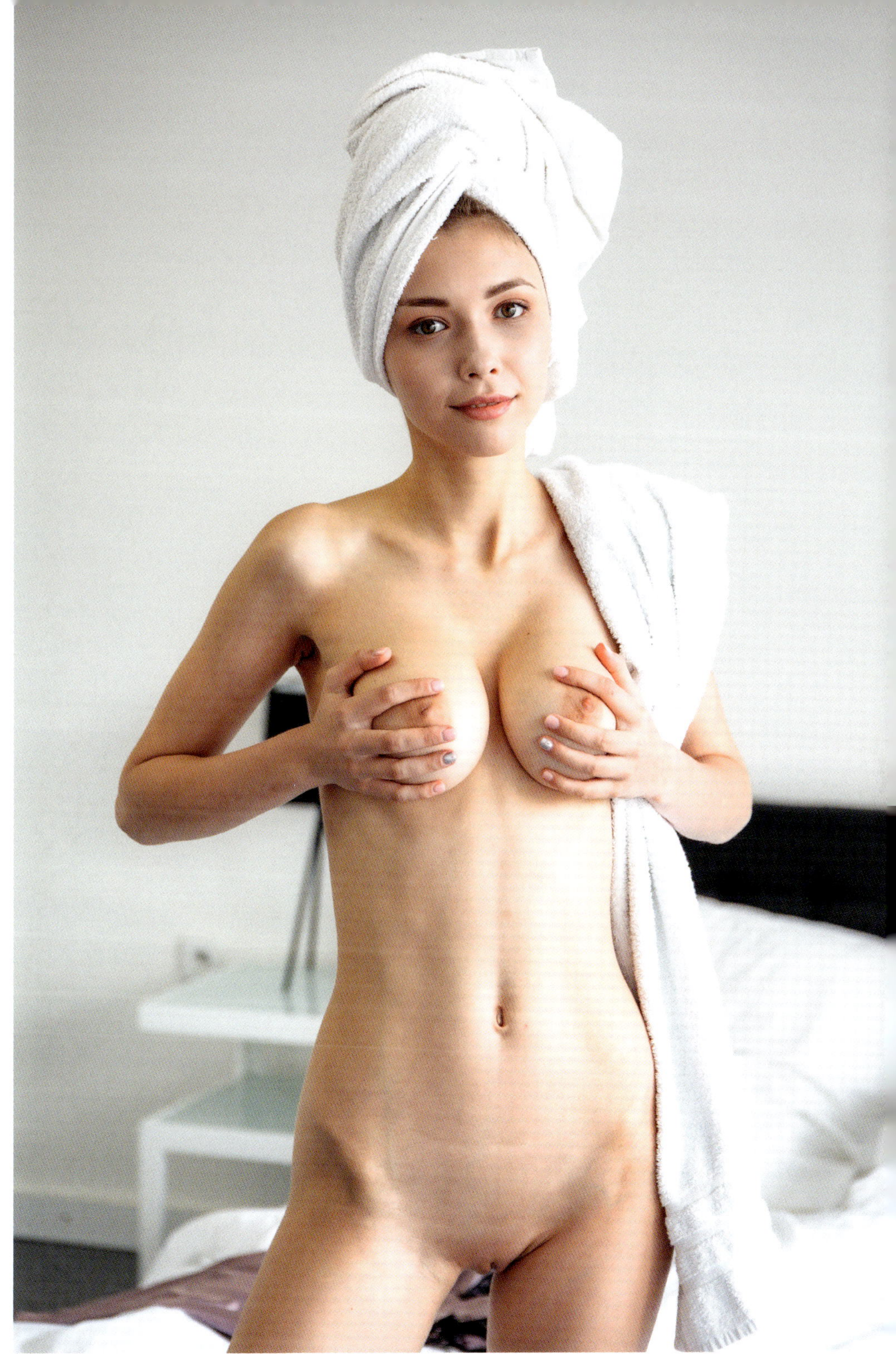

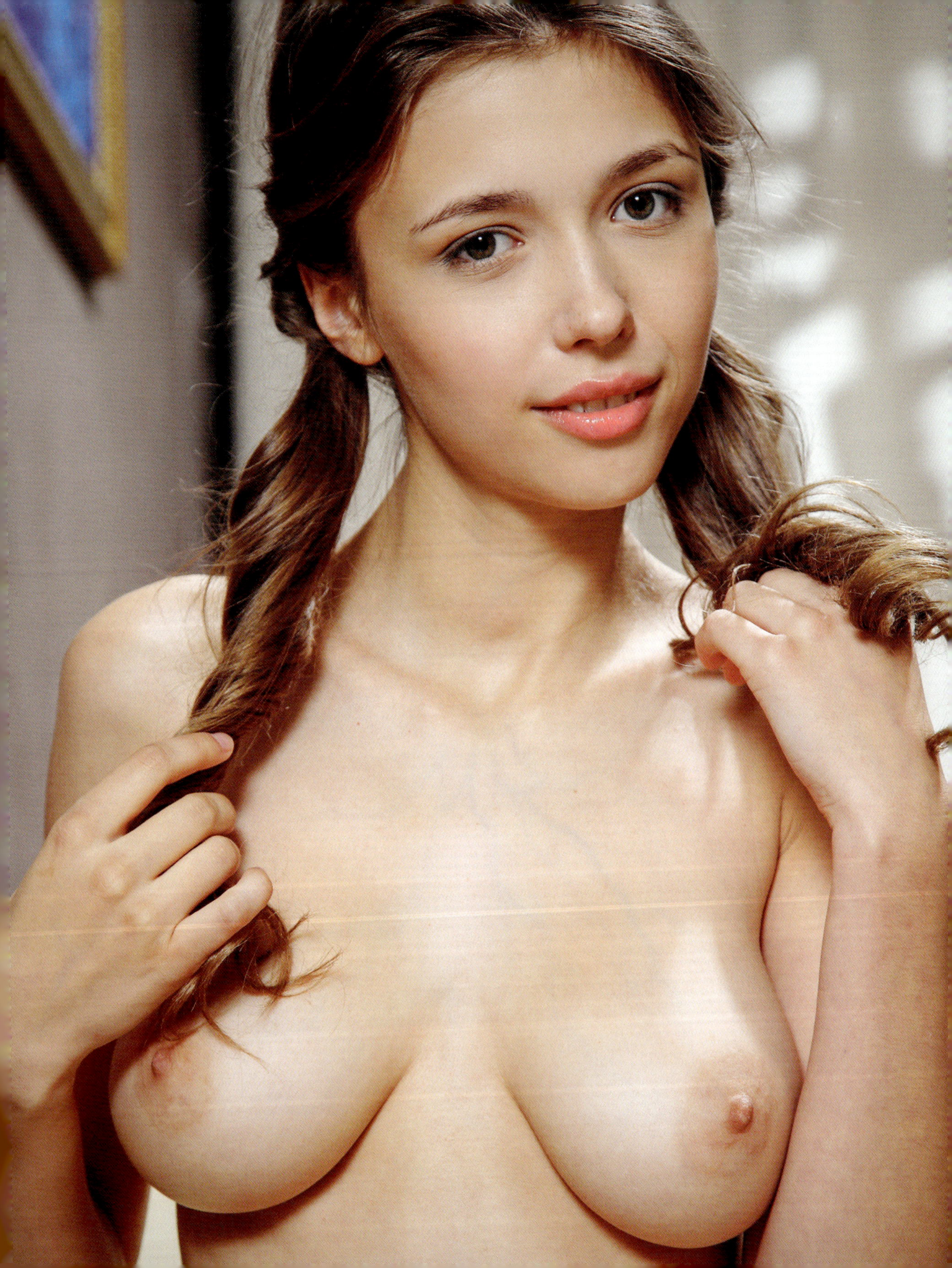

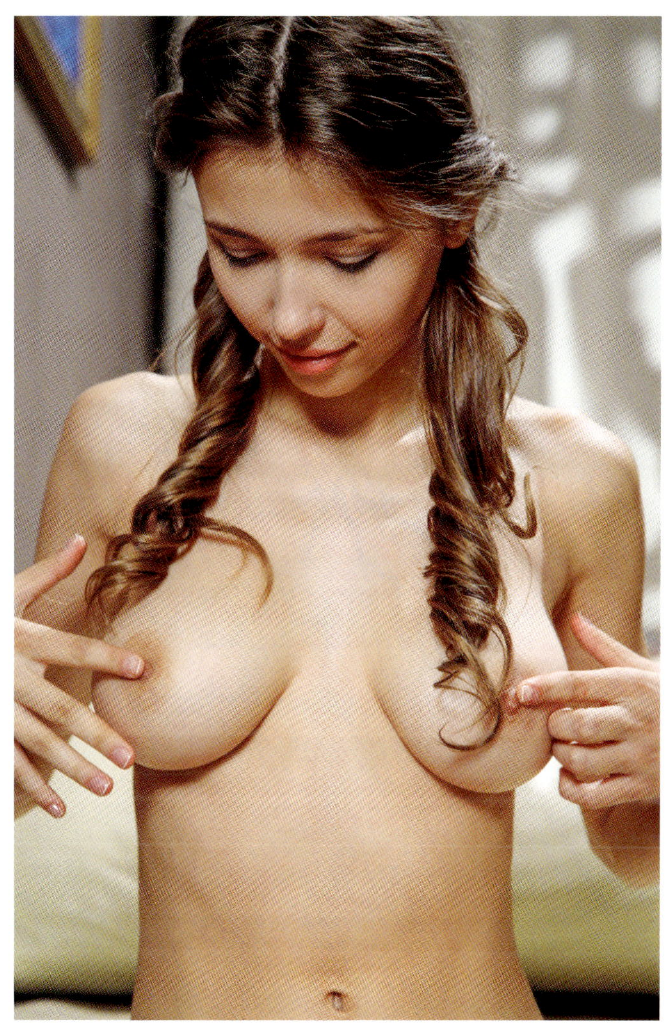

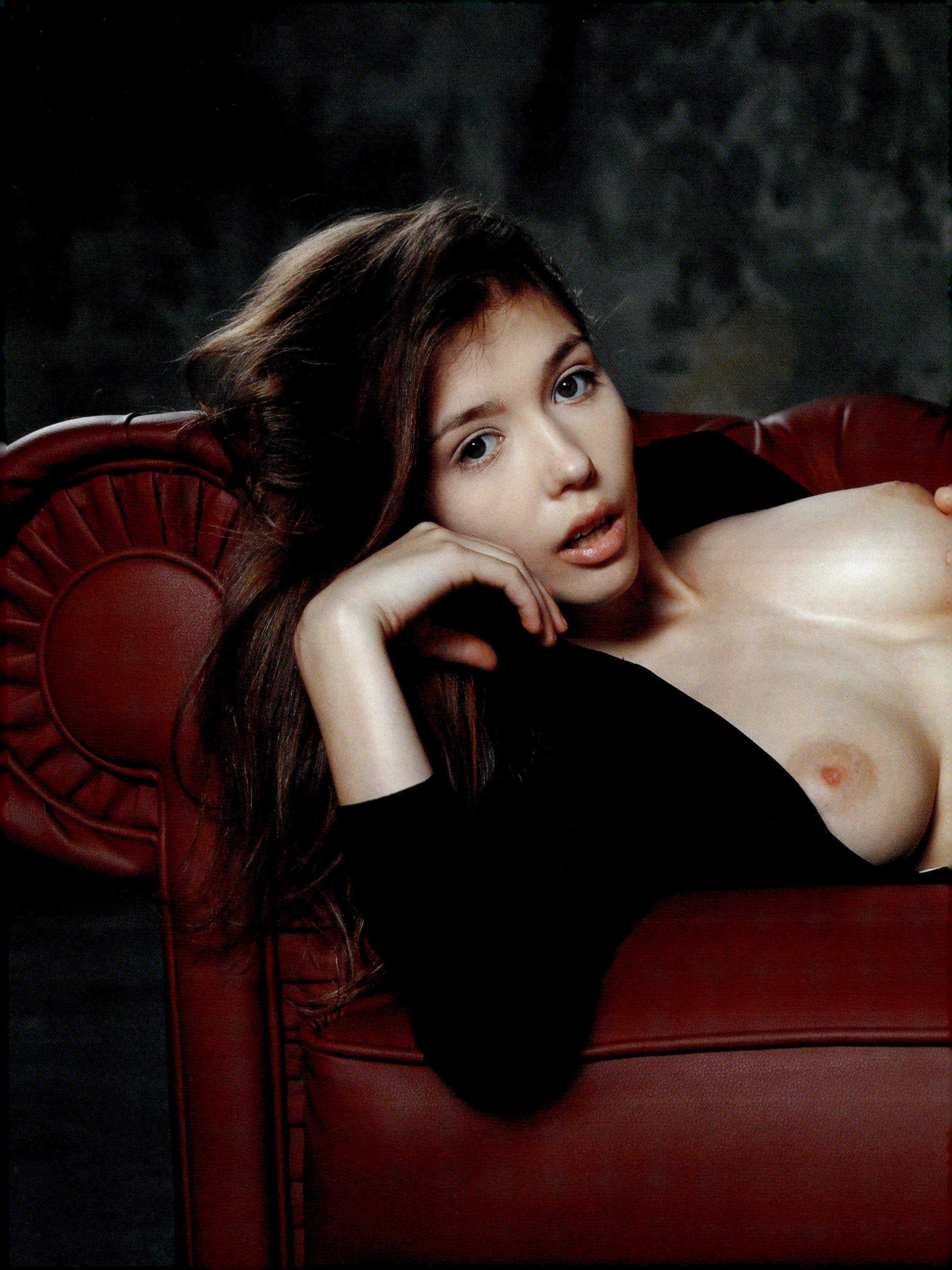

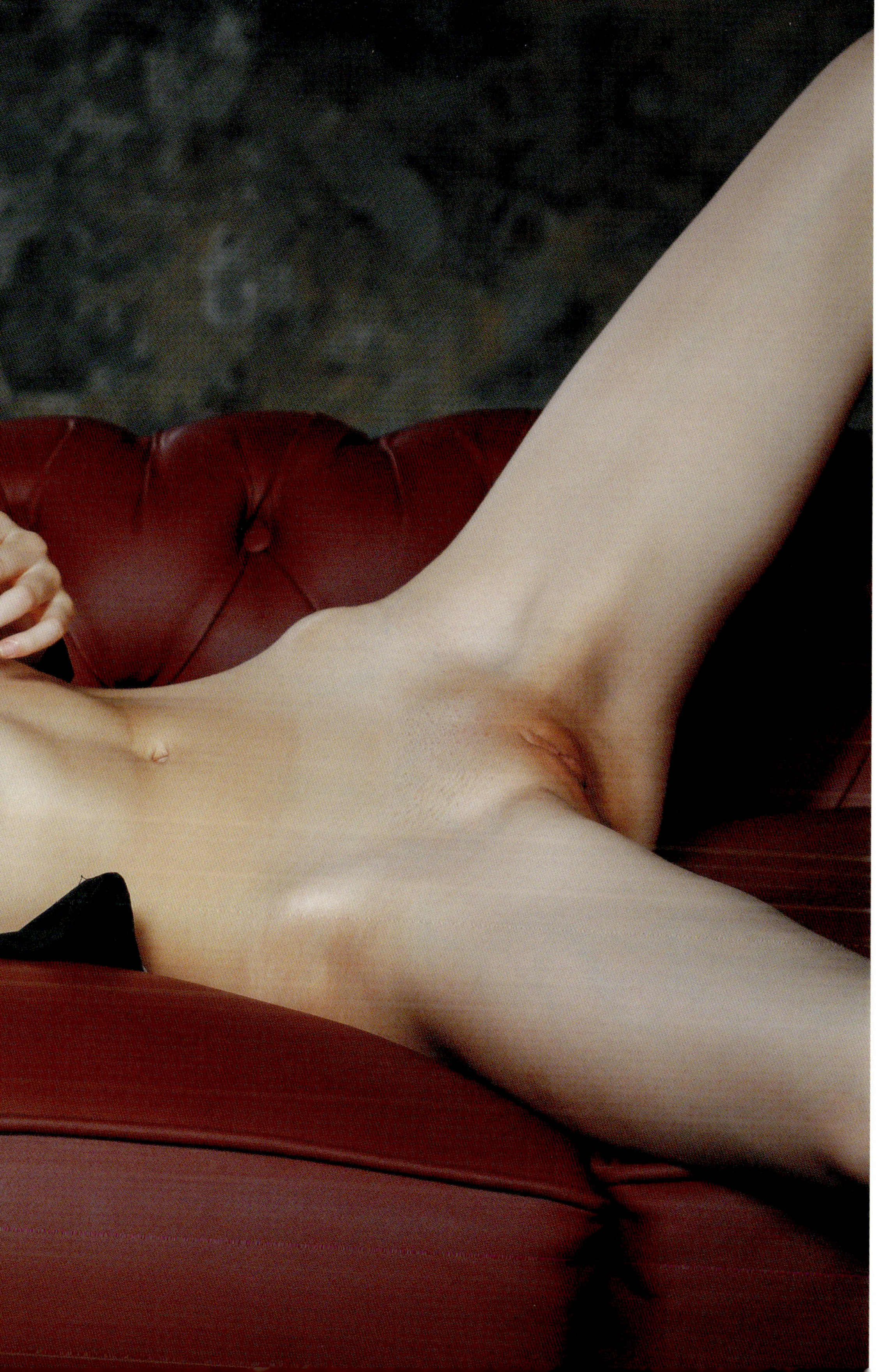

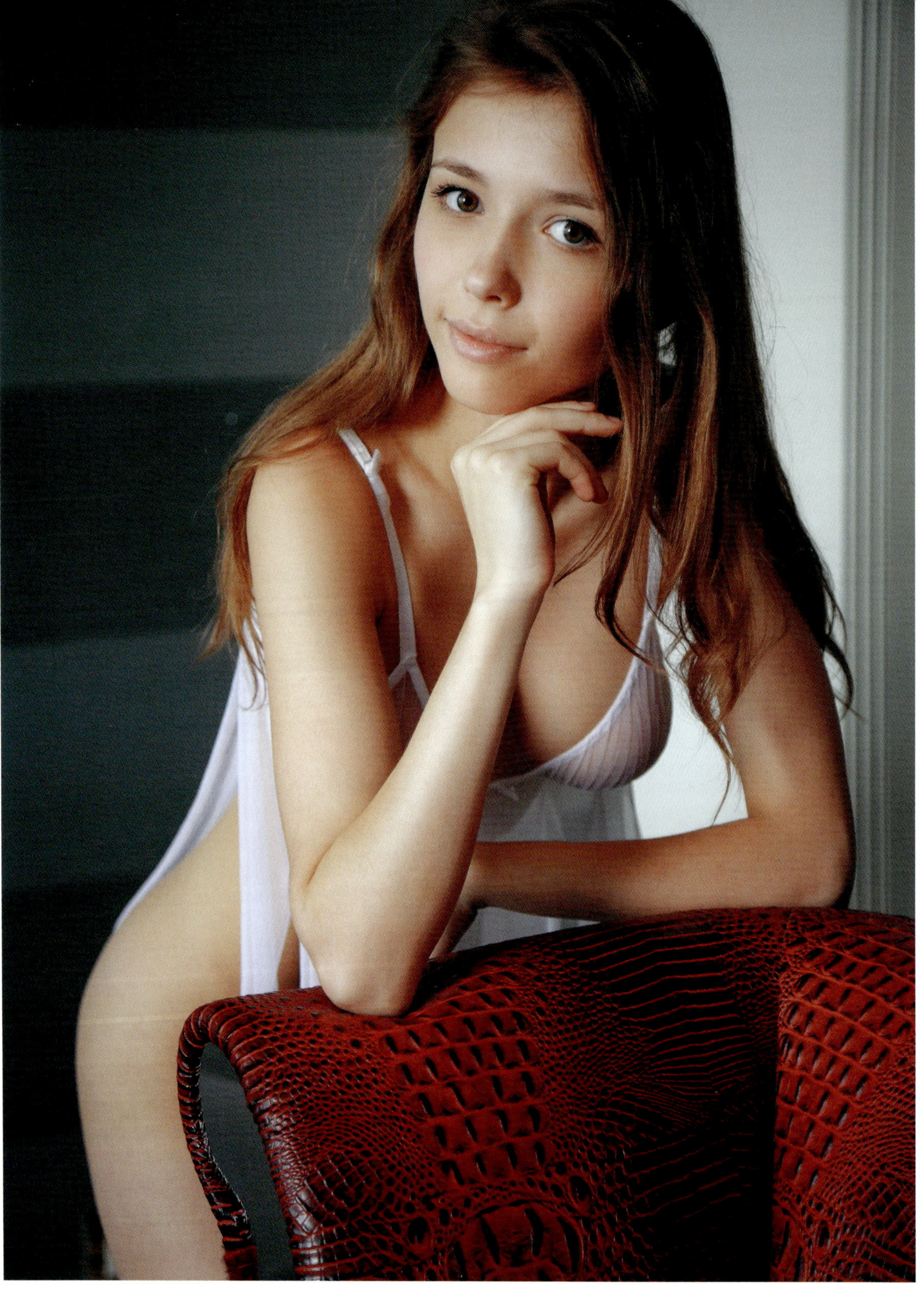

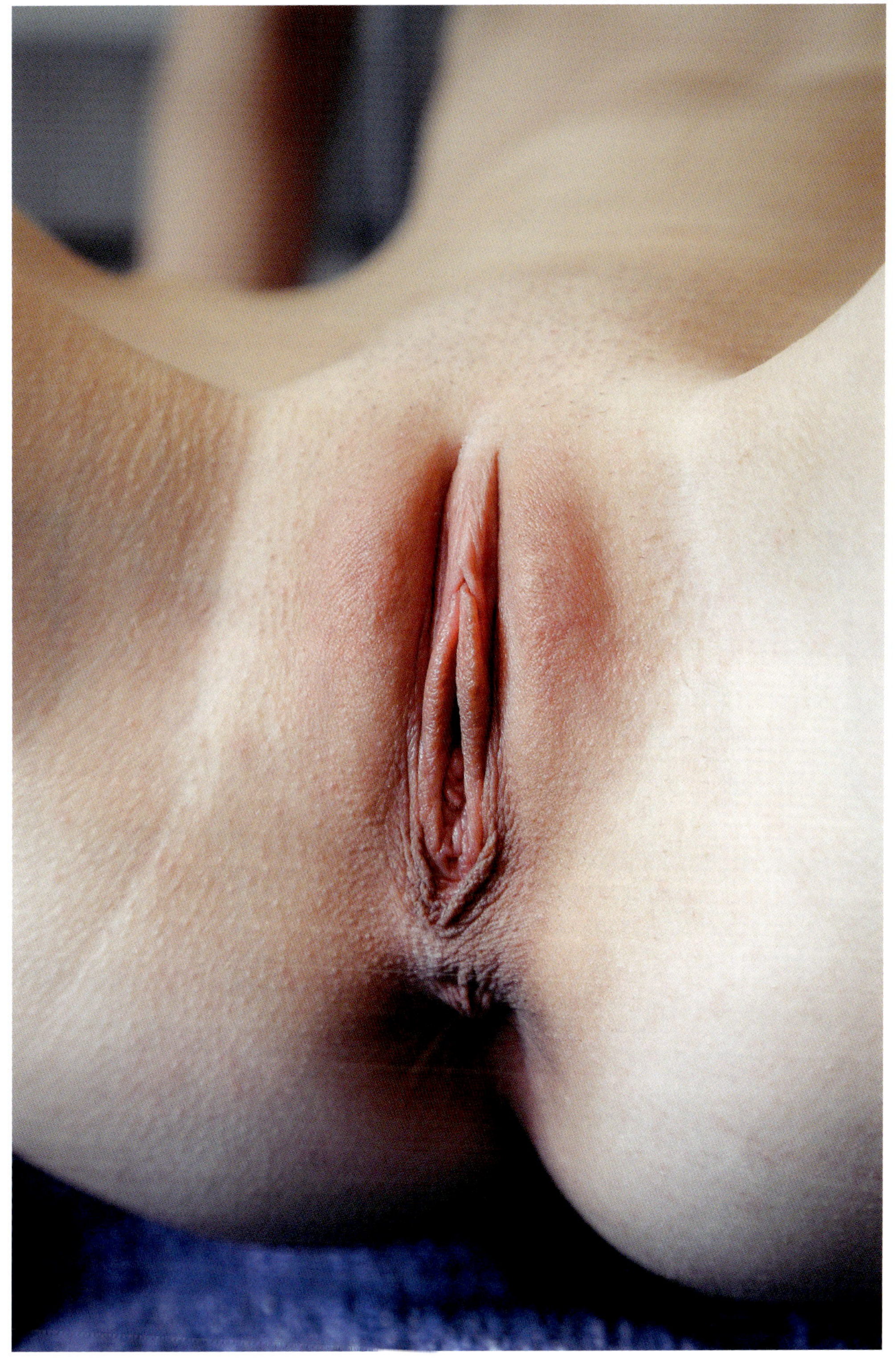

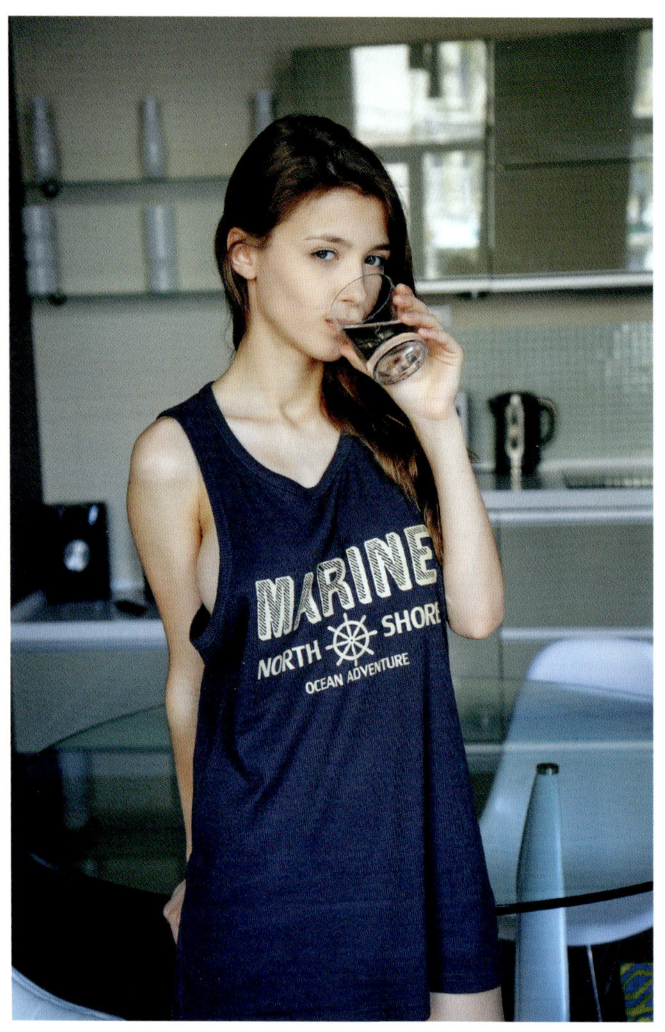
MARINE
NORTH SHORE
OCEAN ADVENTURE

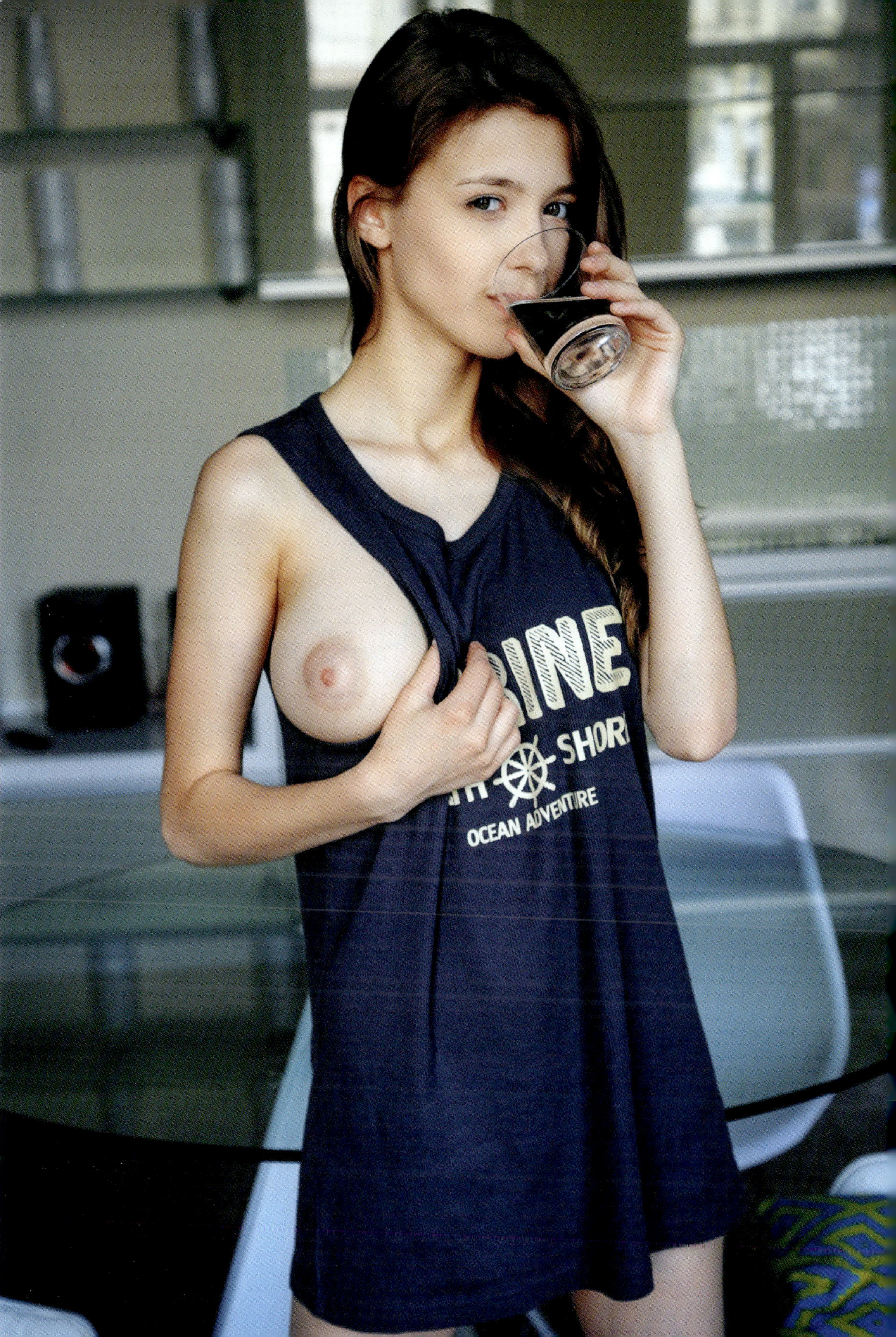
OCEAN ADVENTURE

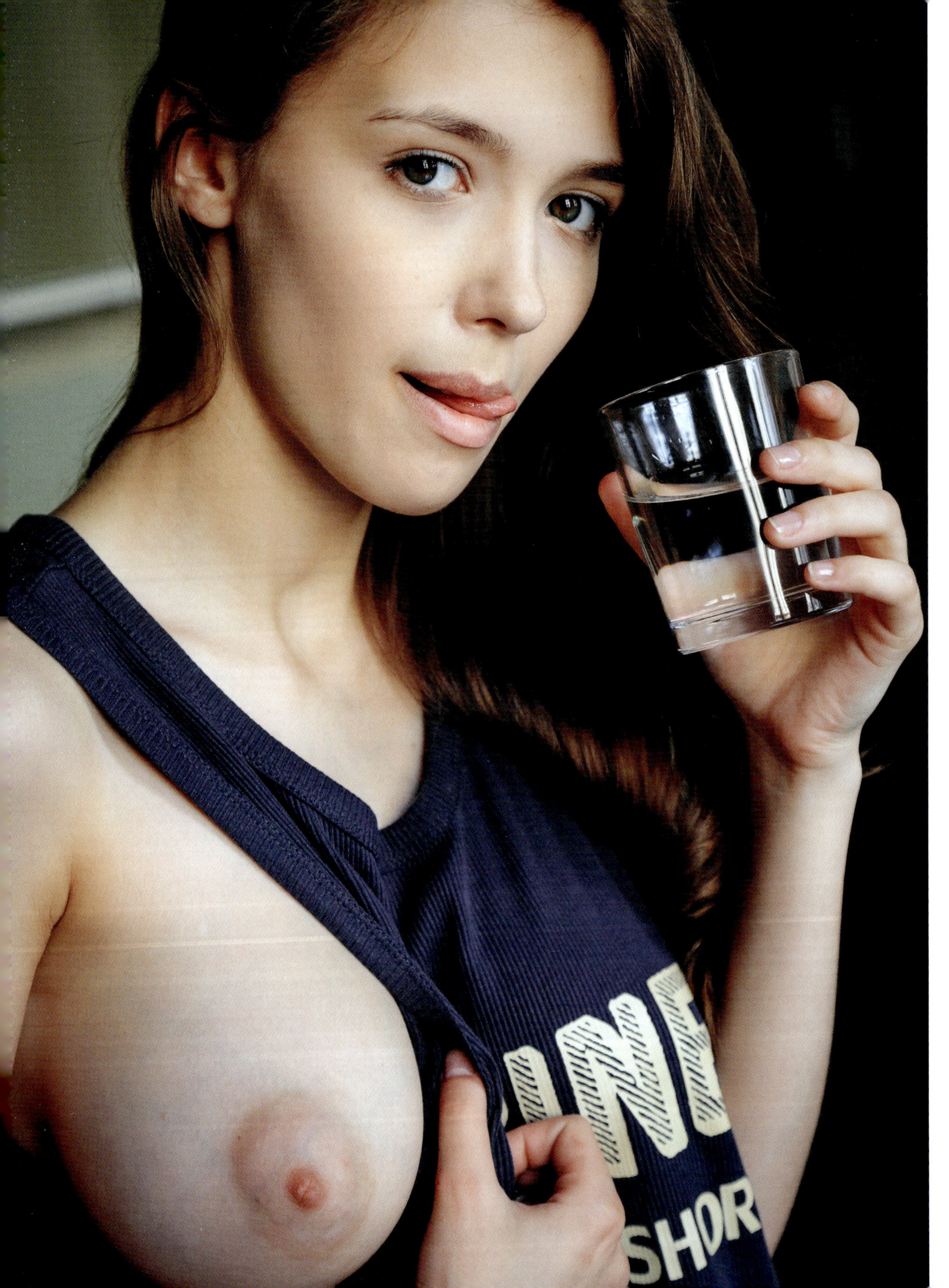

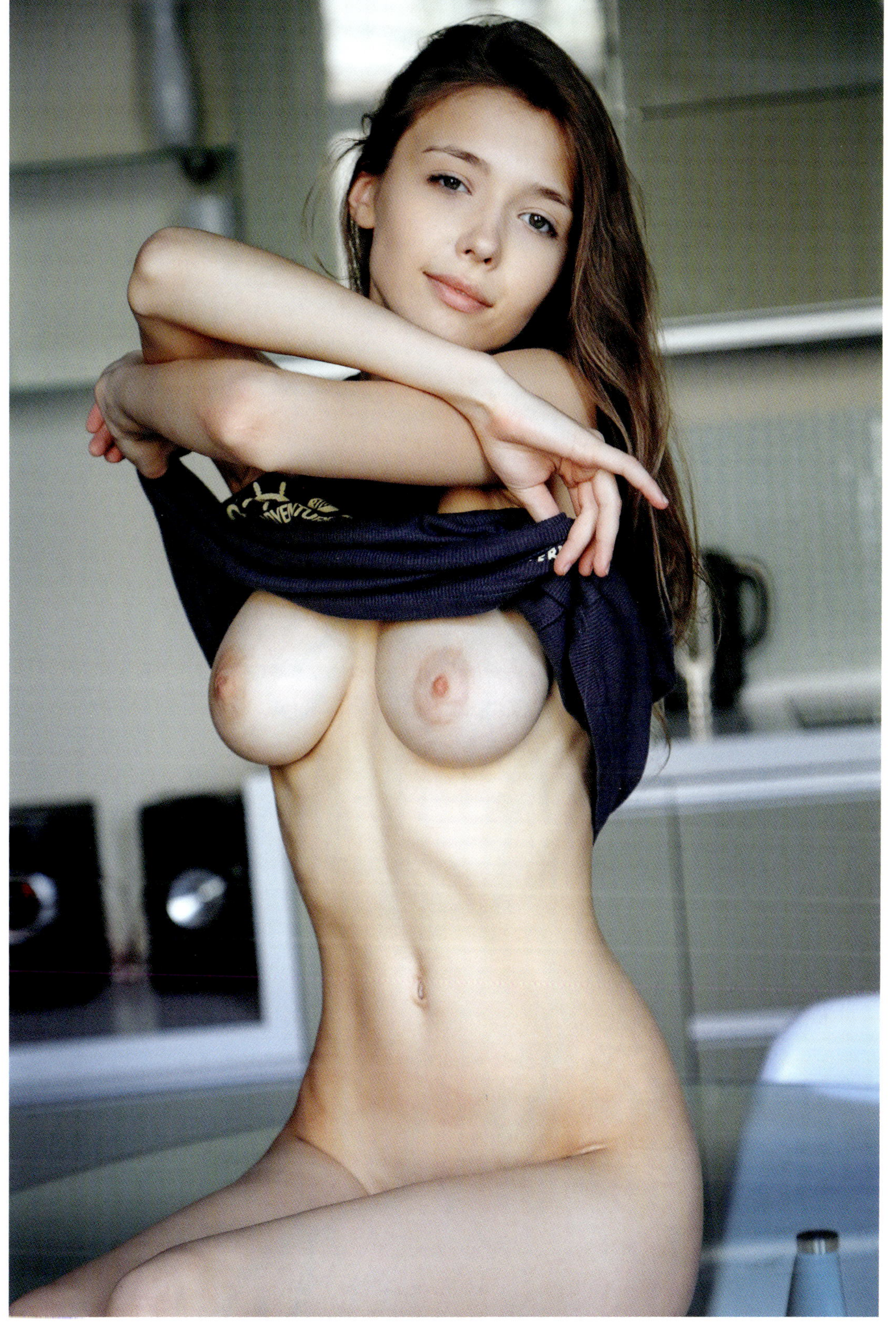

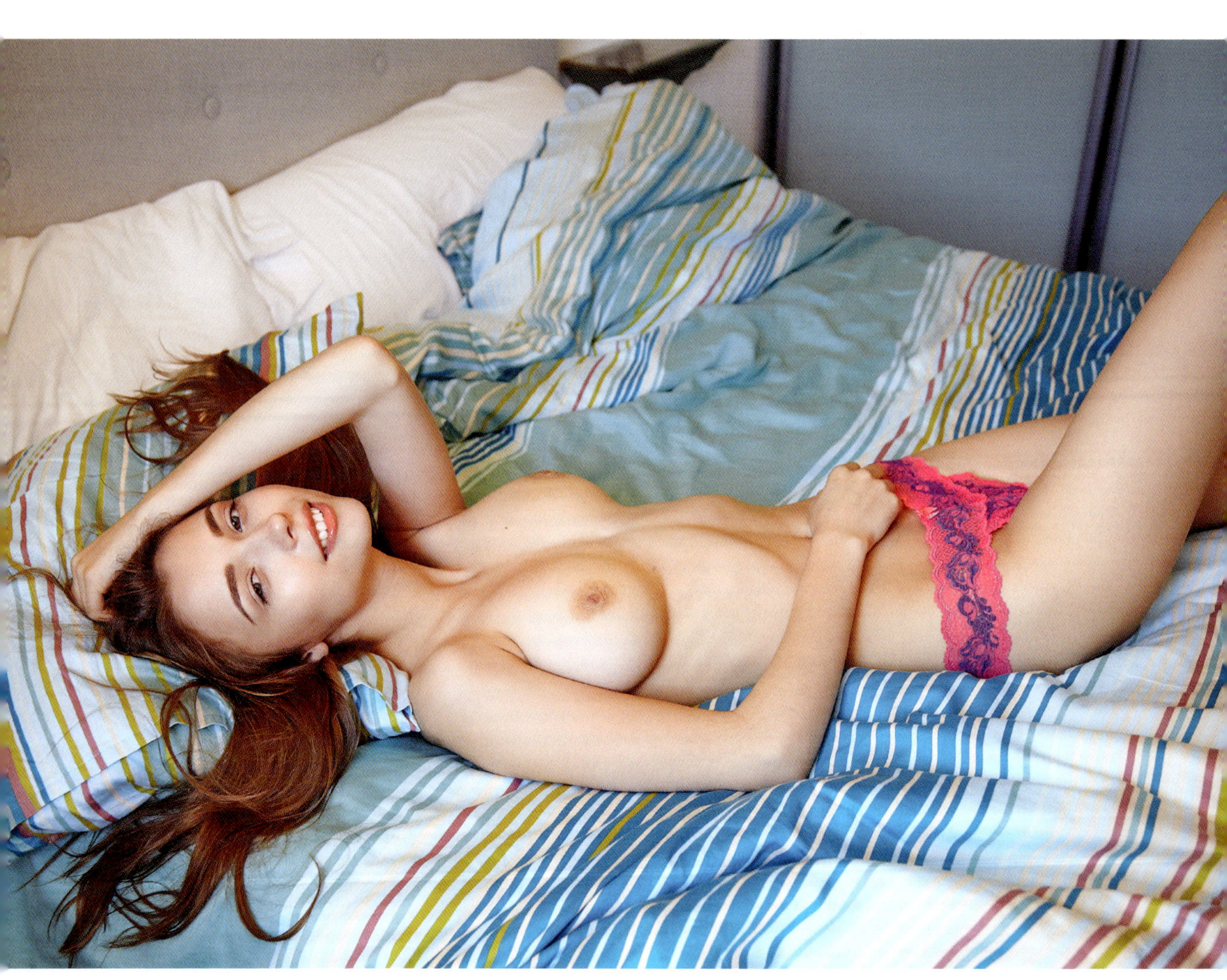

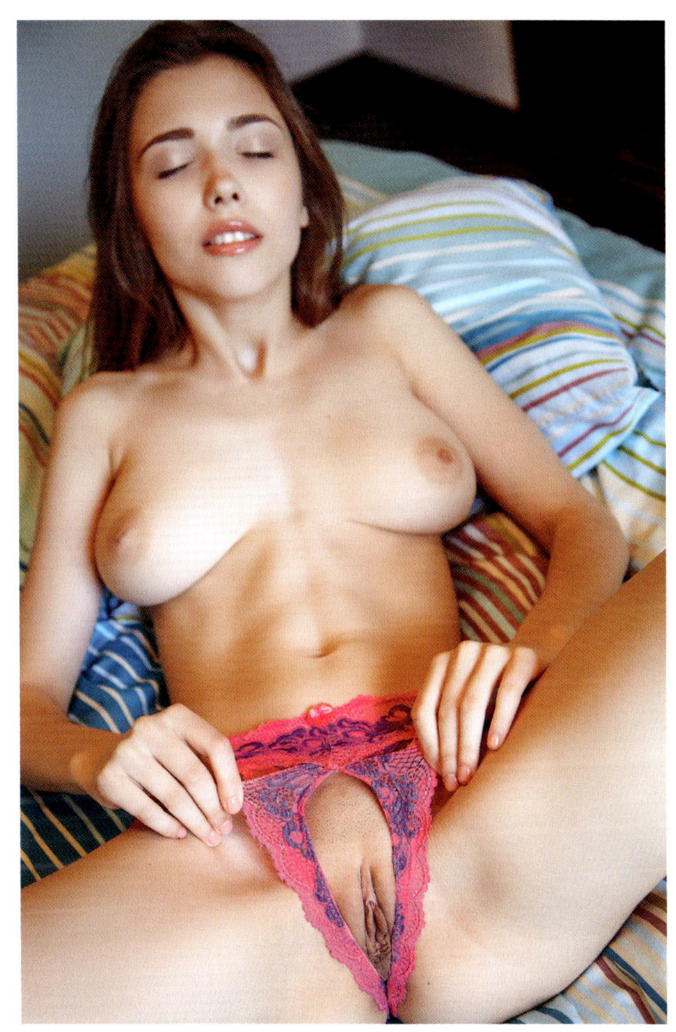

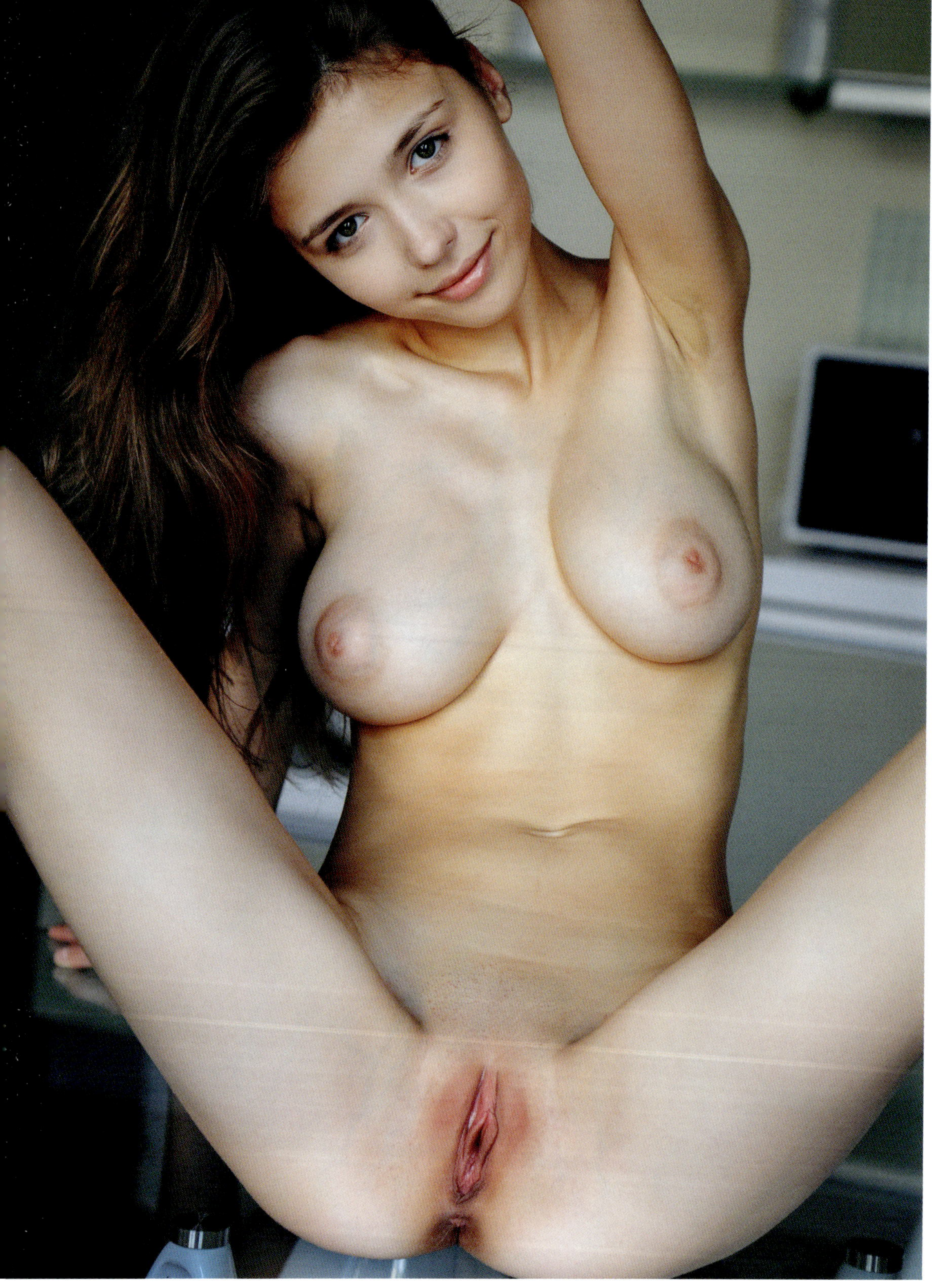

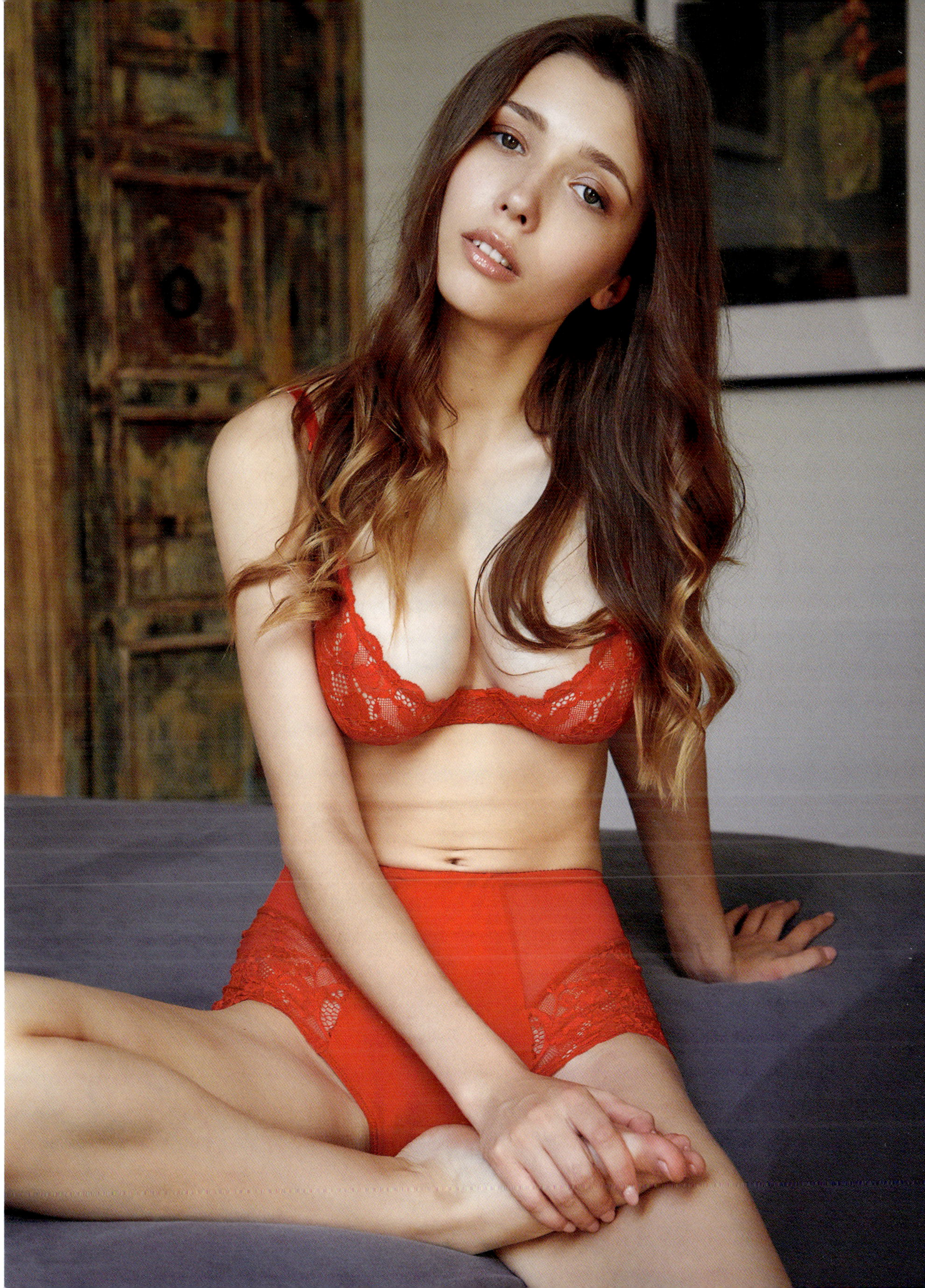

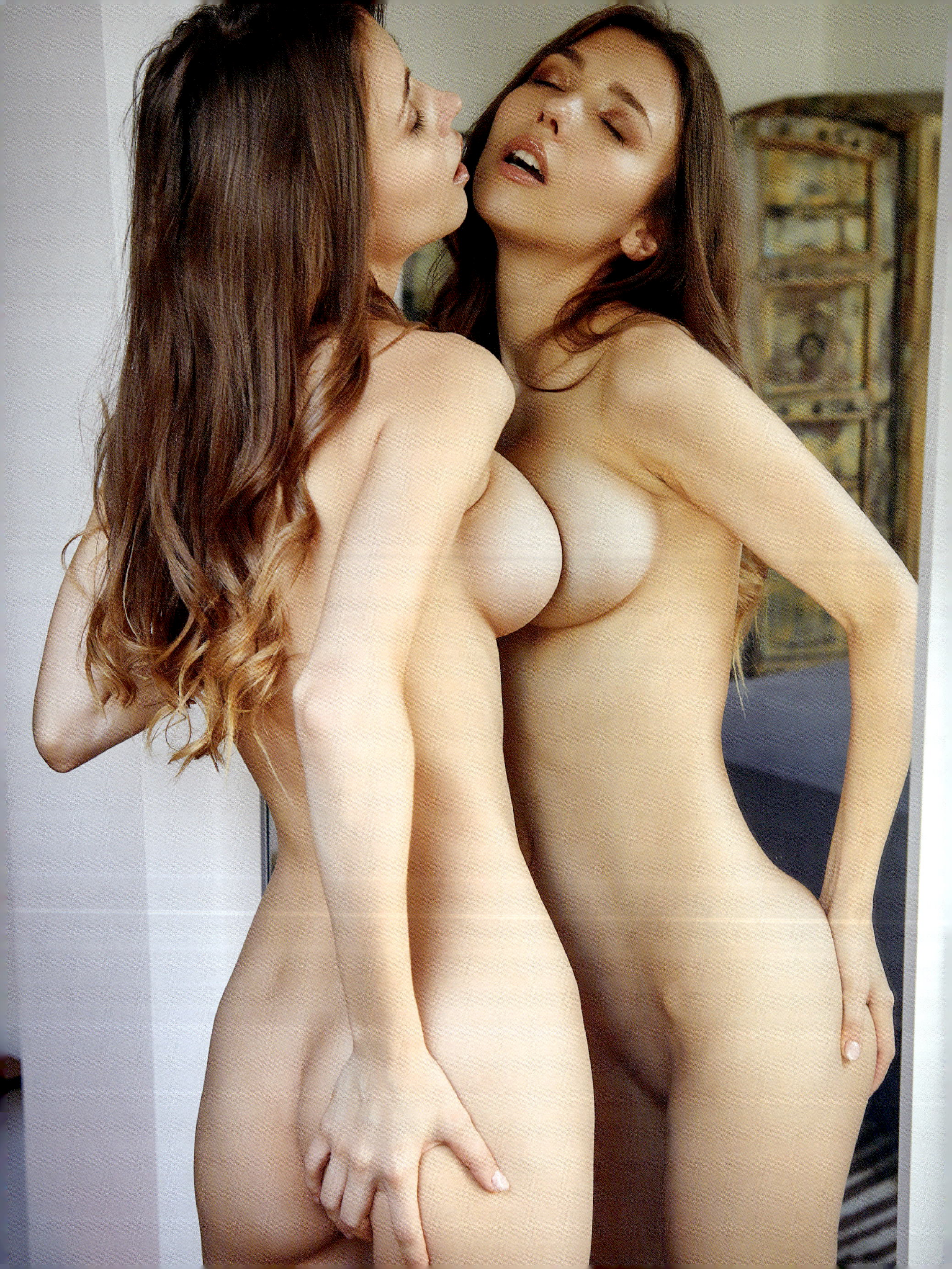

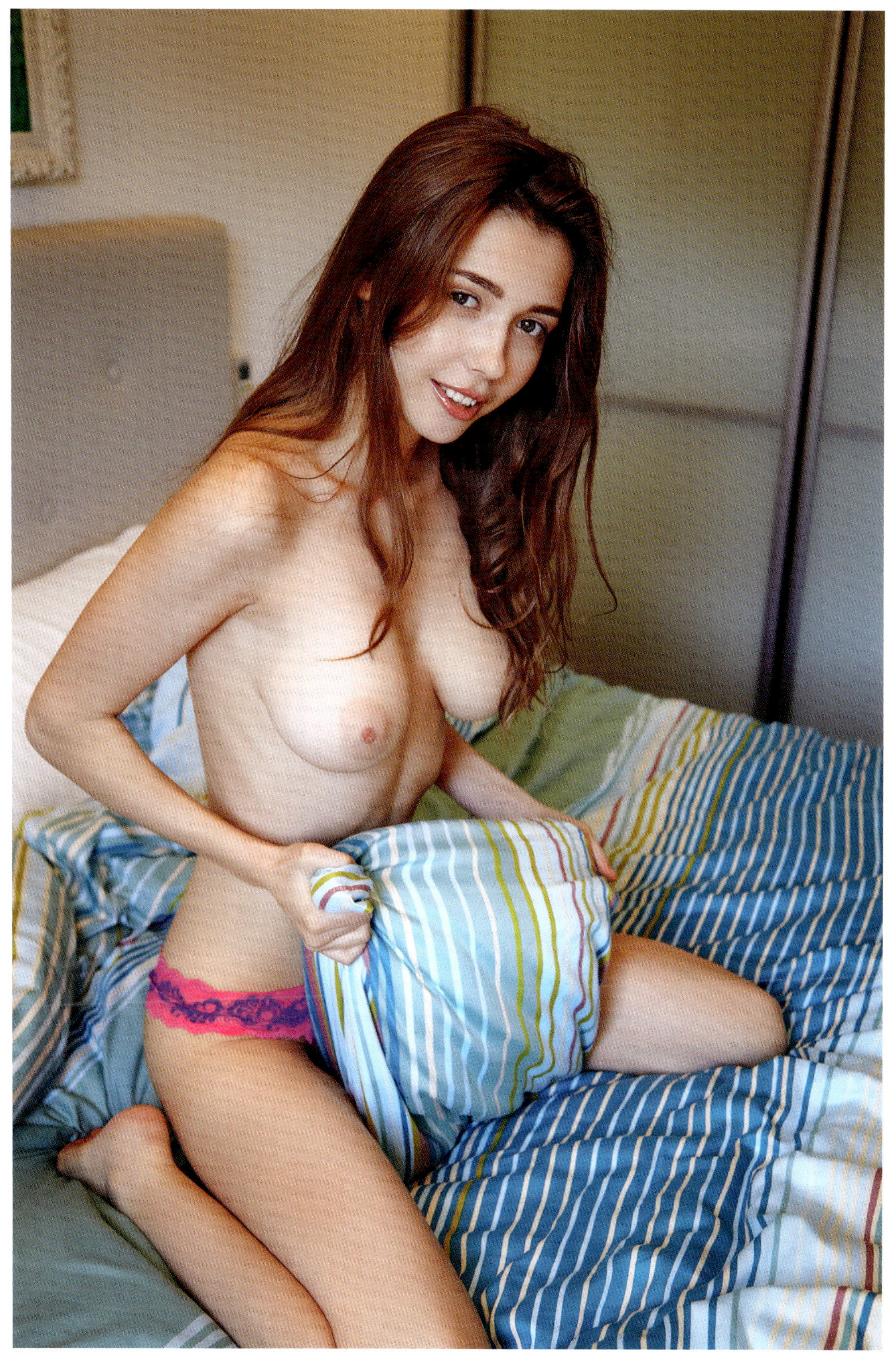

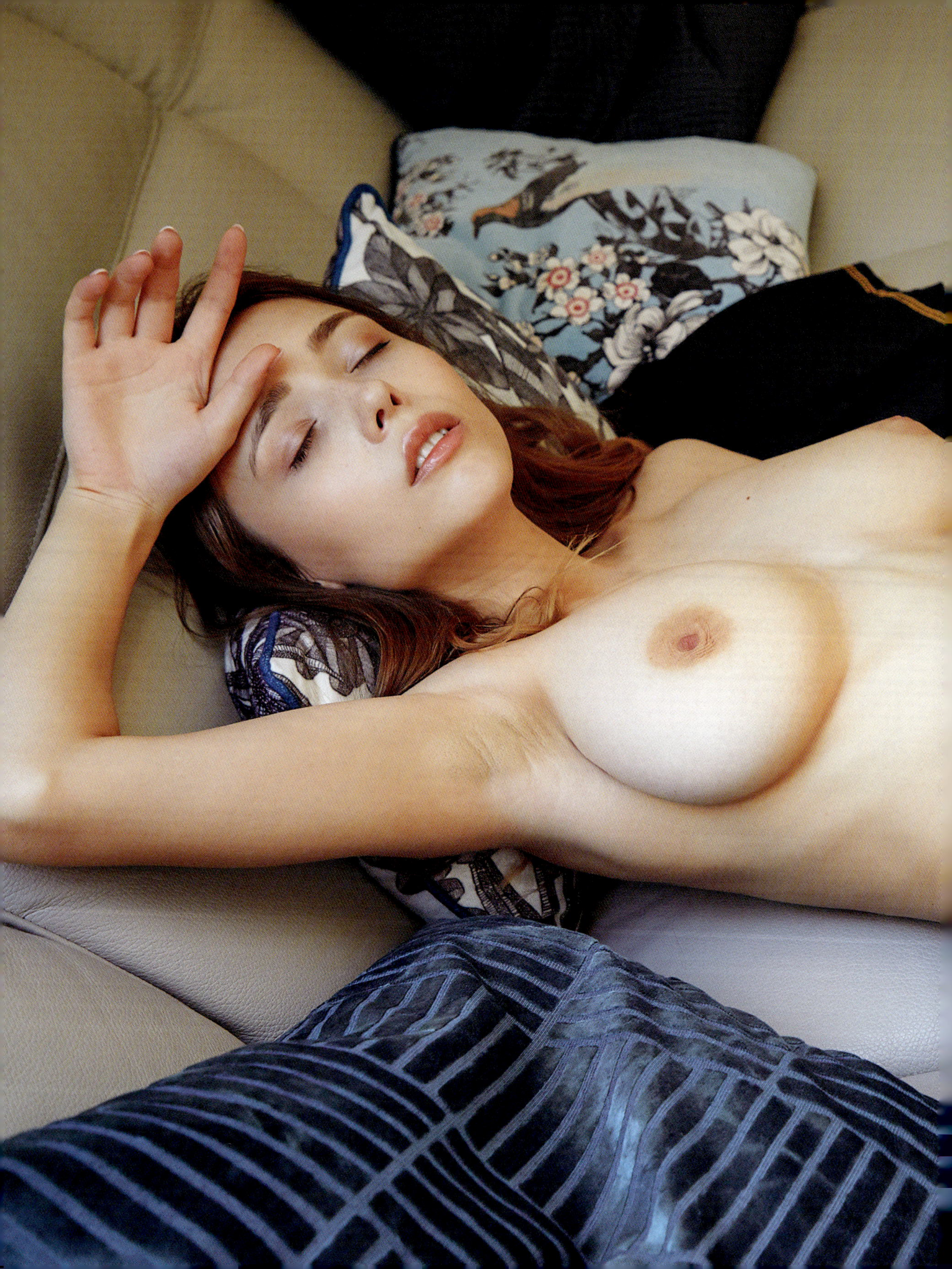

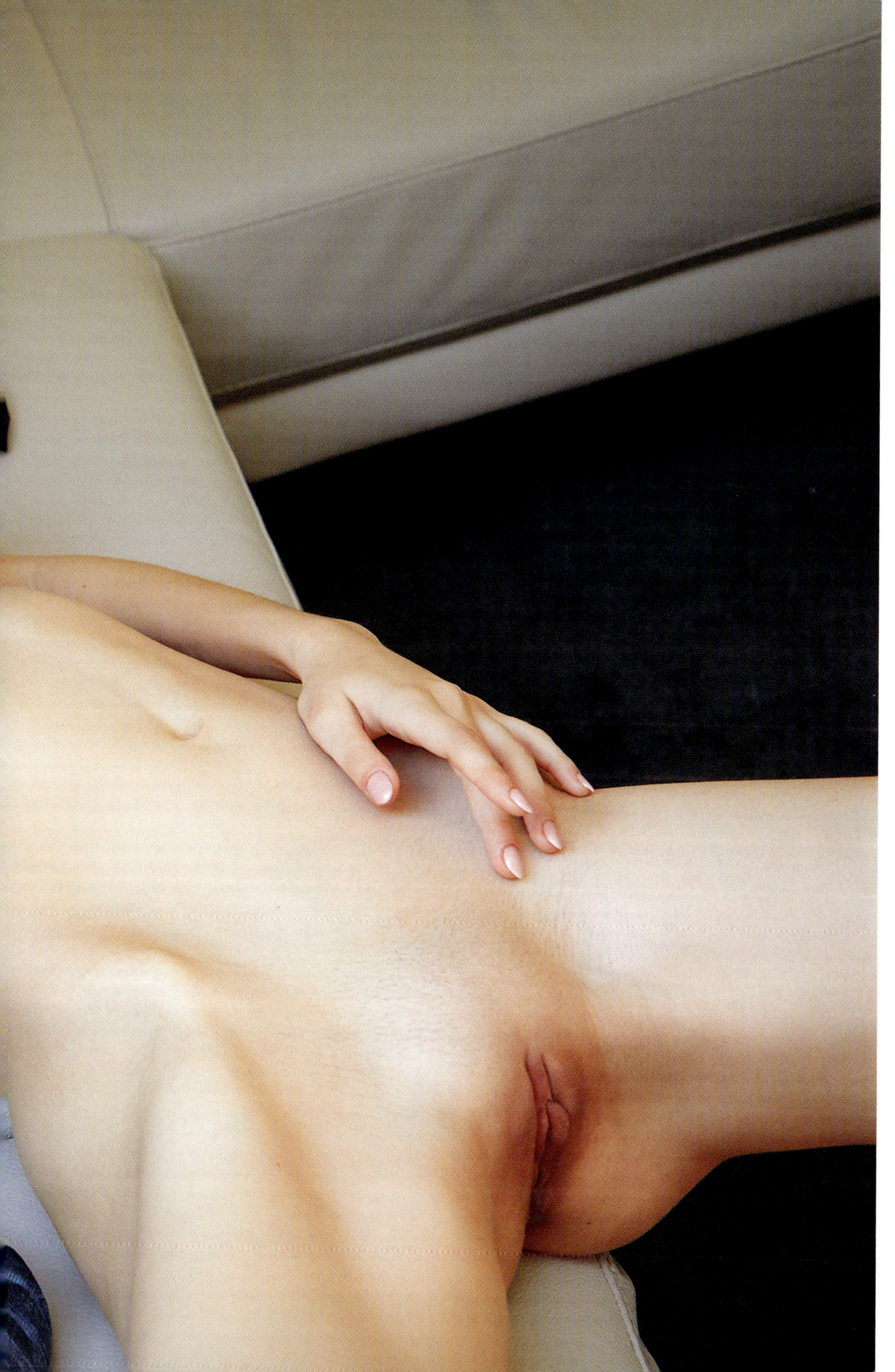

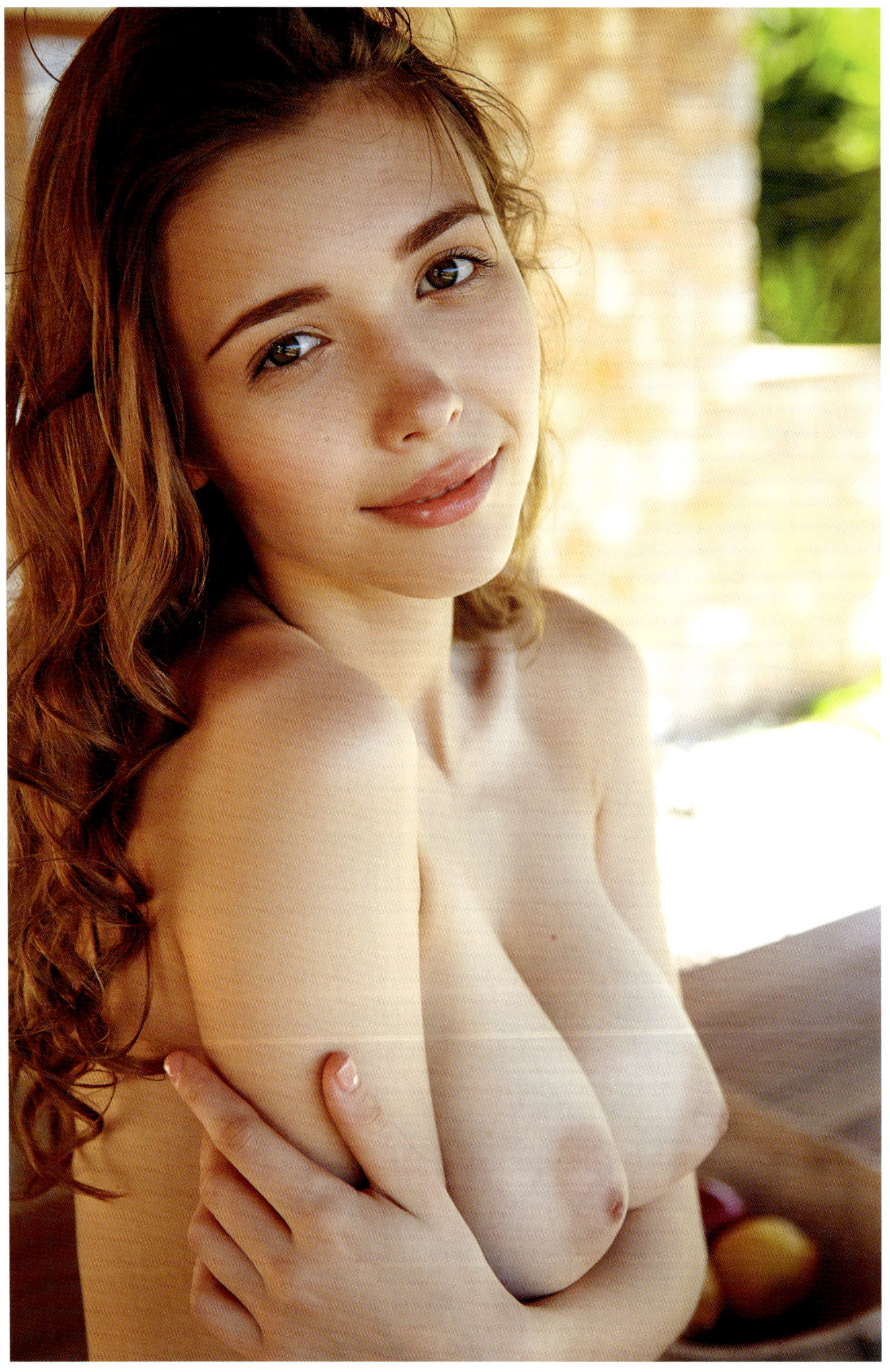

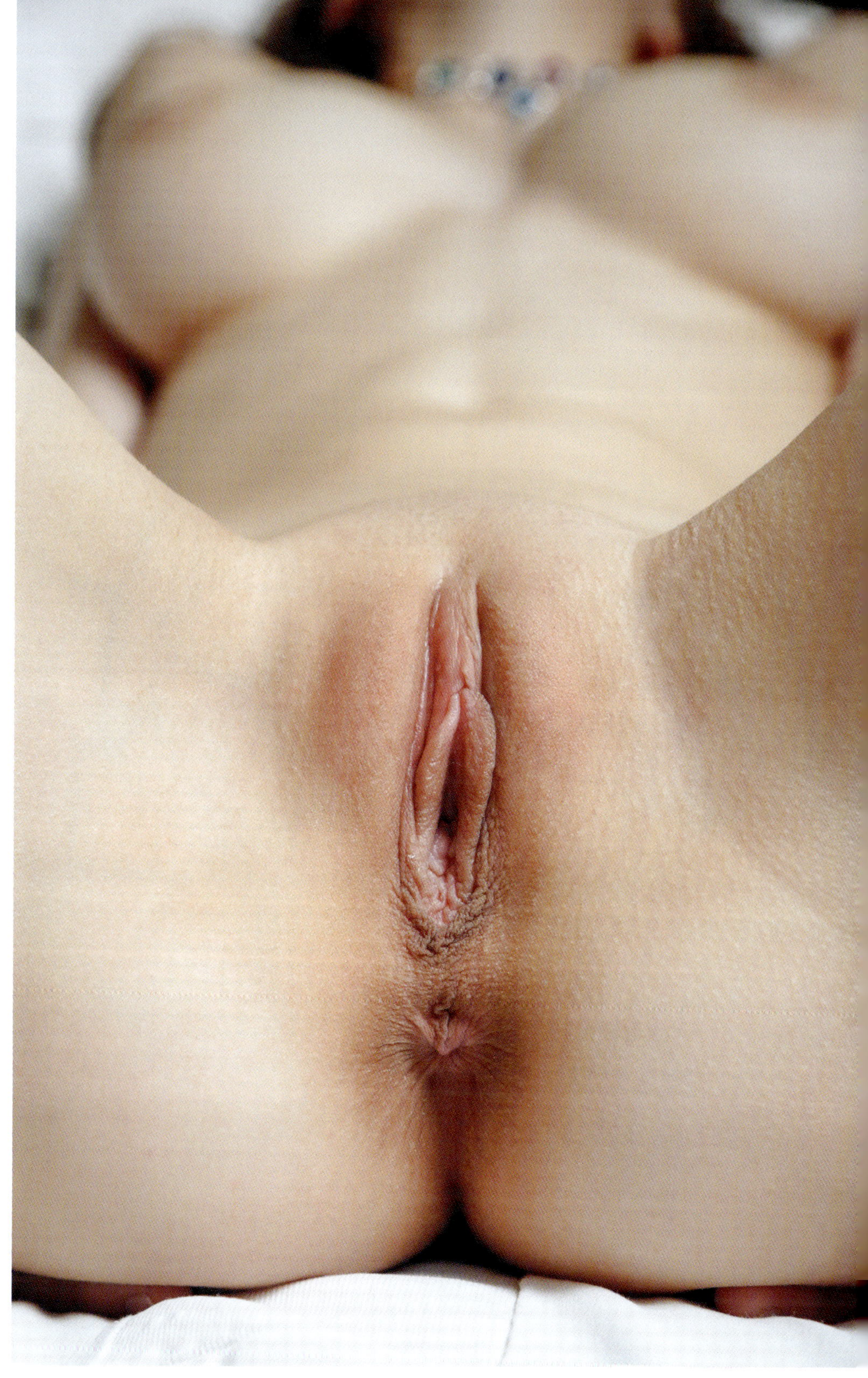

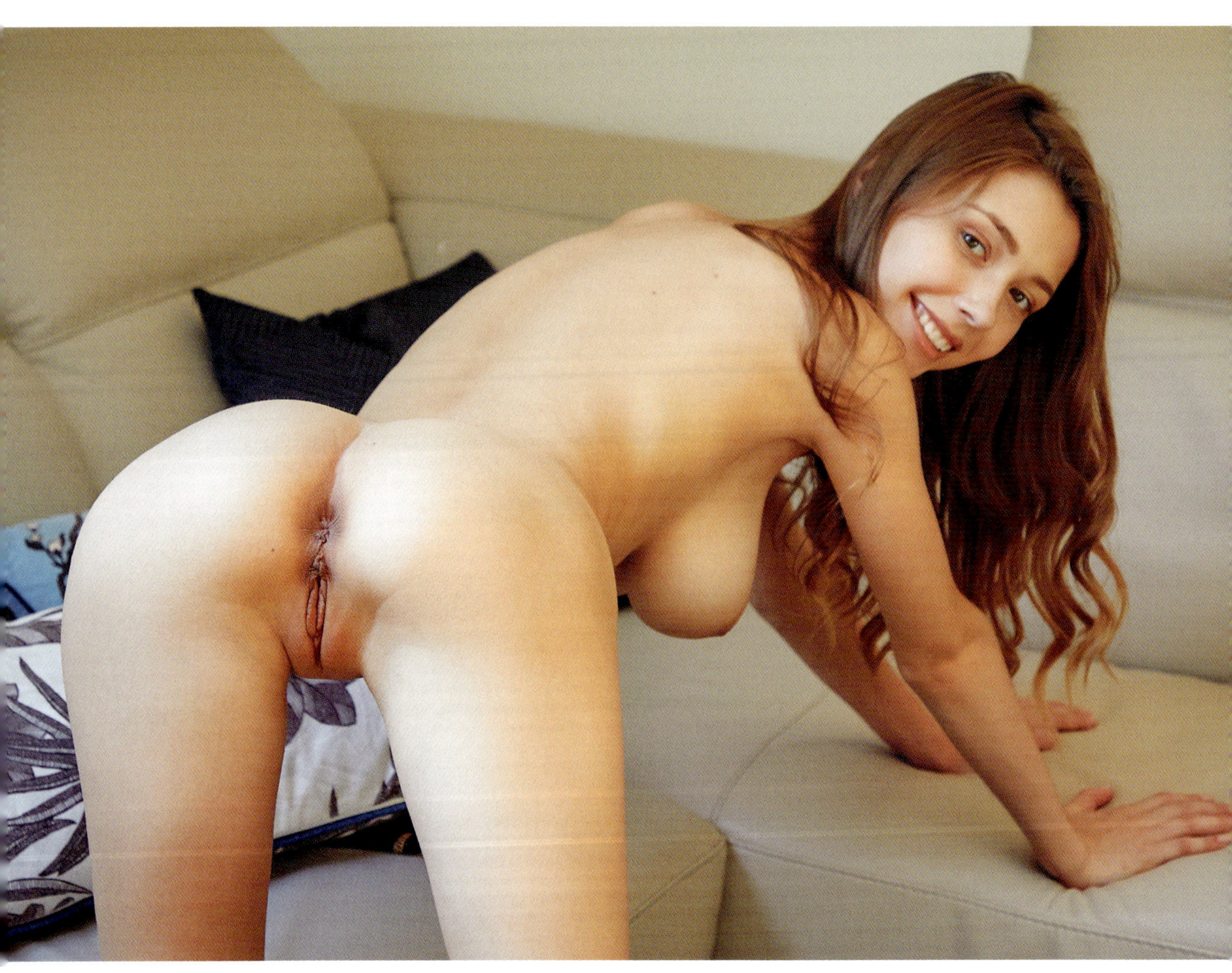

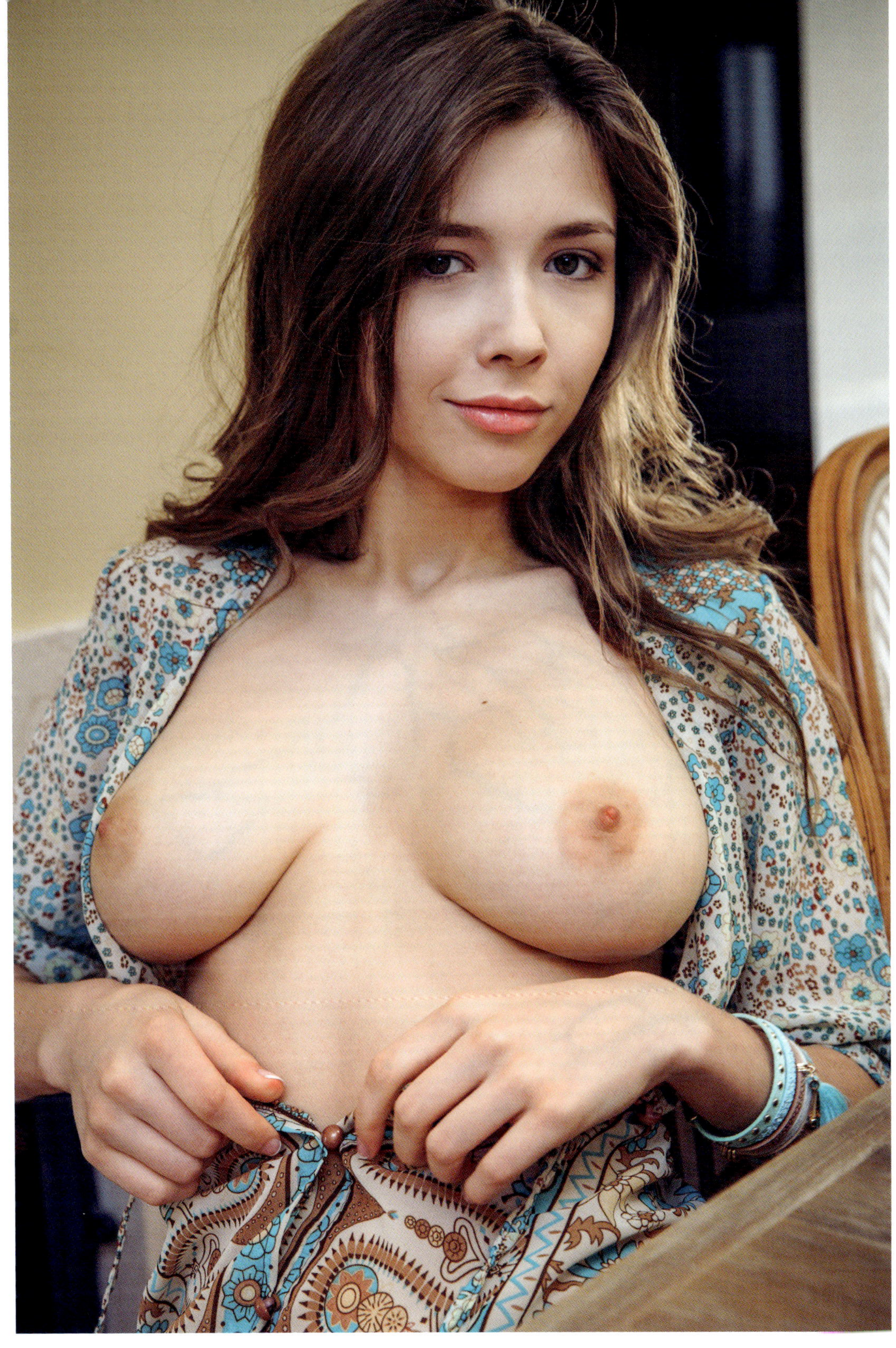

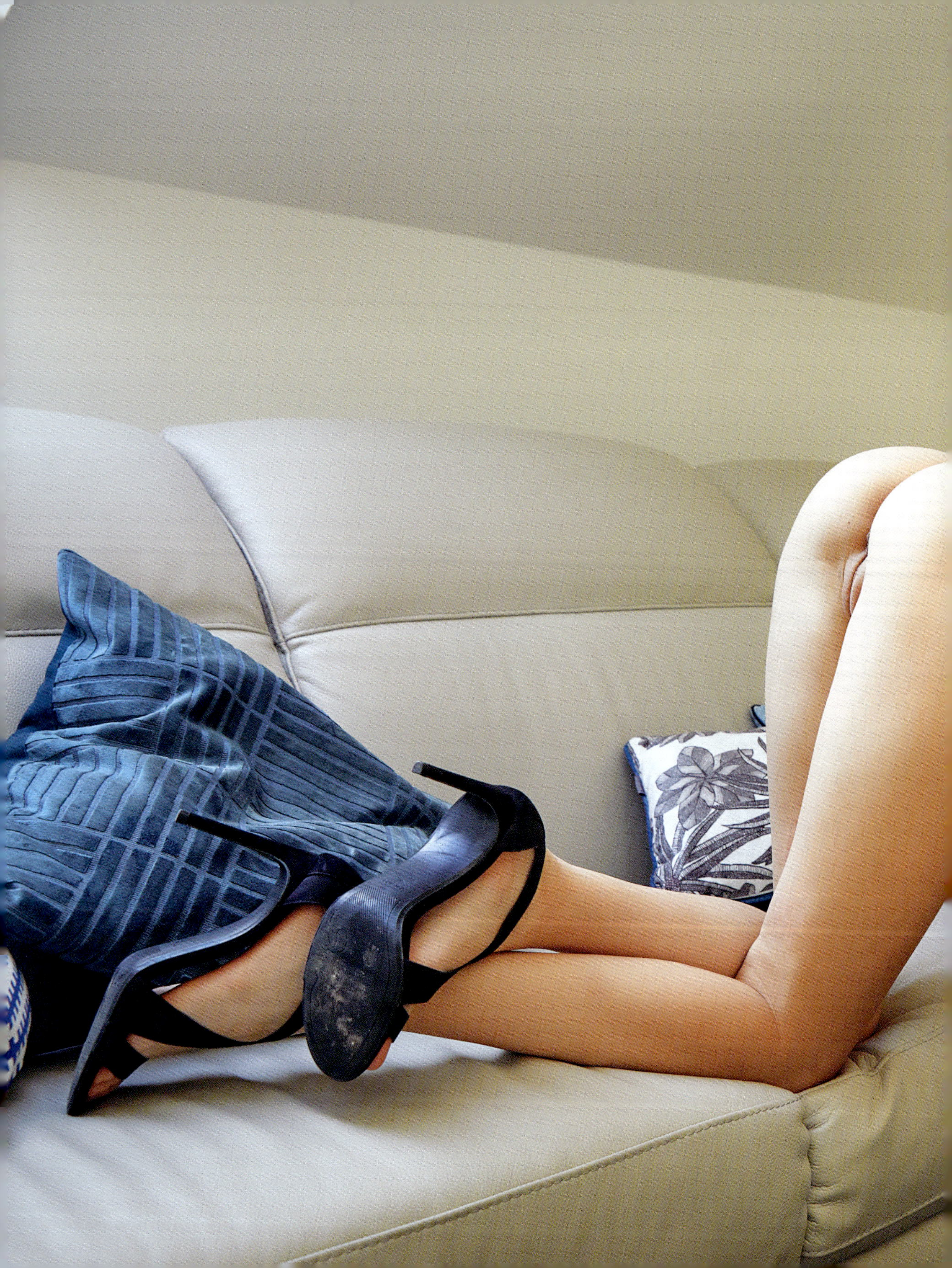

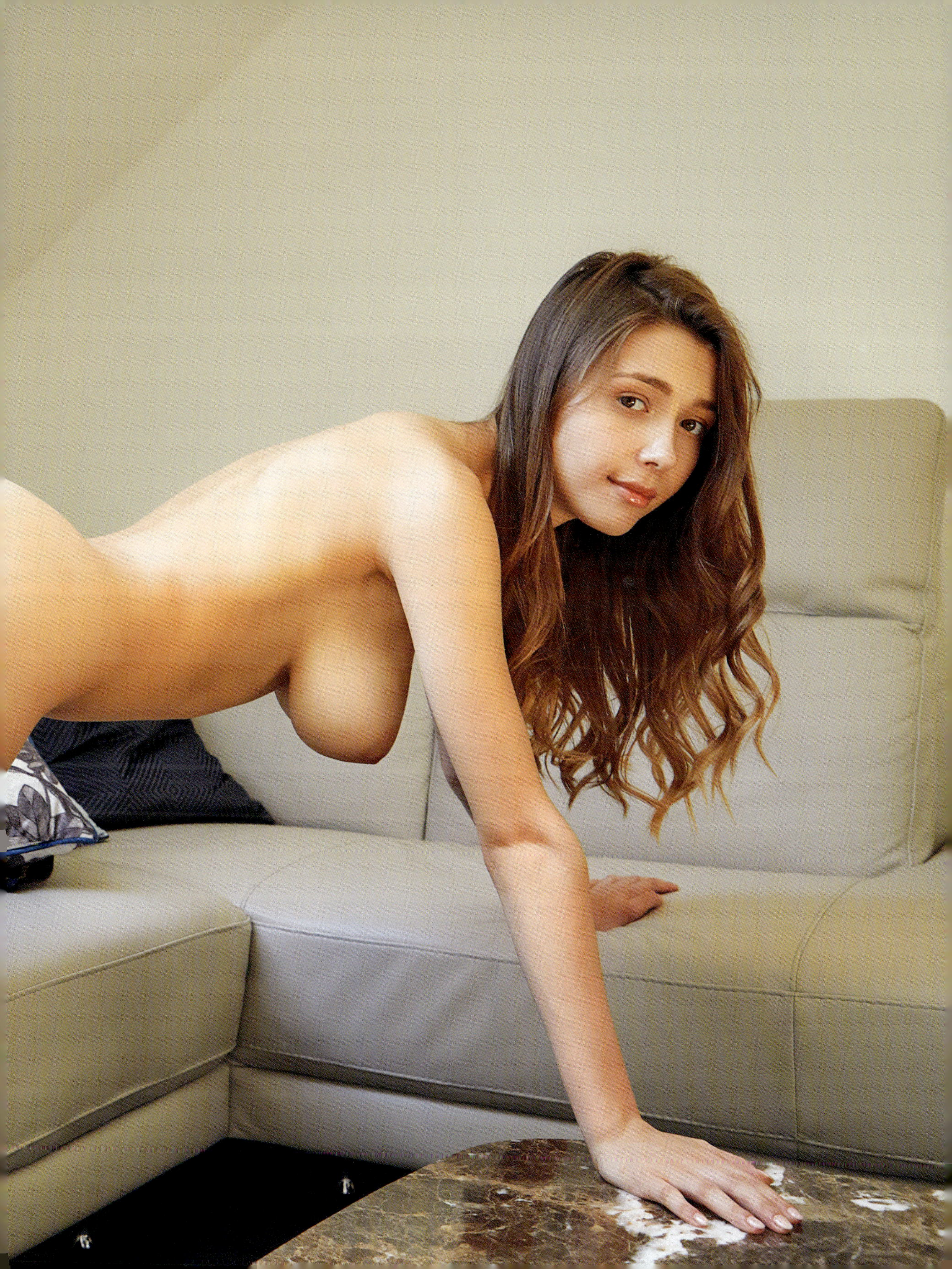

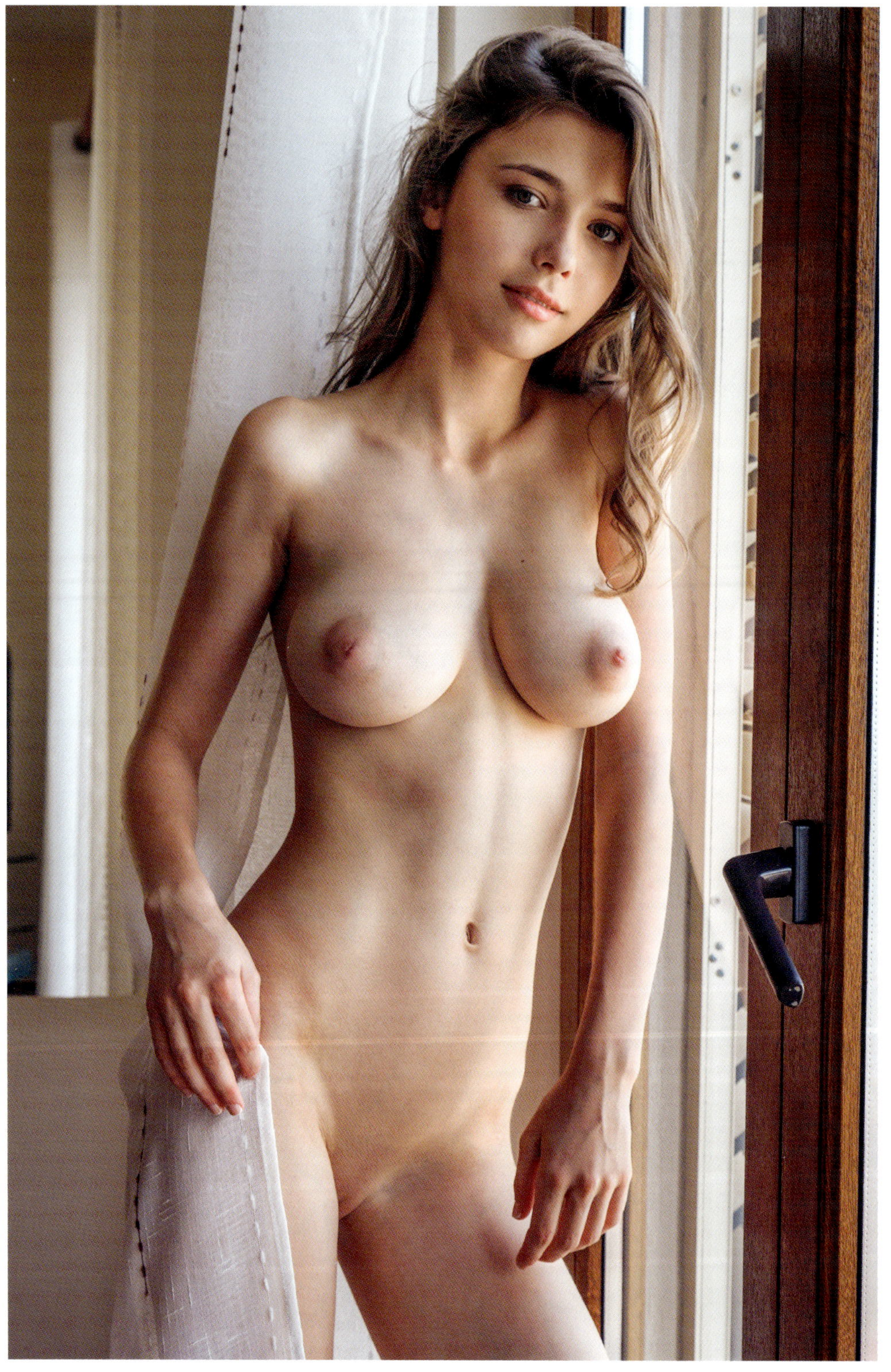

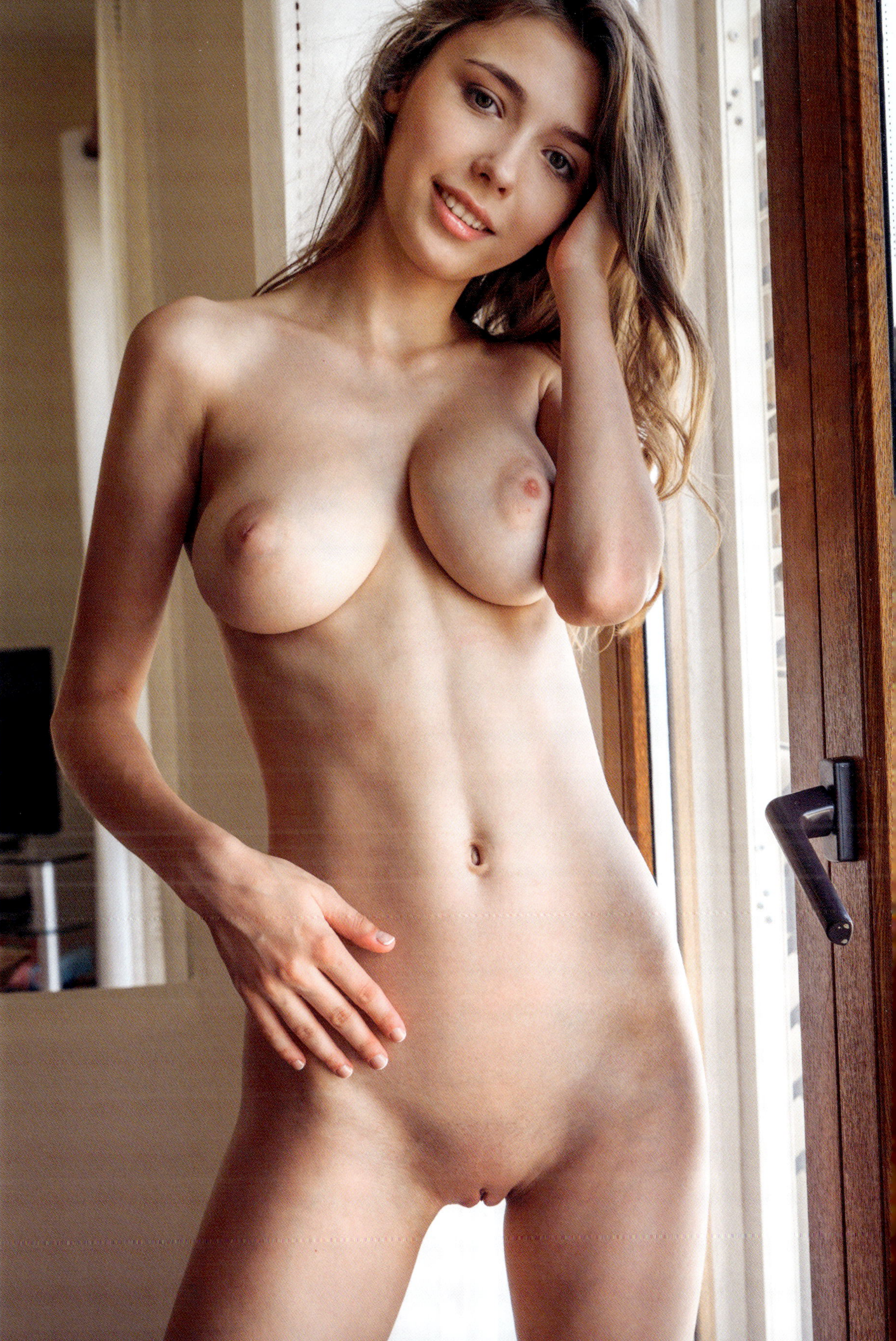

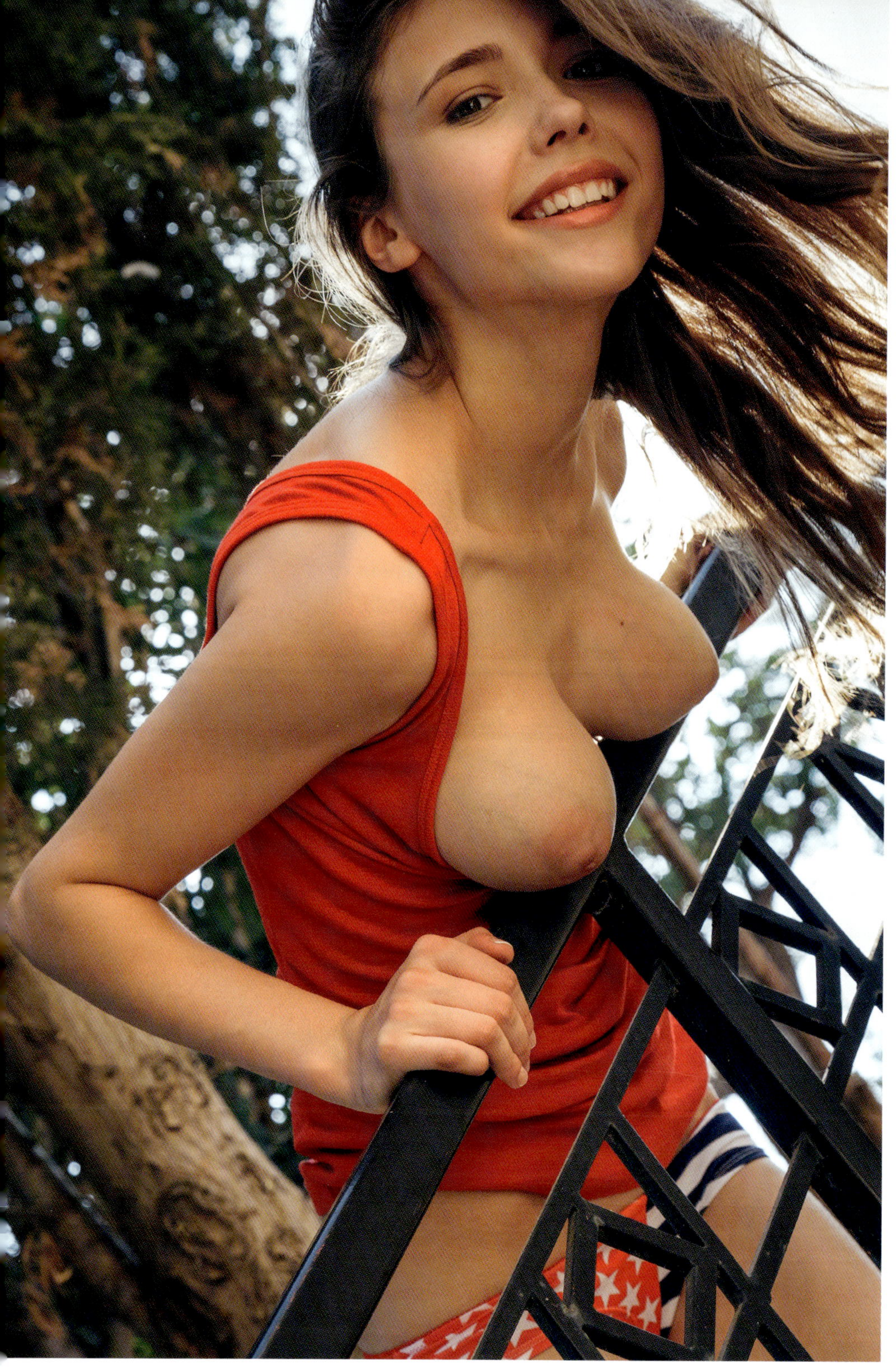

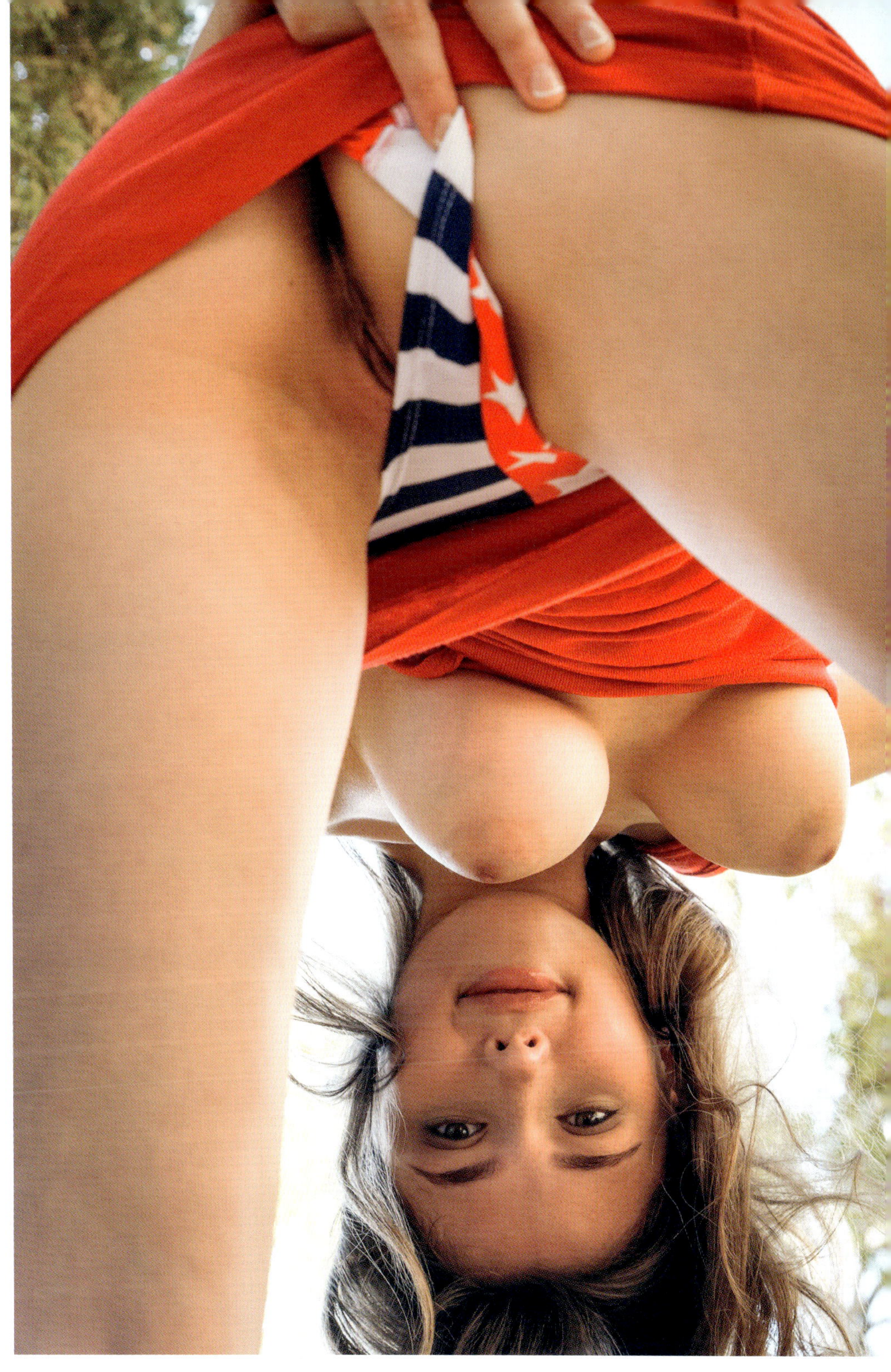

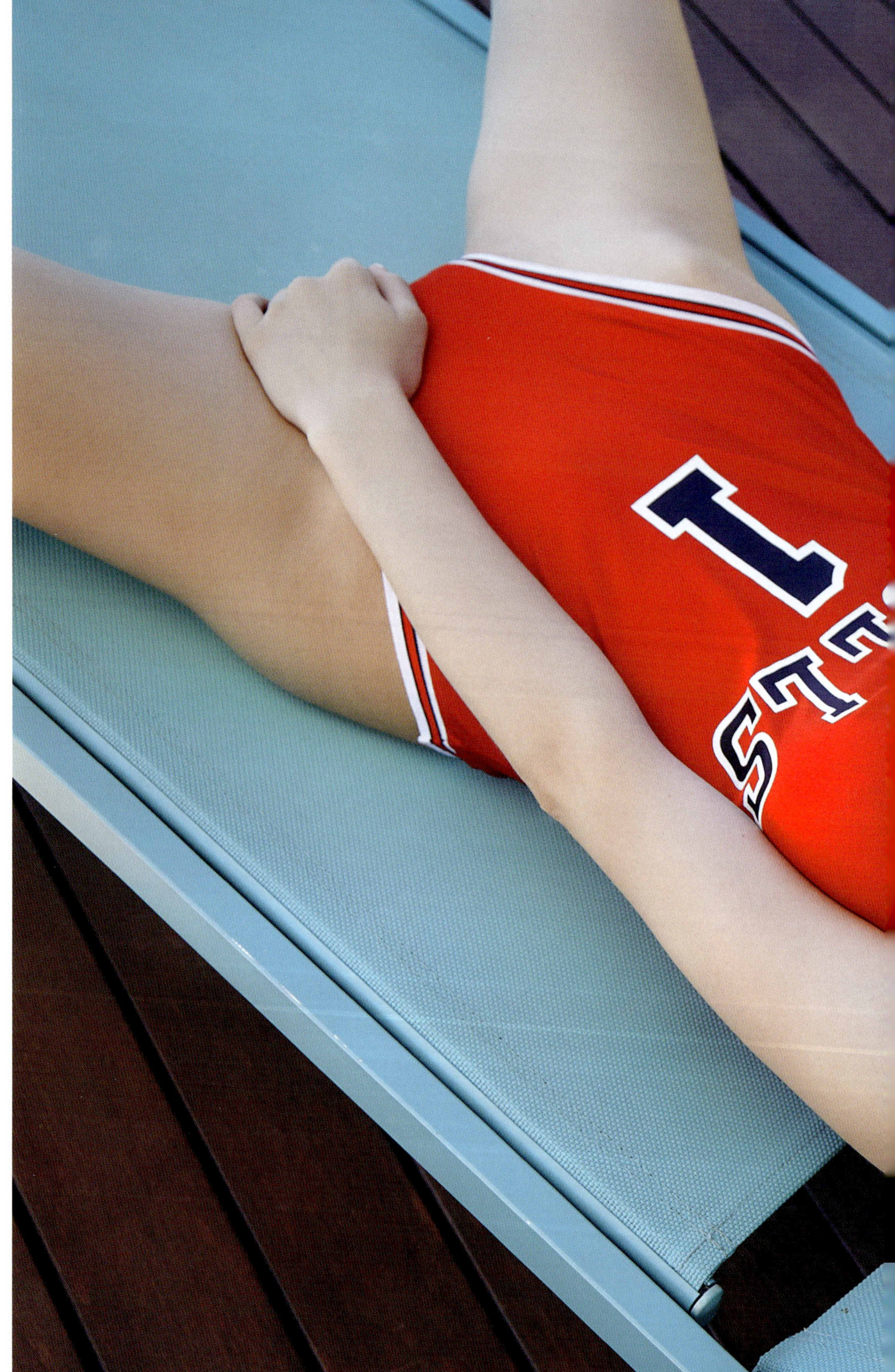

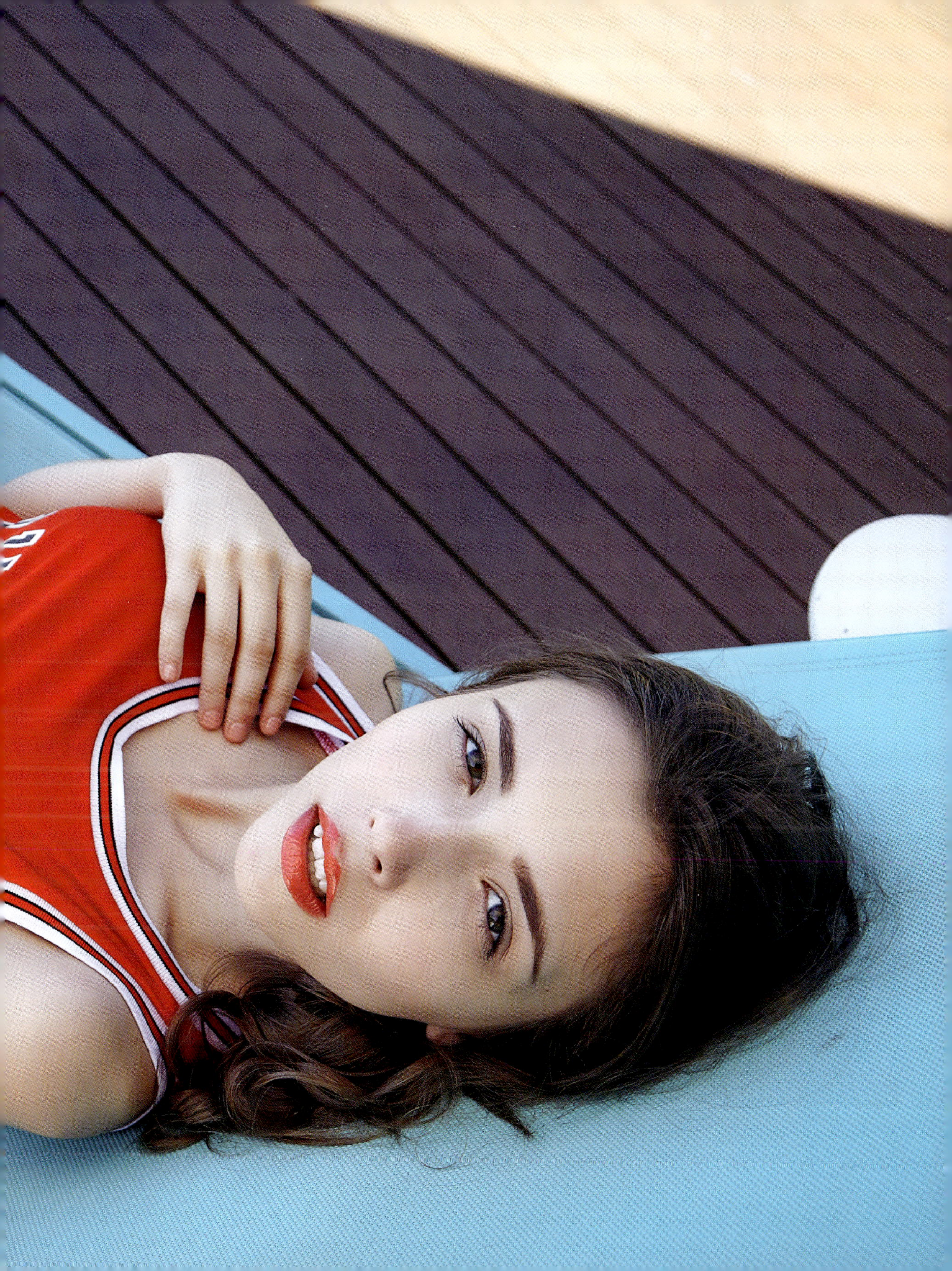

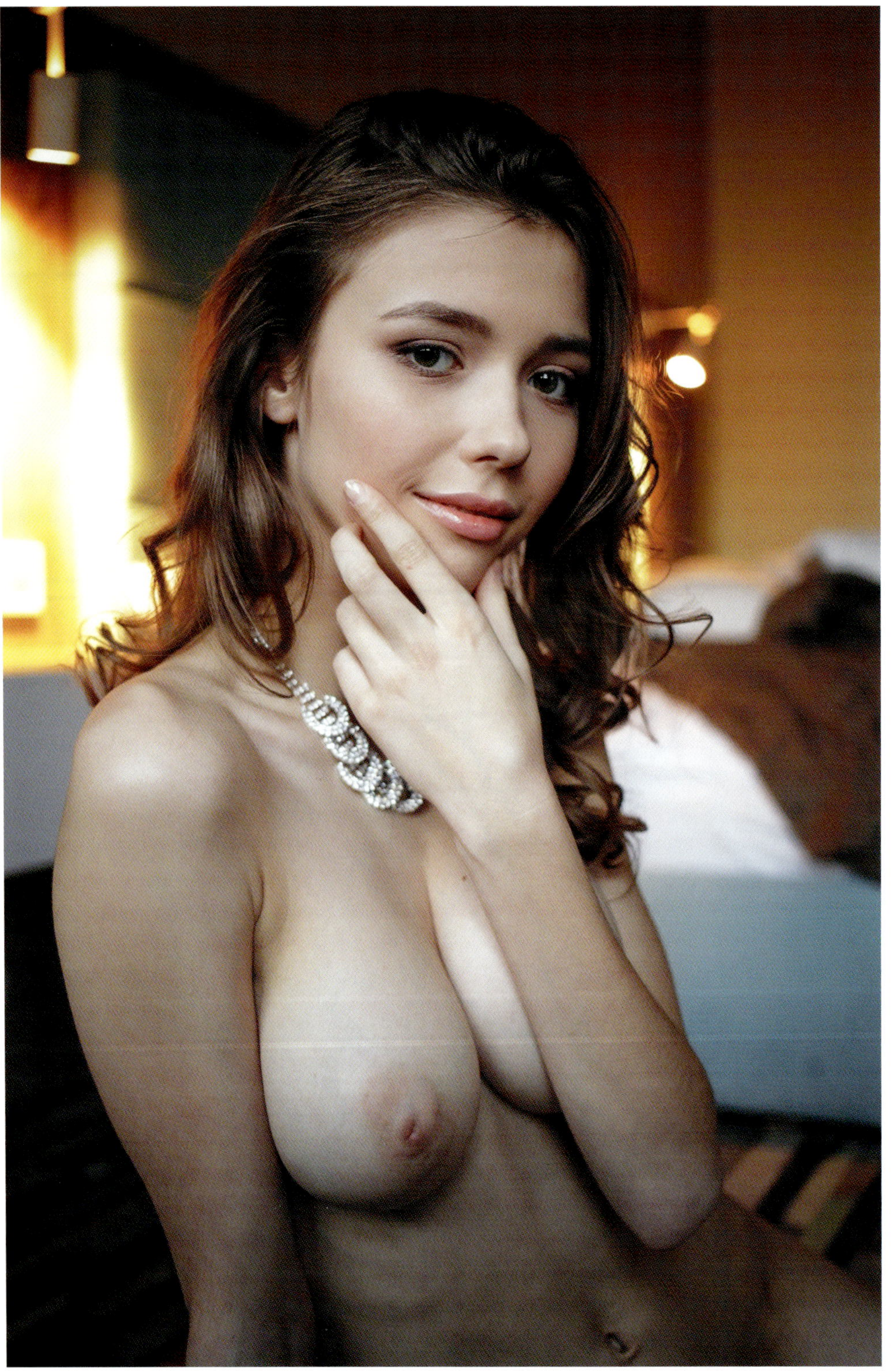

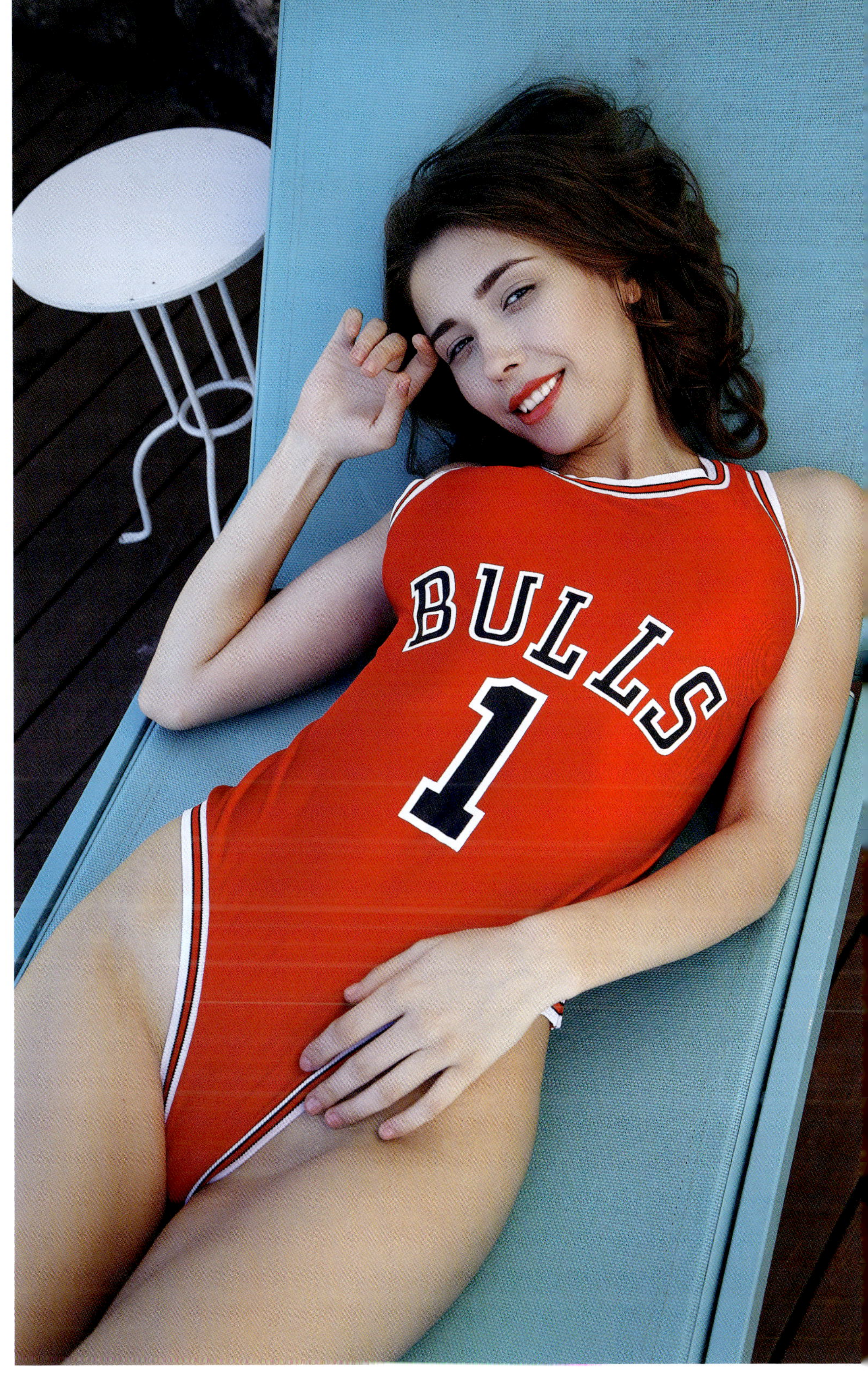
BULLS
1

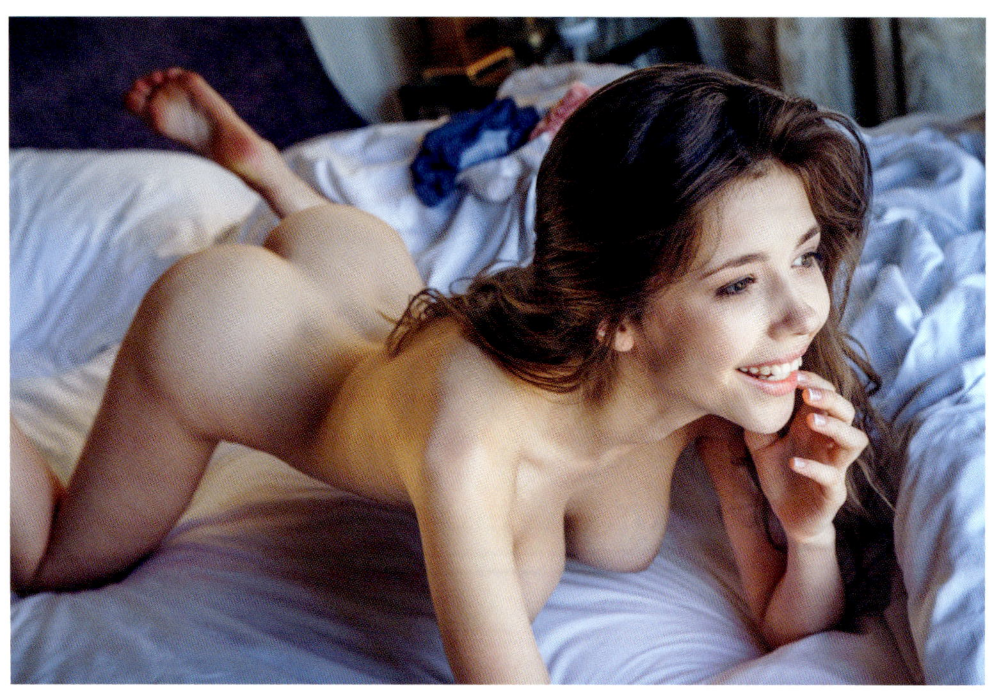

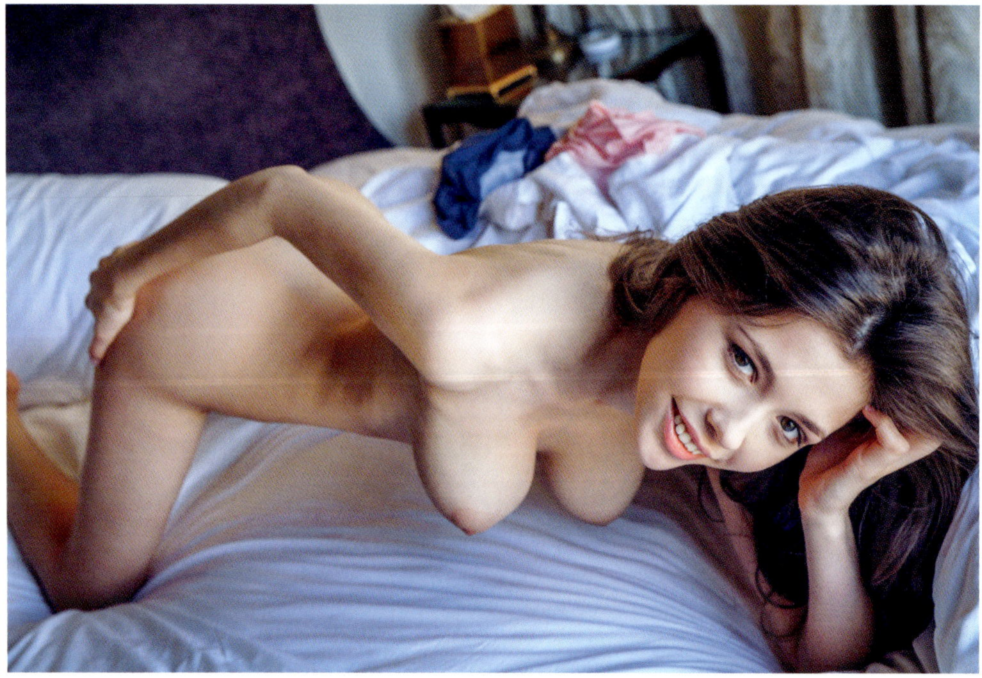

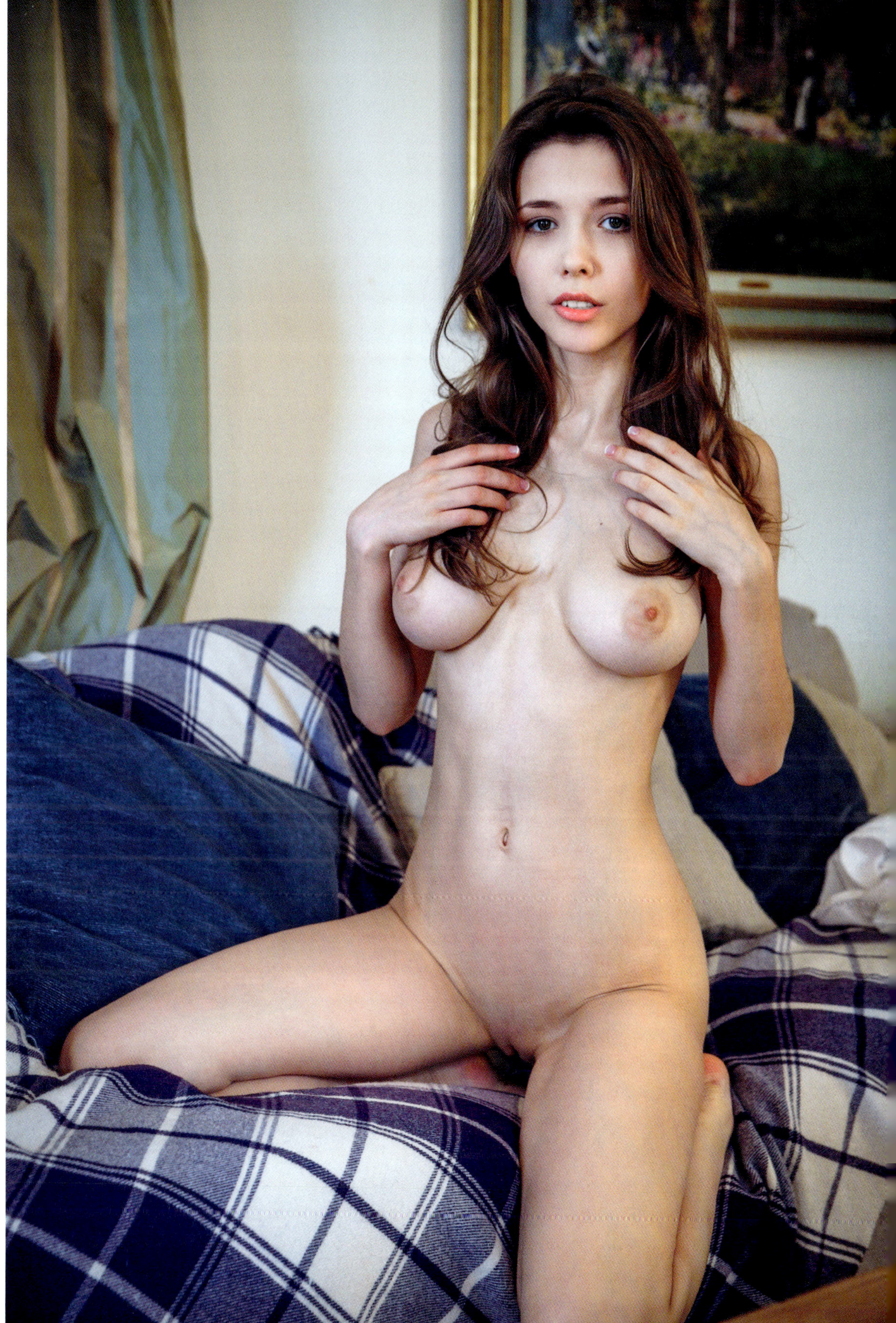

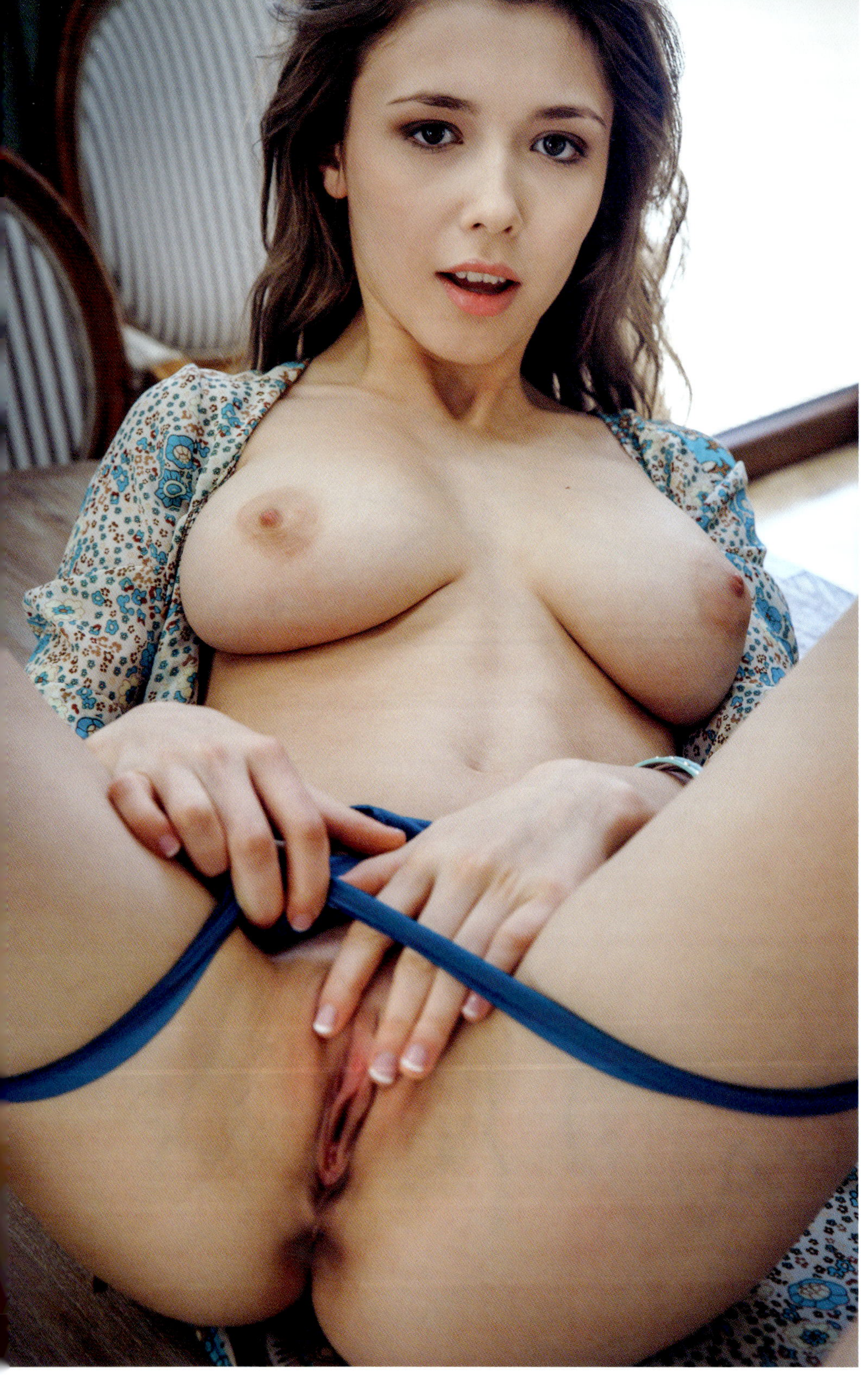

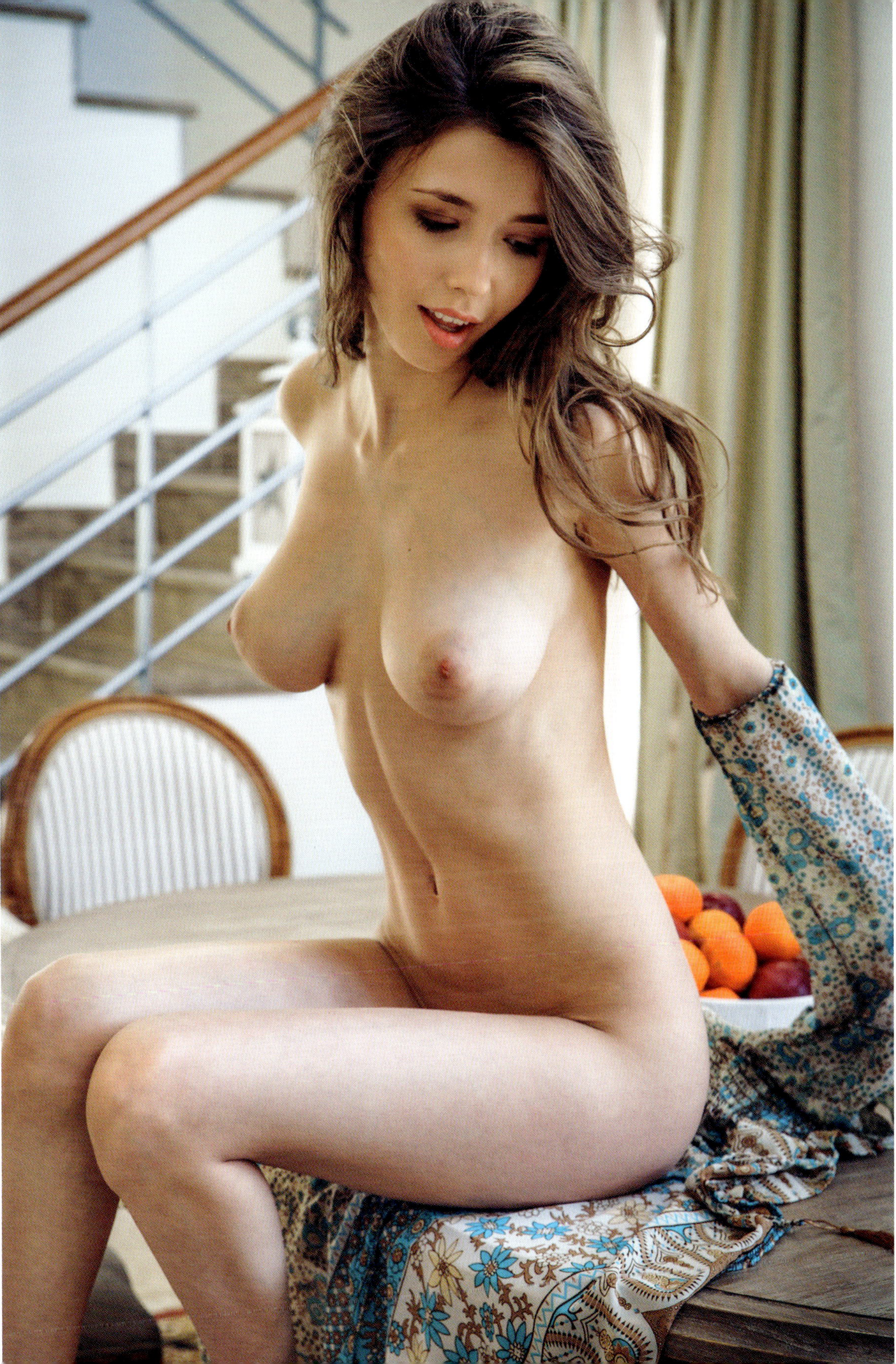

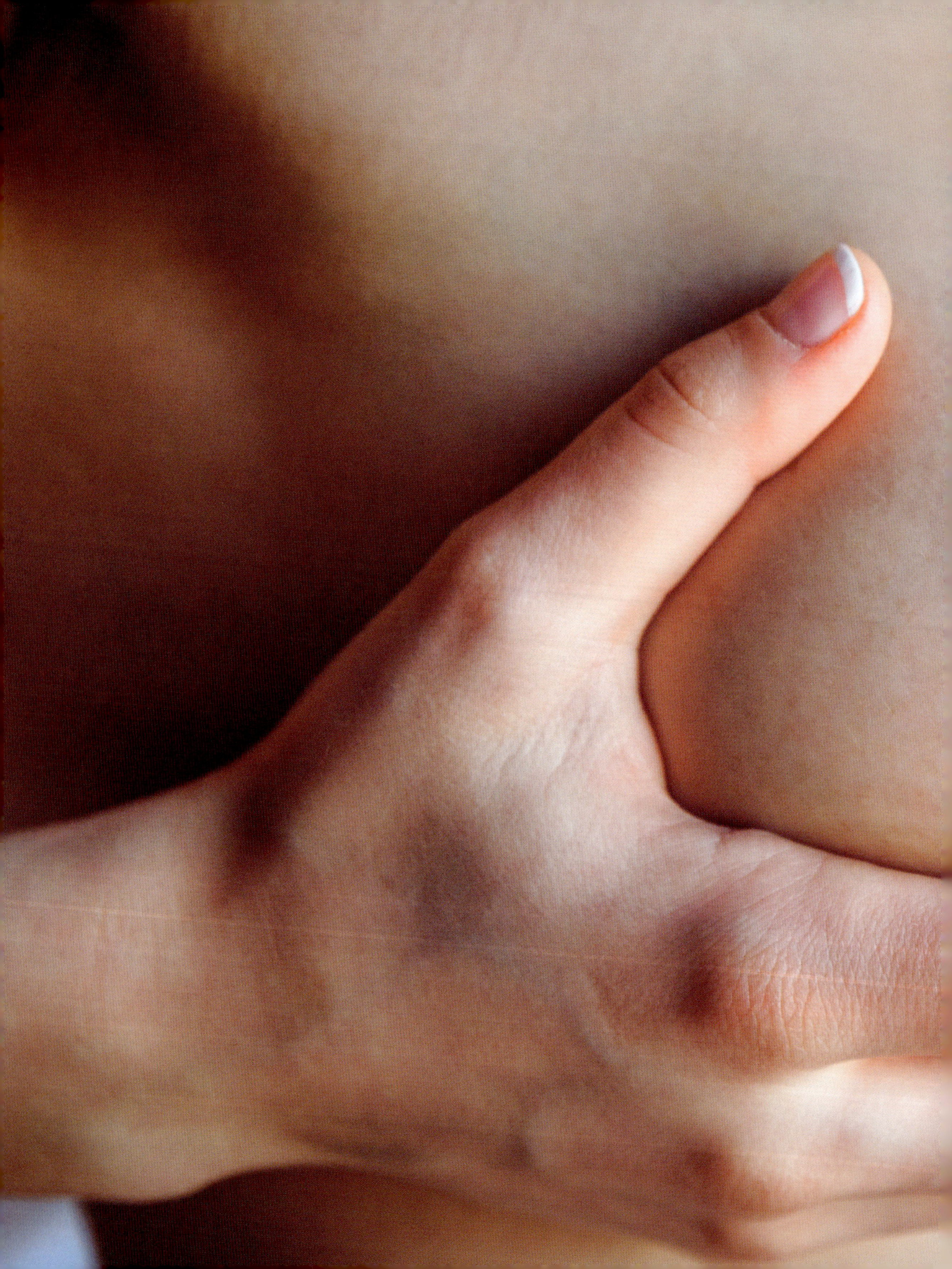

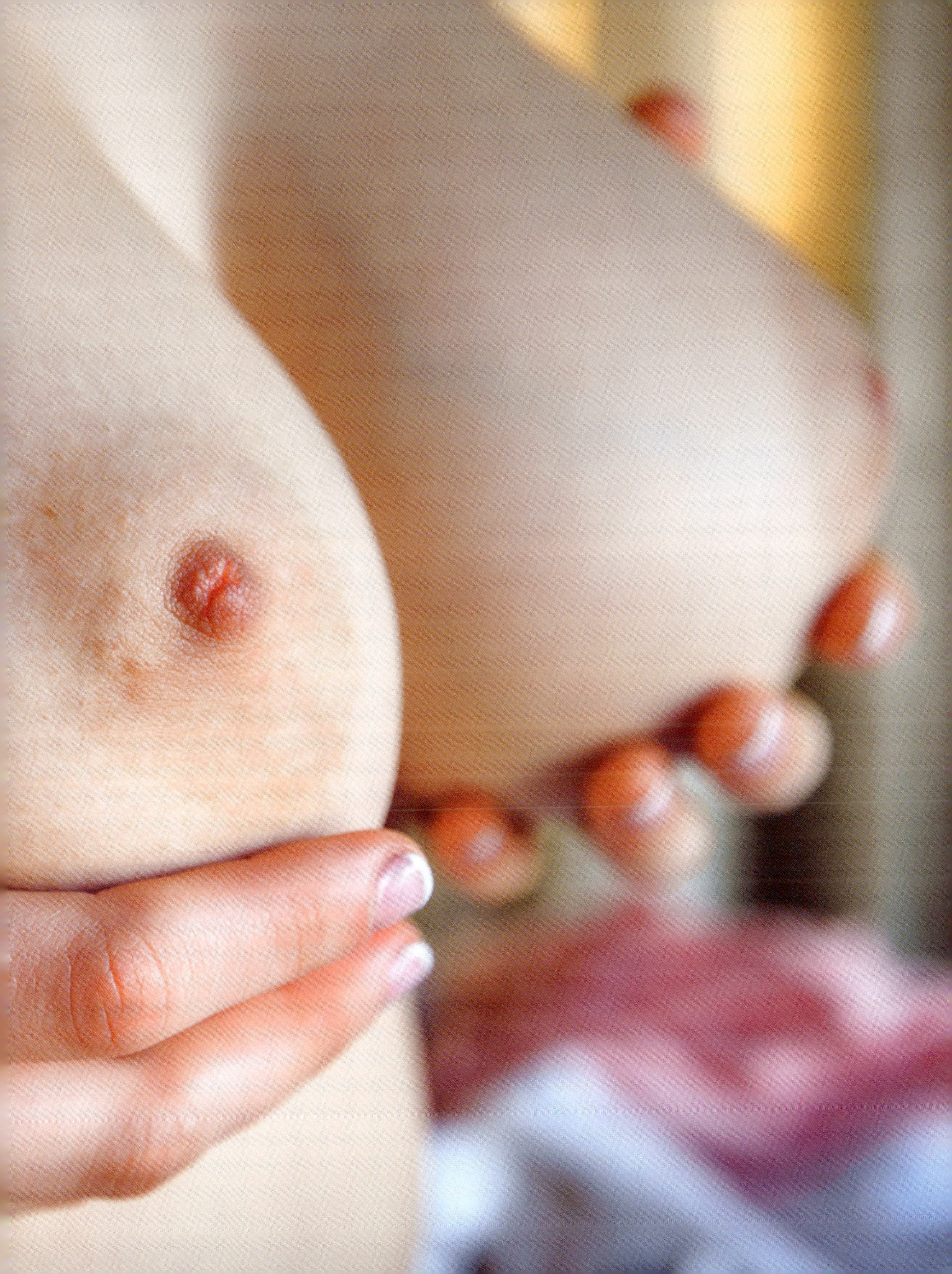

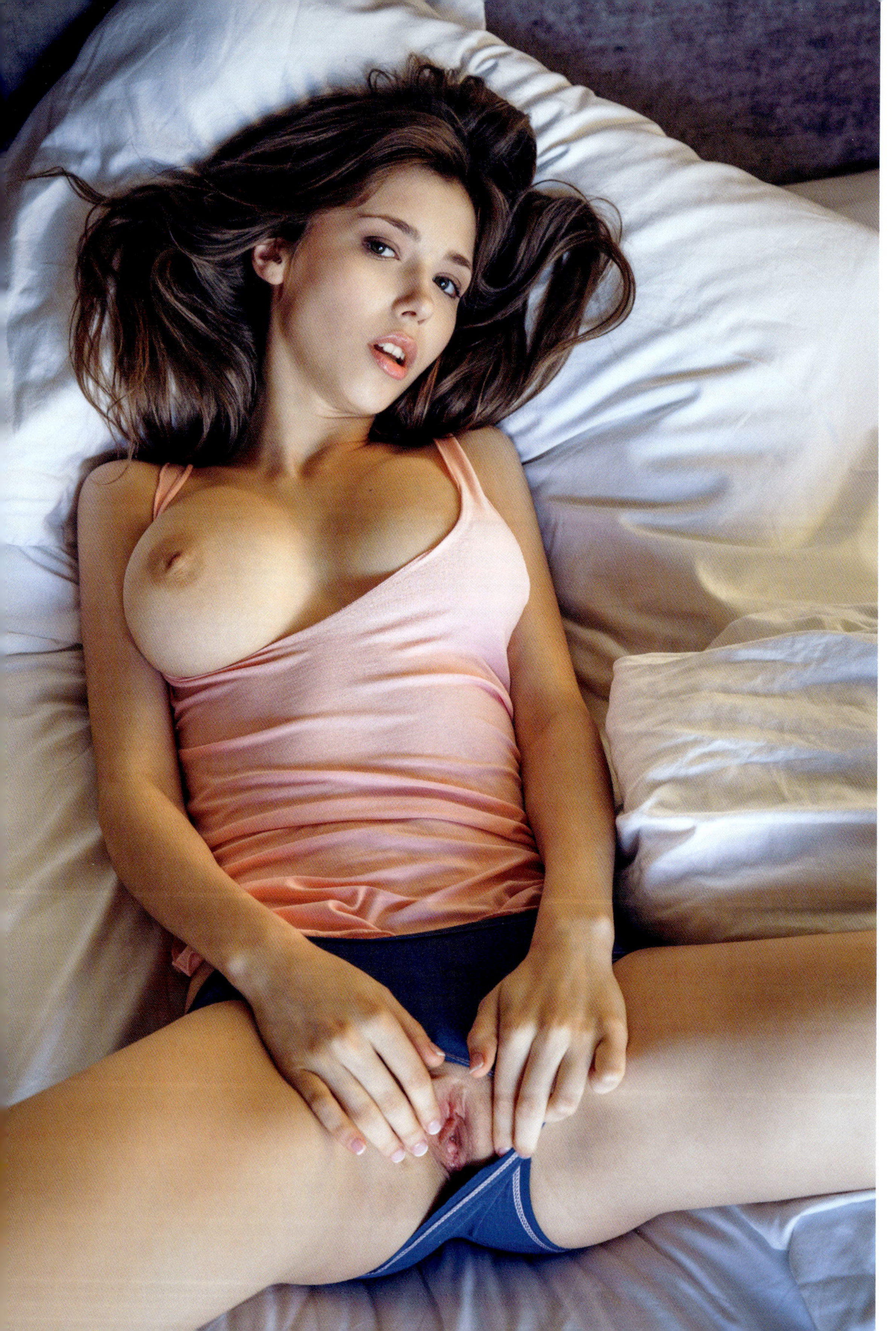

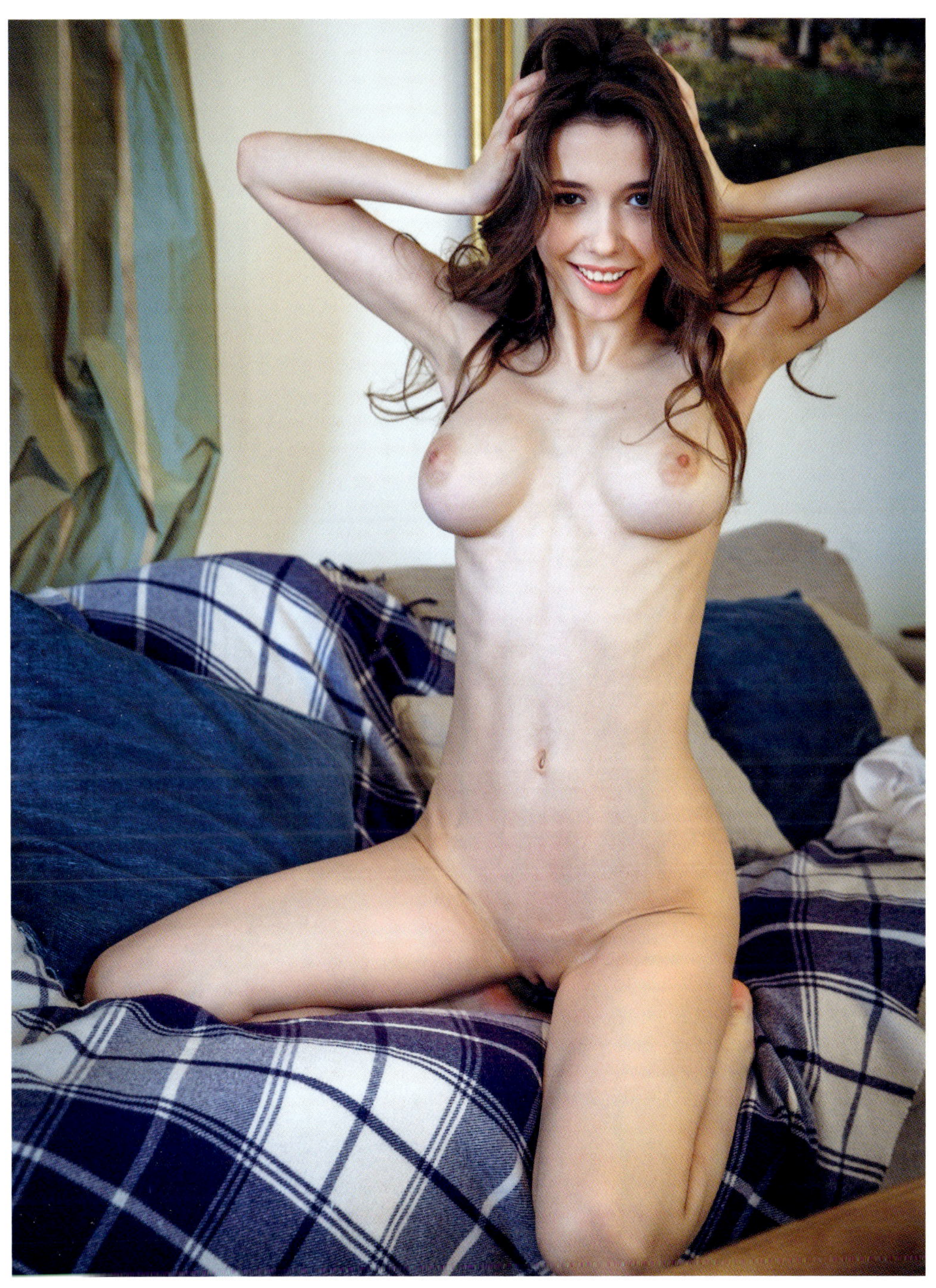

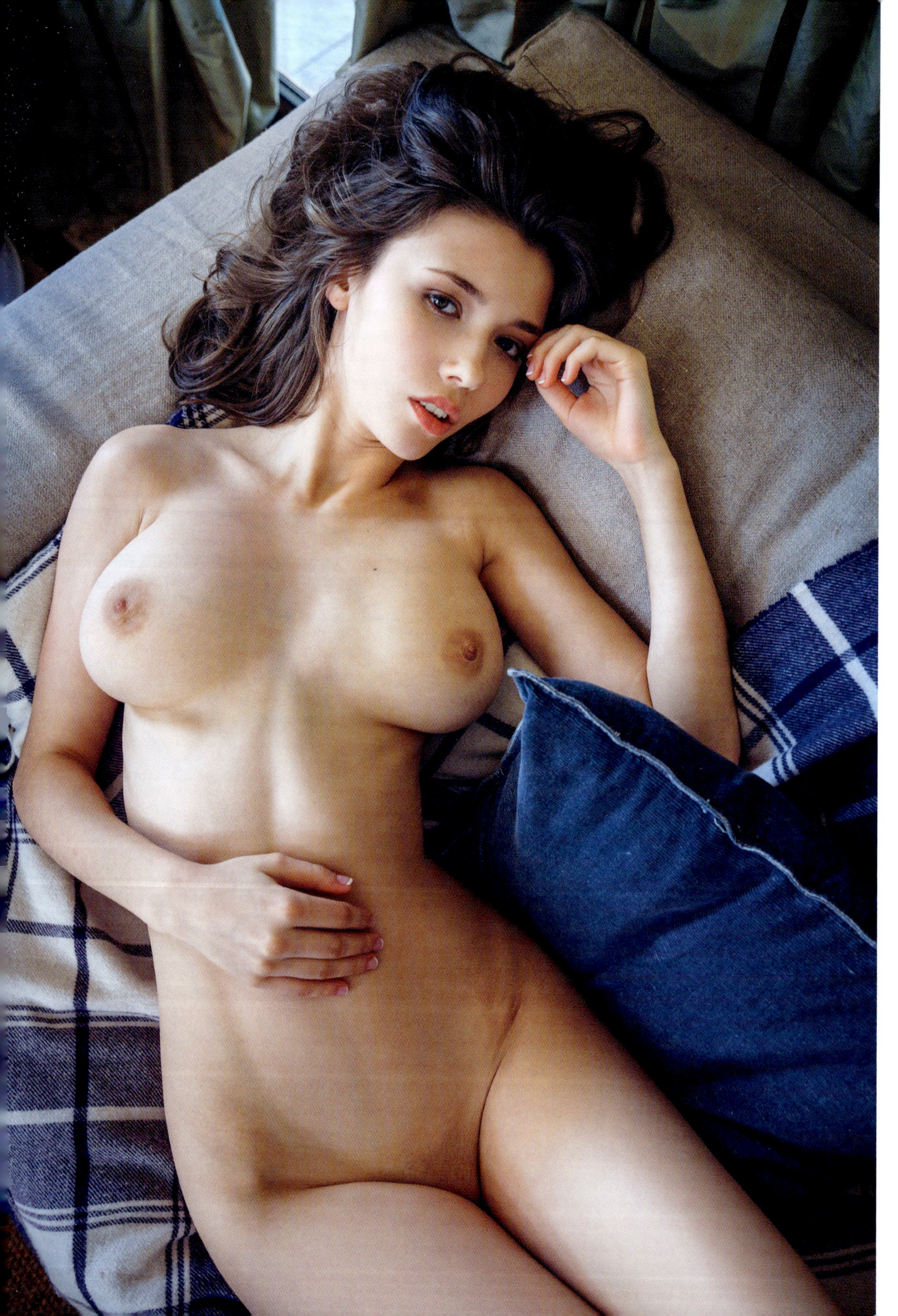

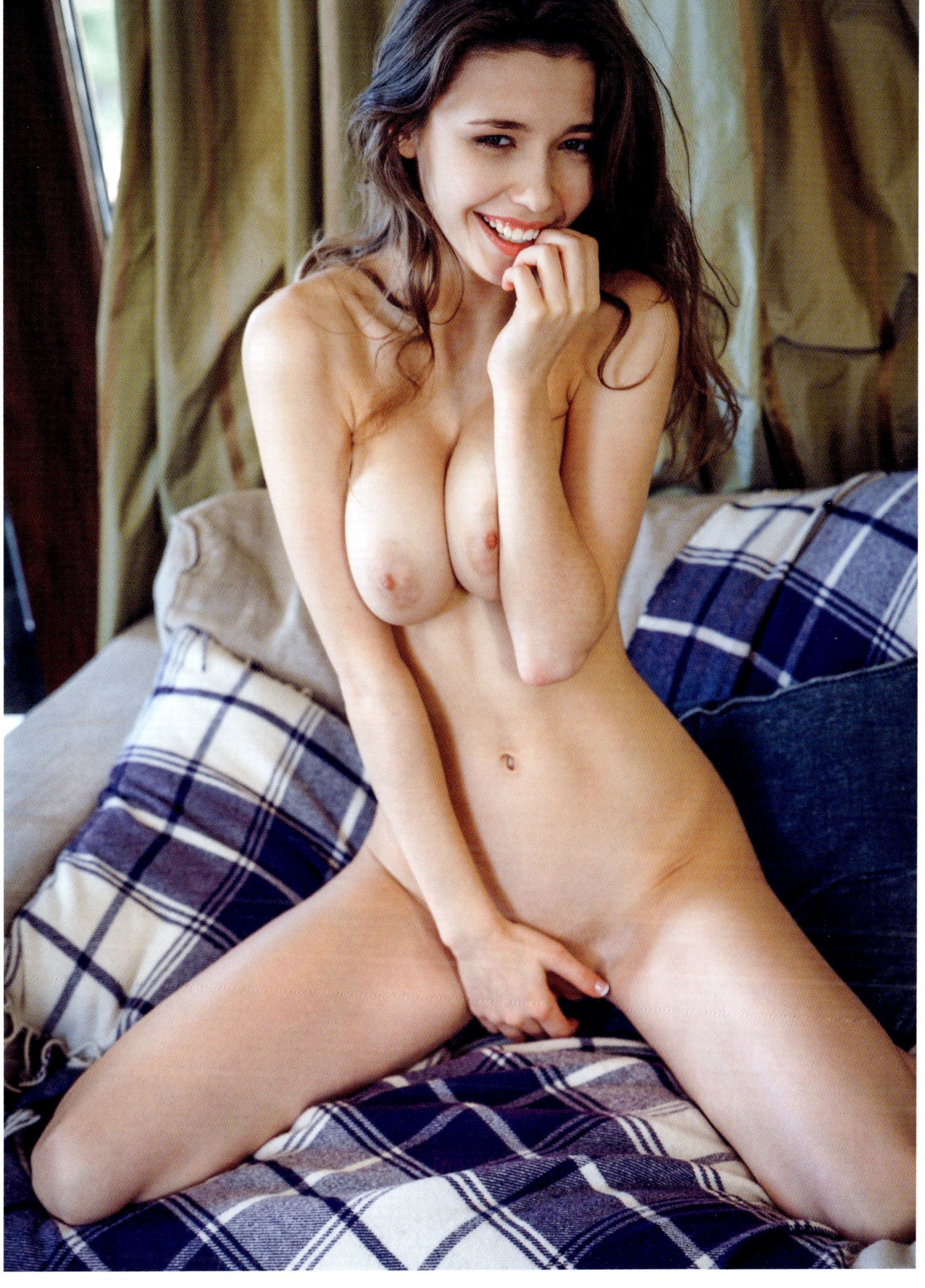

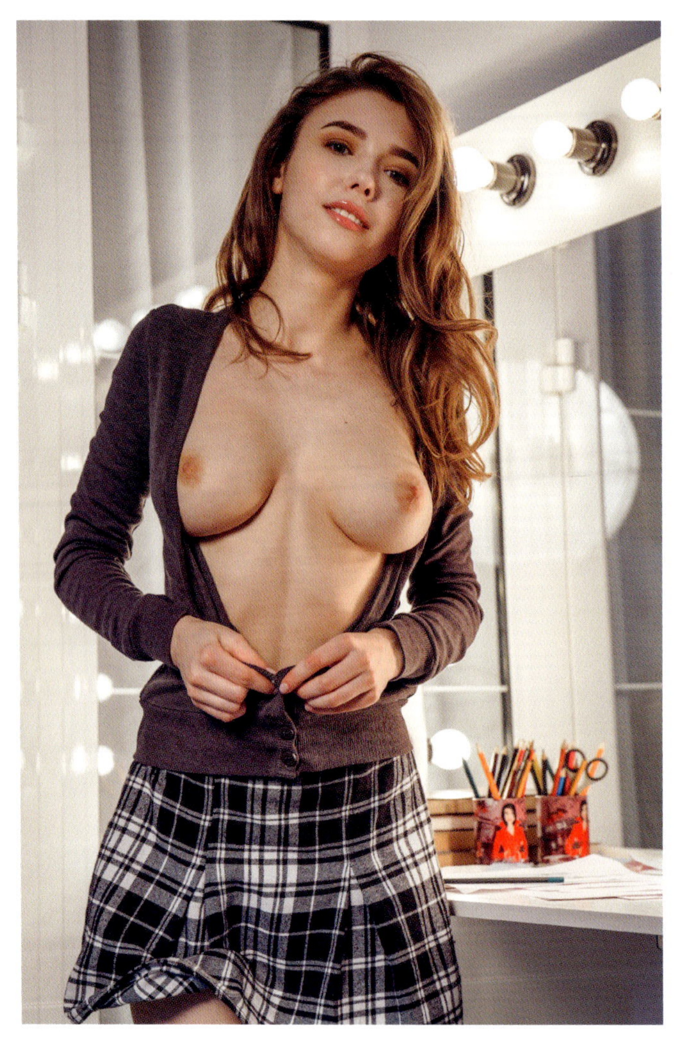

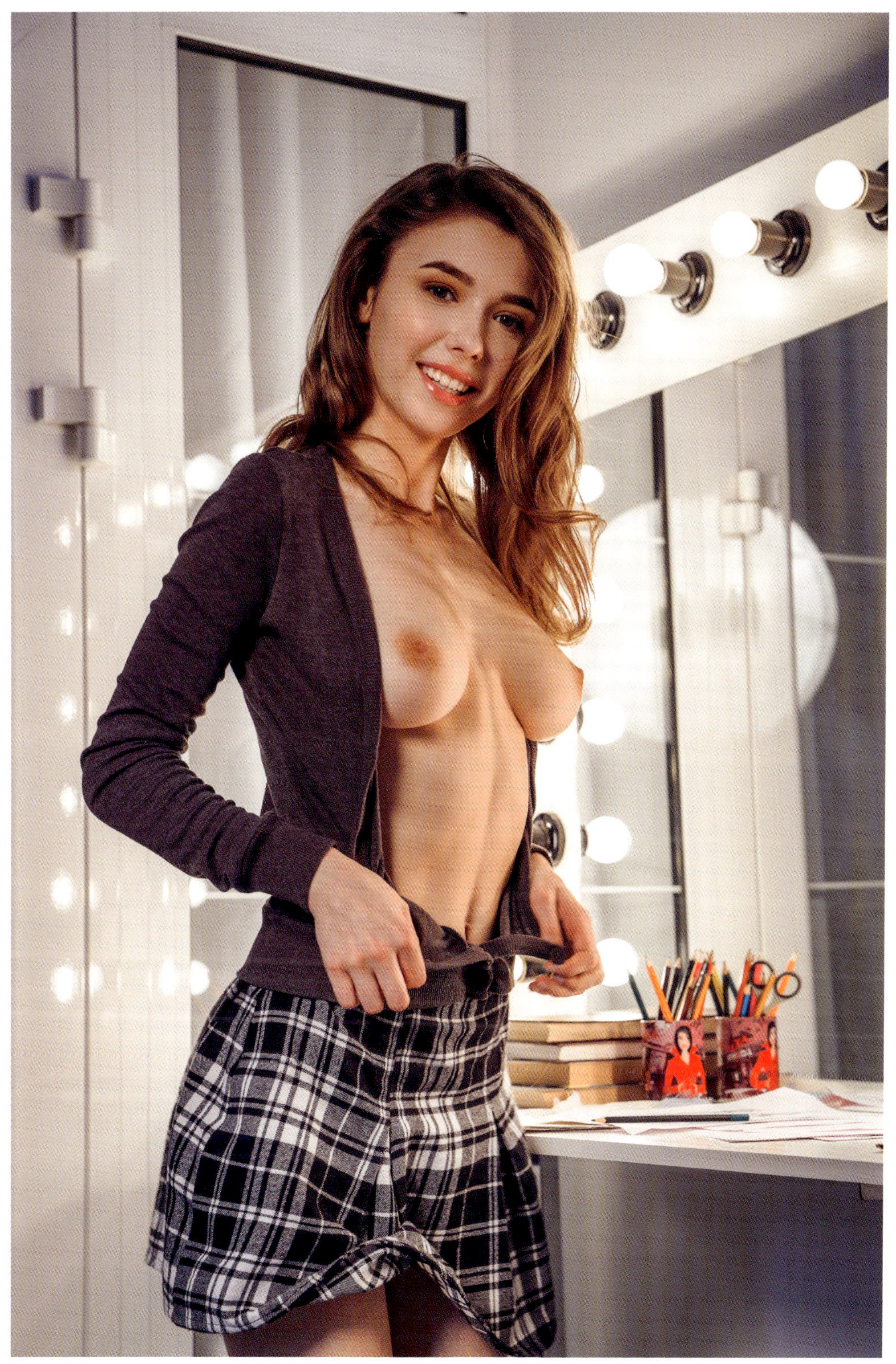

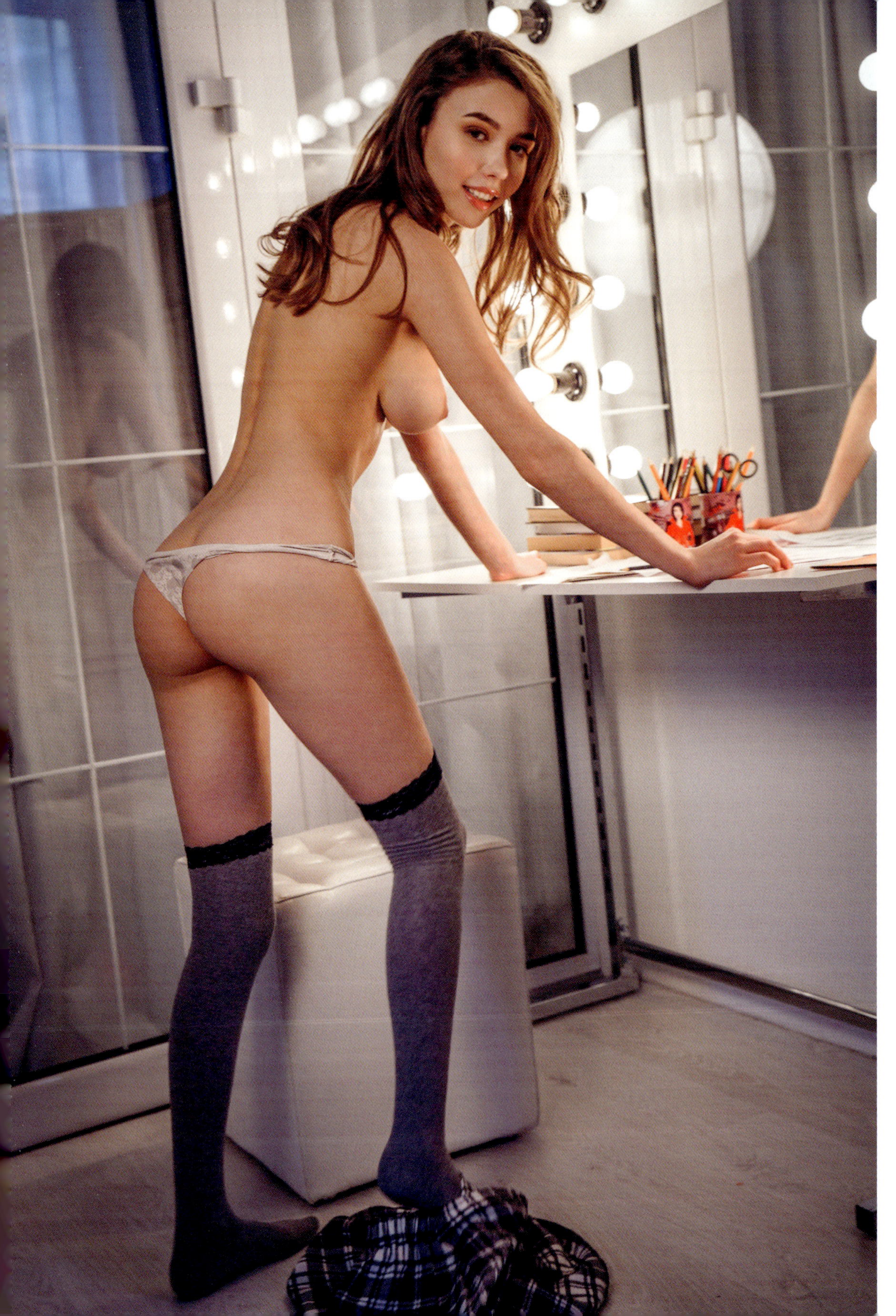

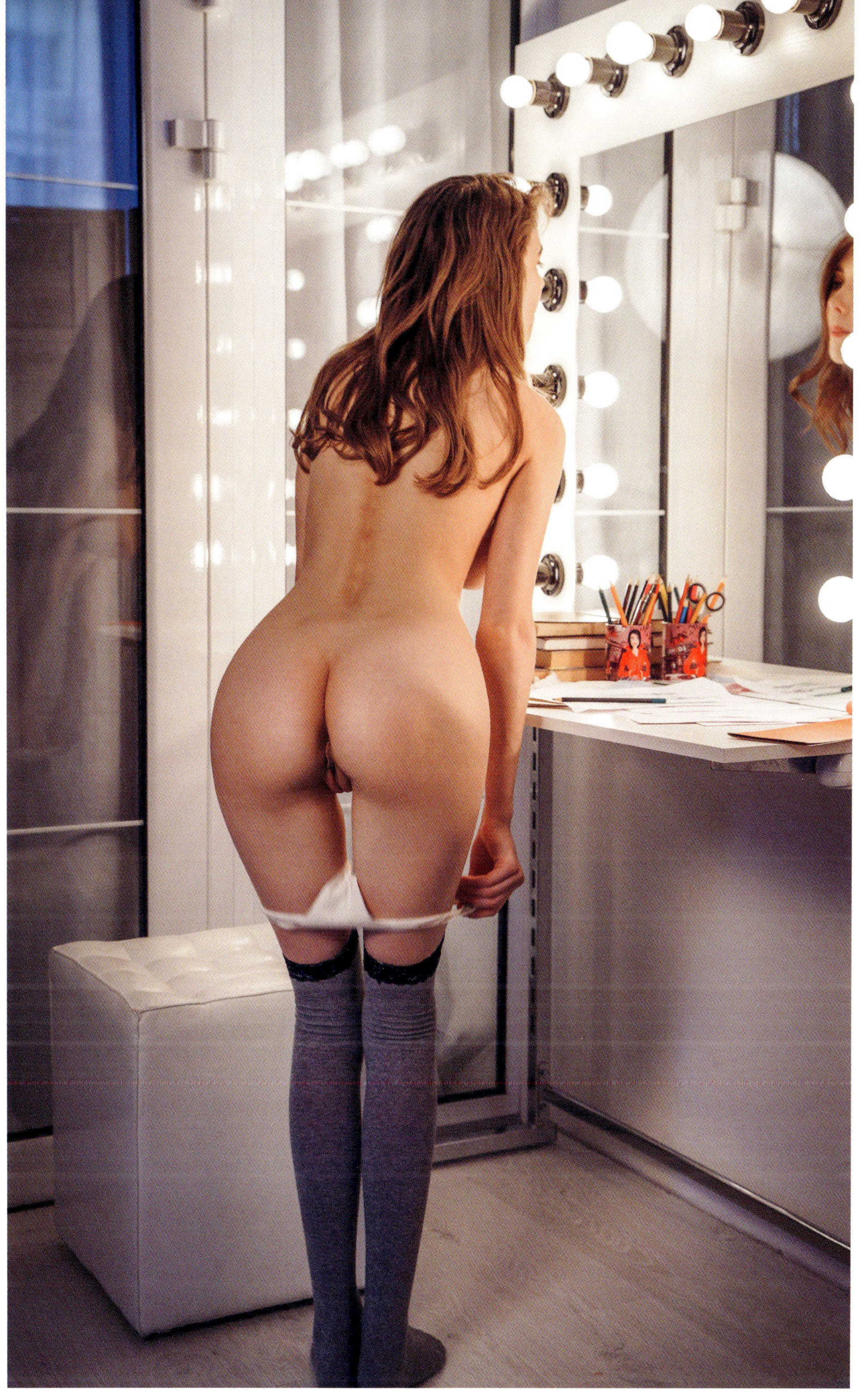

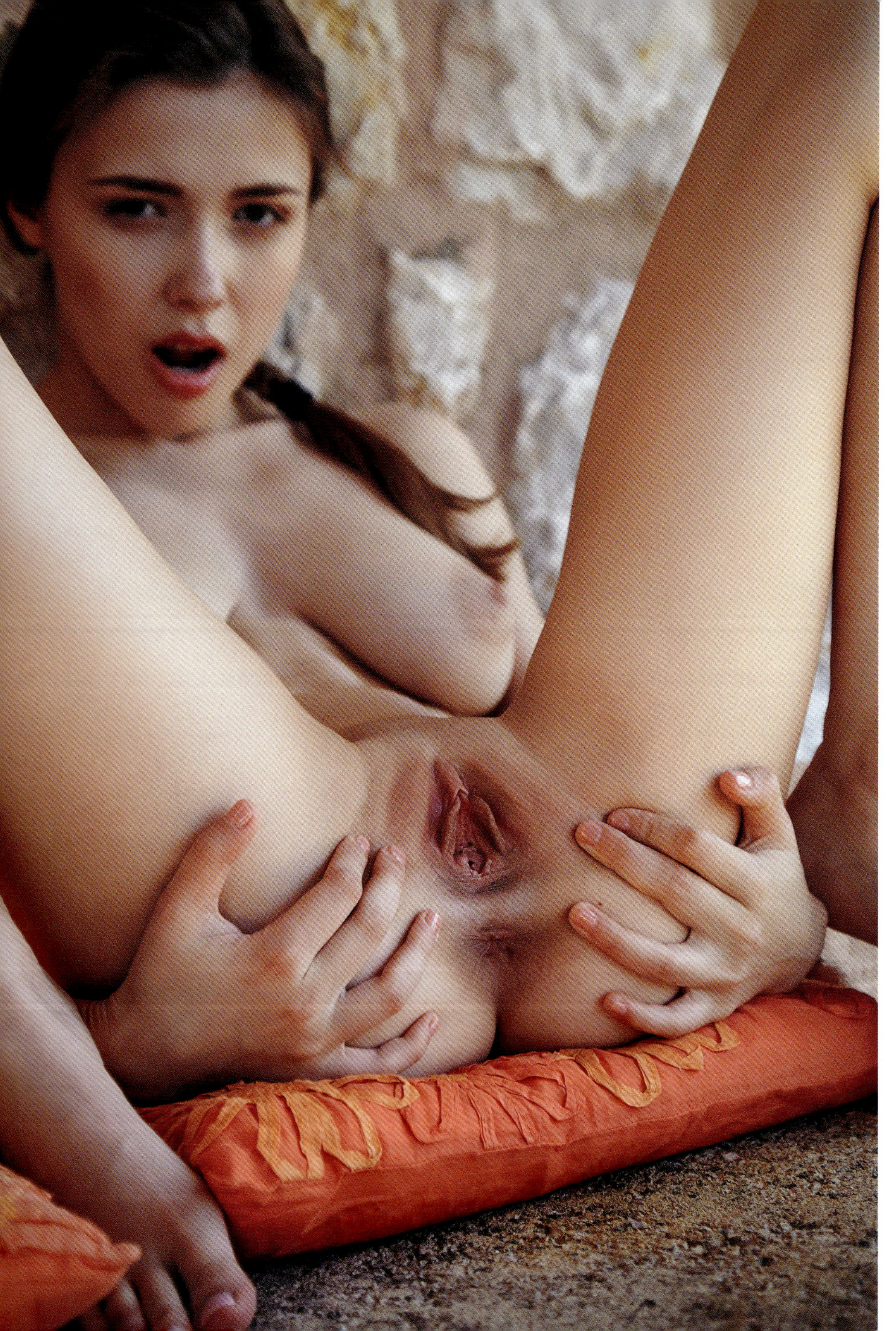

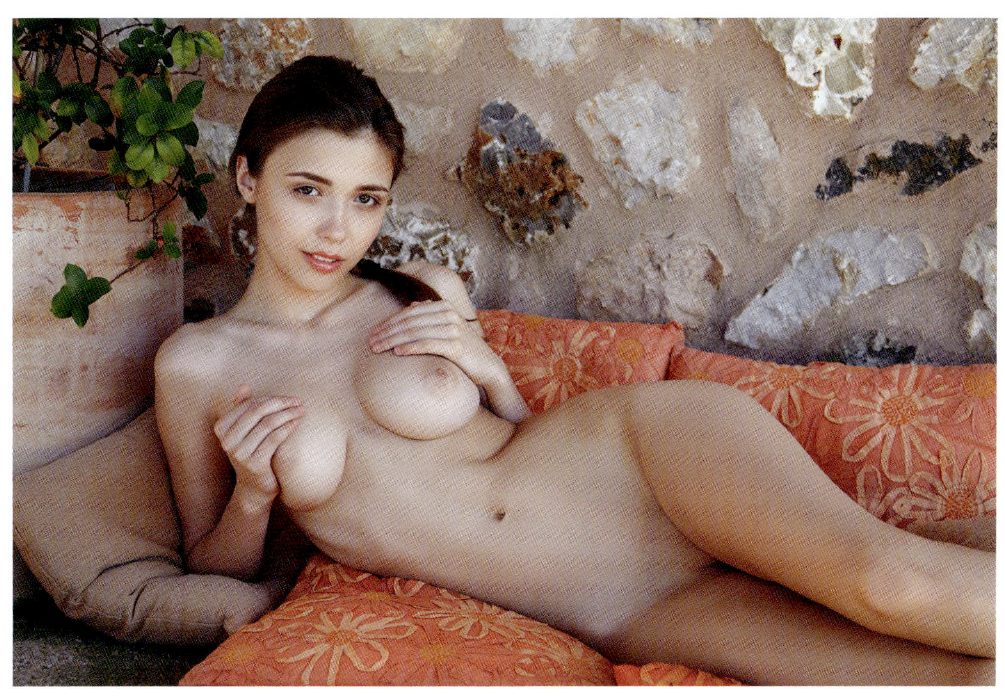

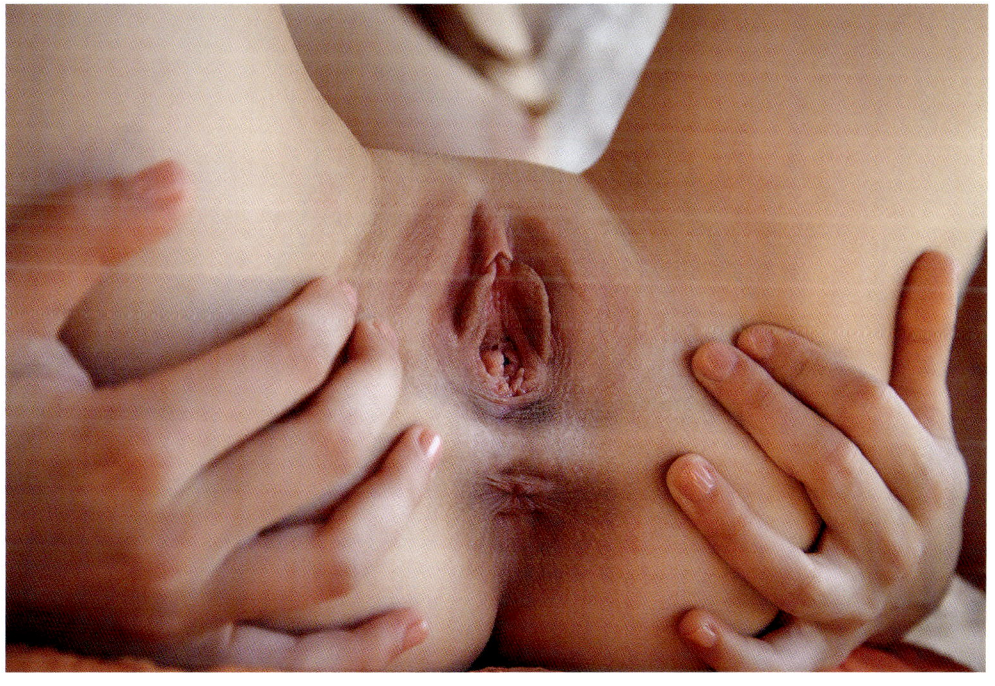

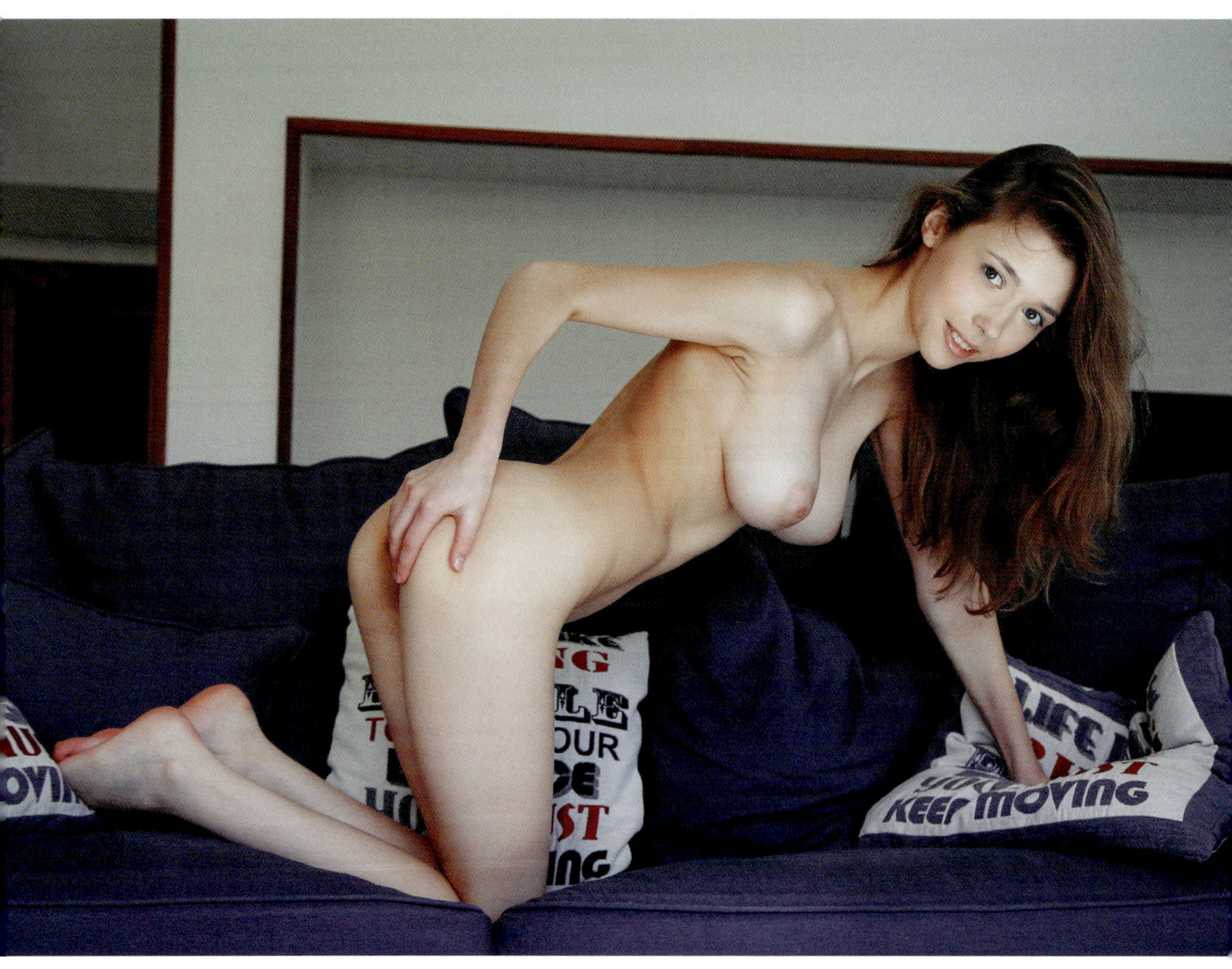
KEEP MOVING

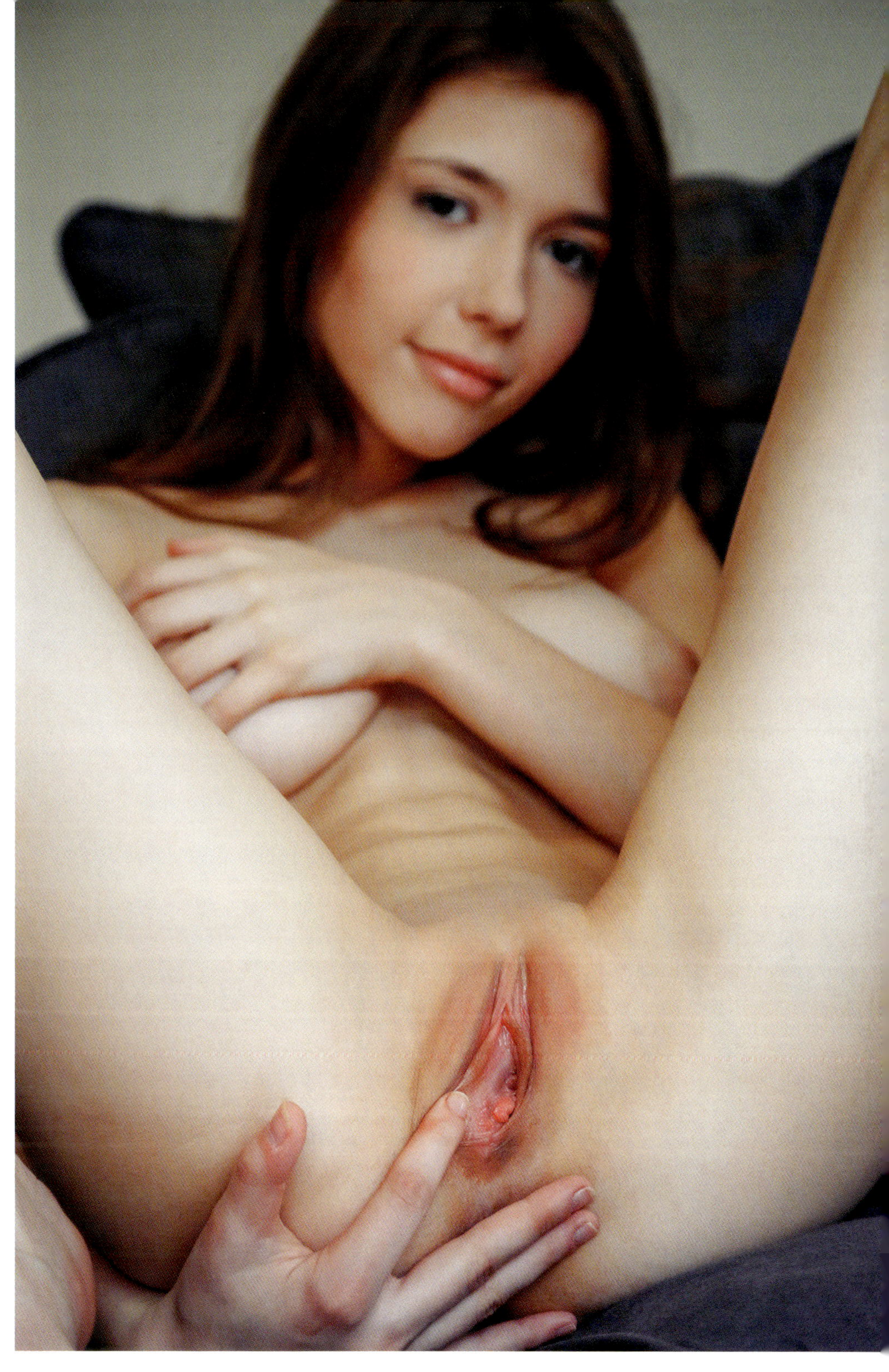

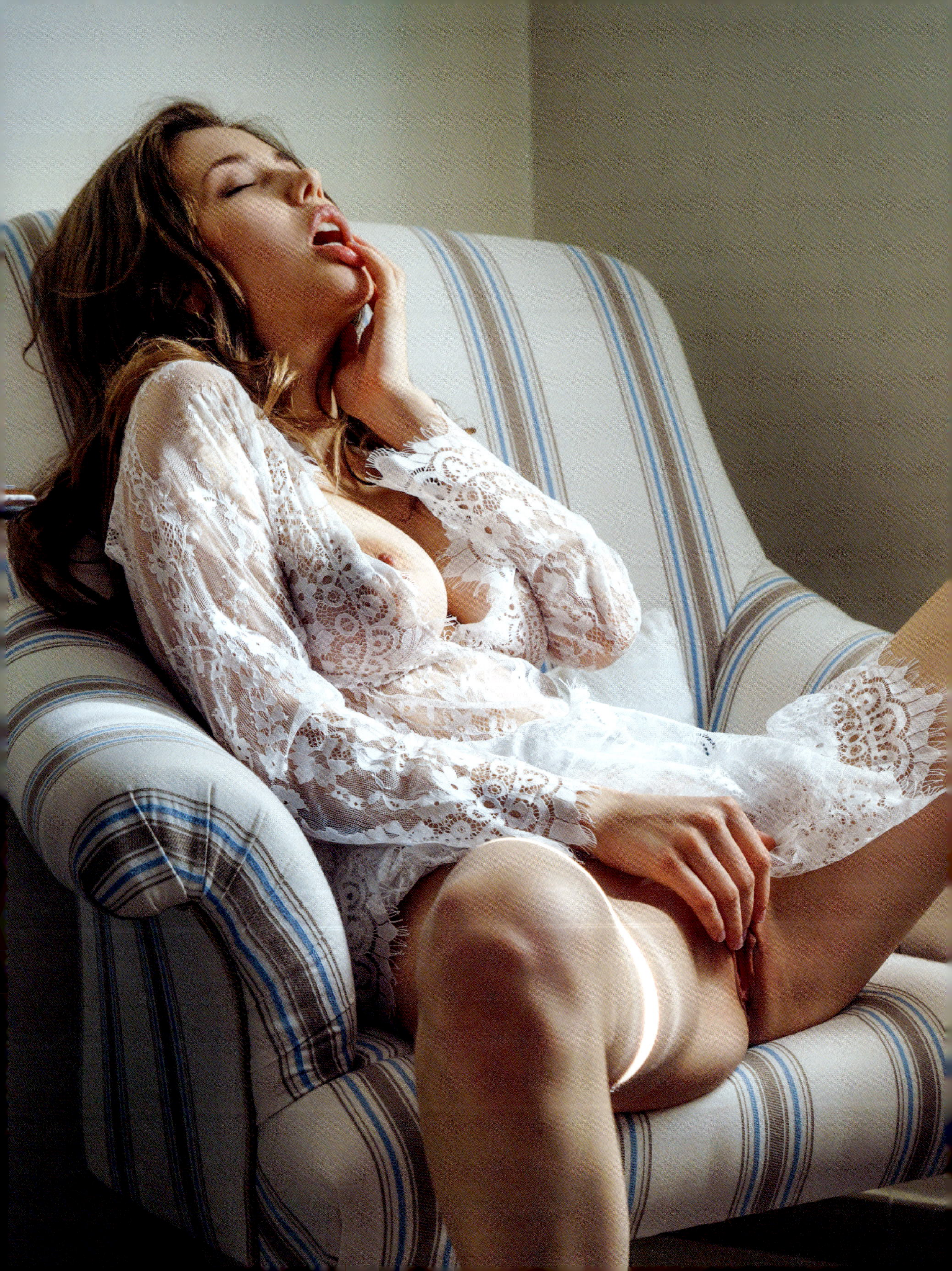

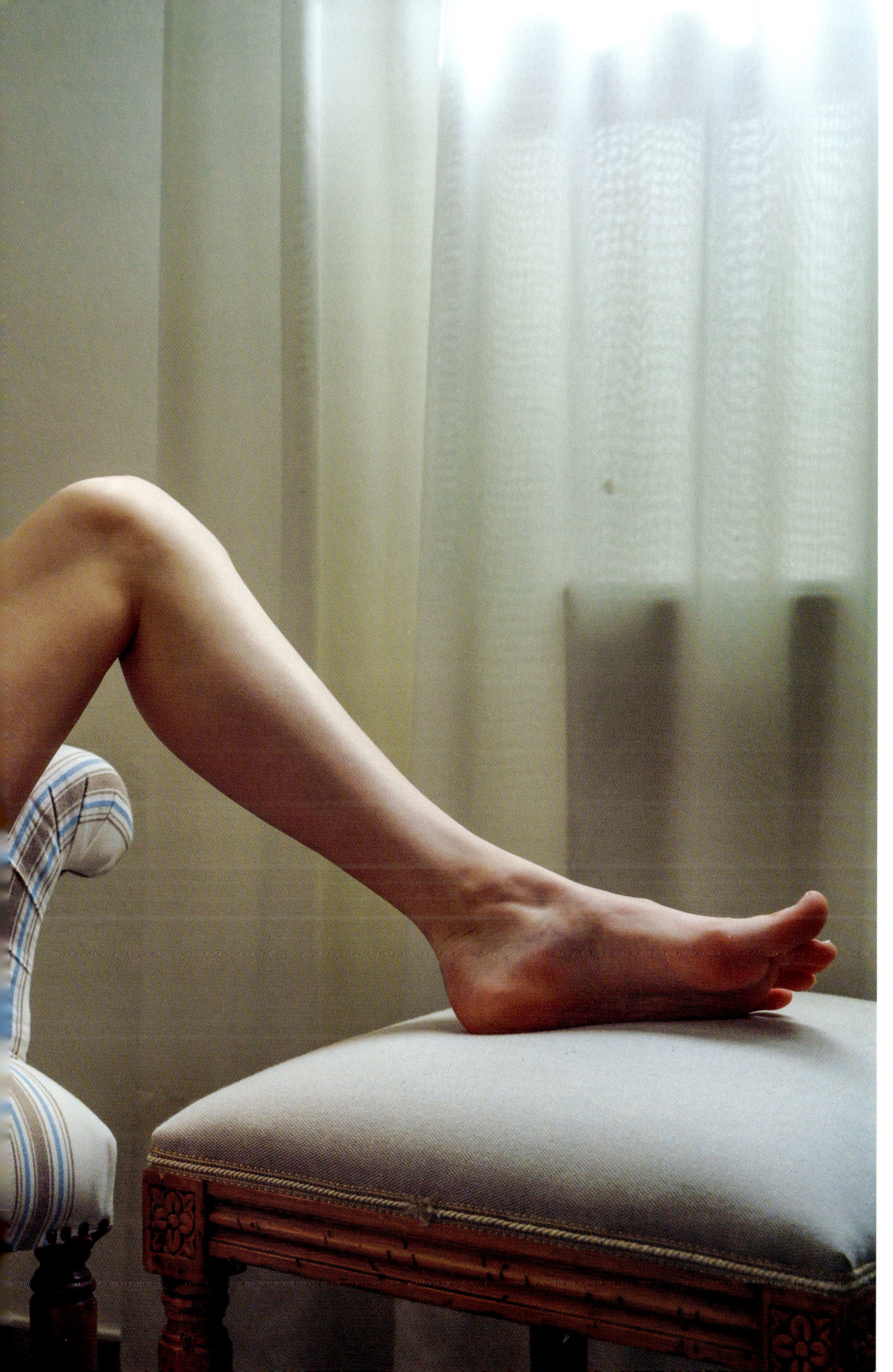

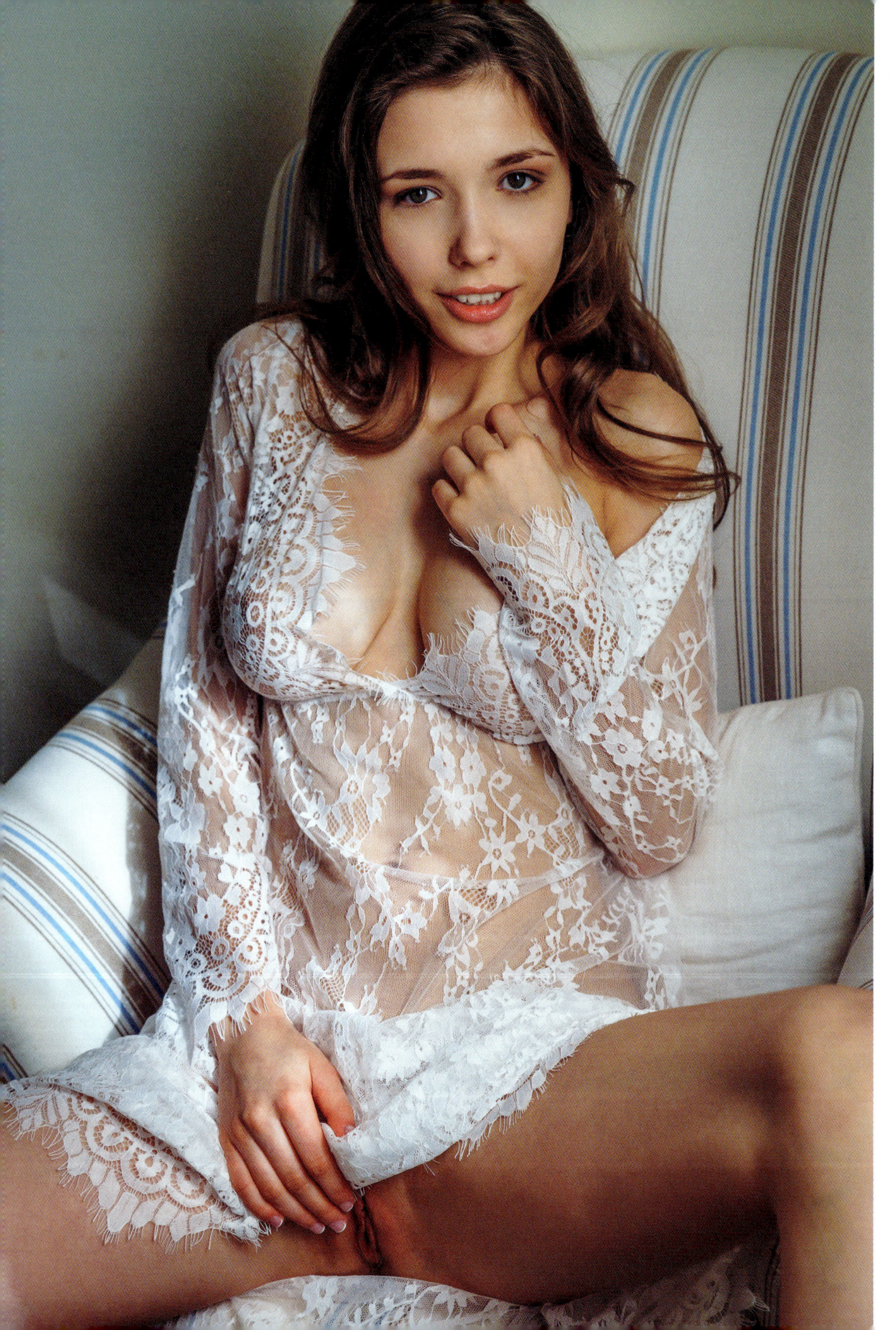

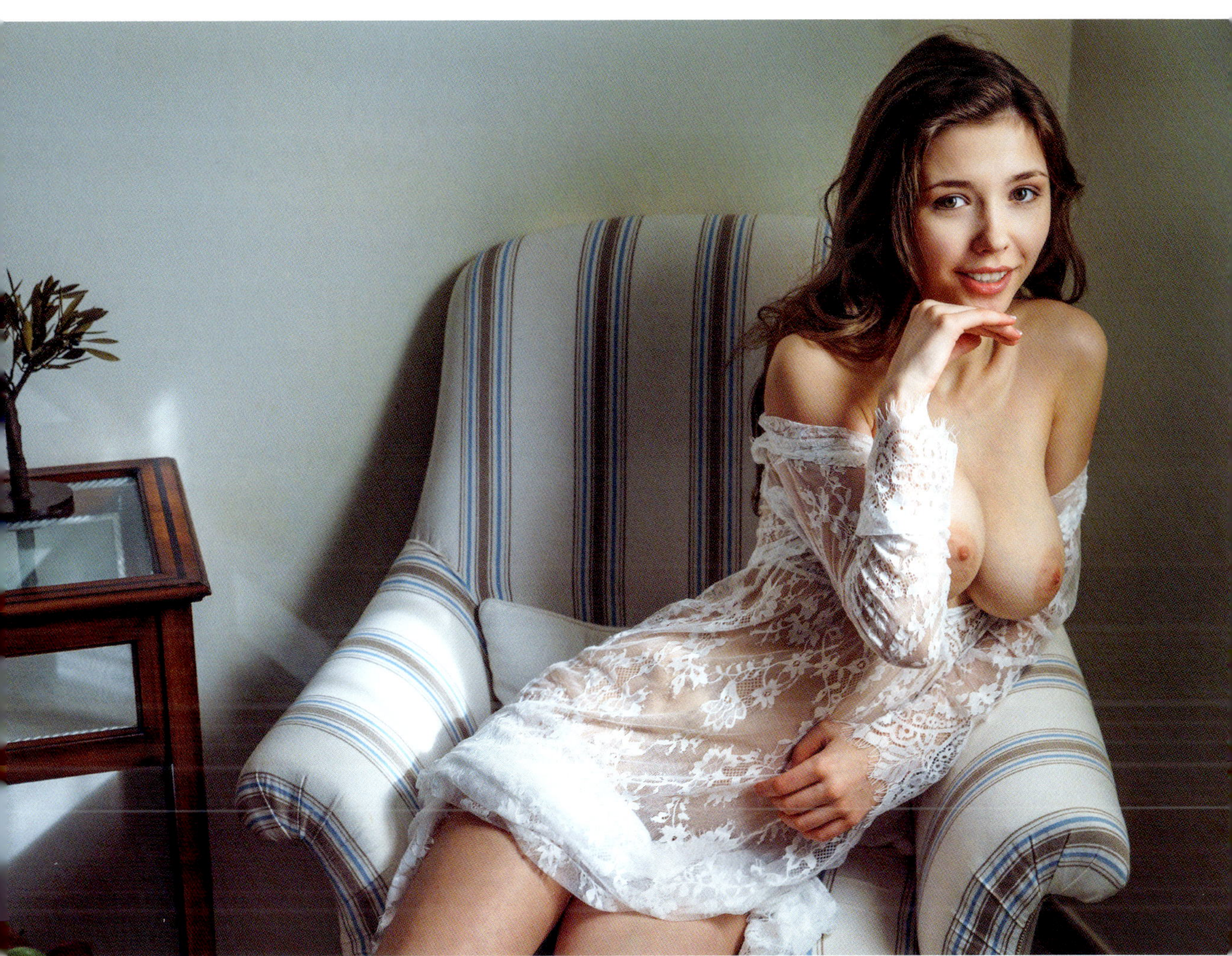

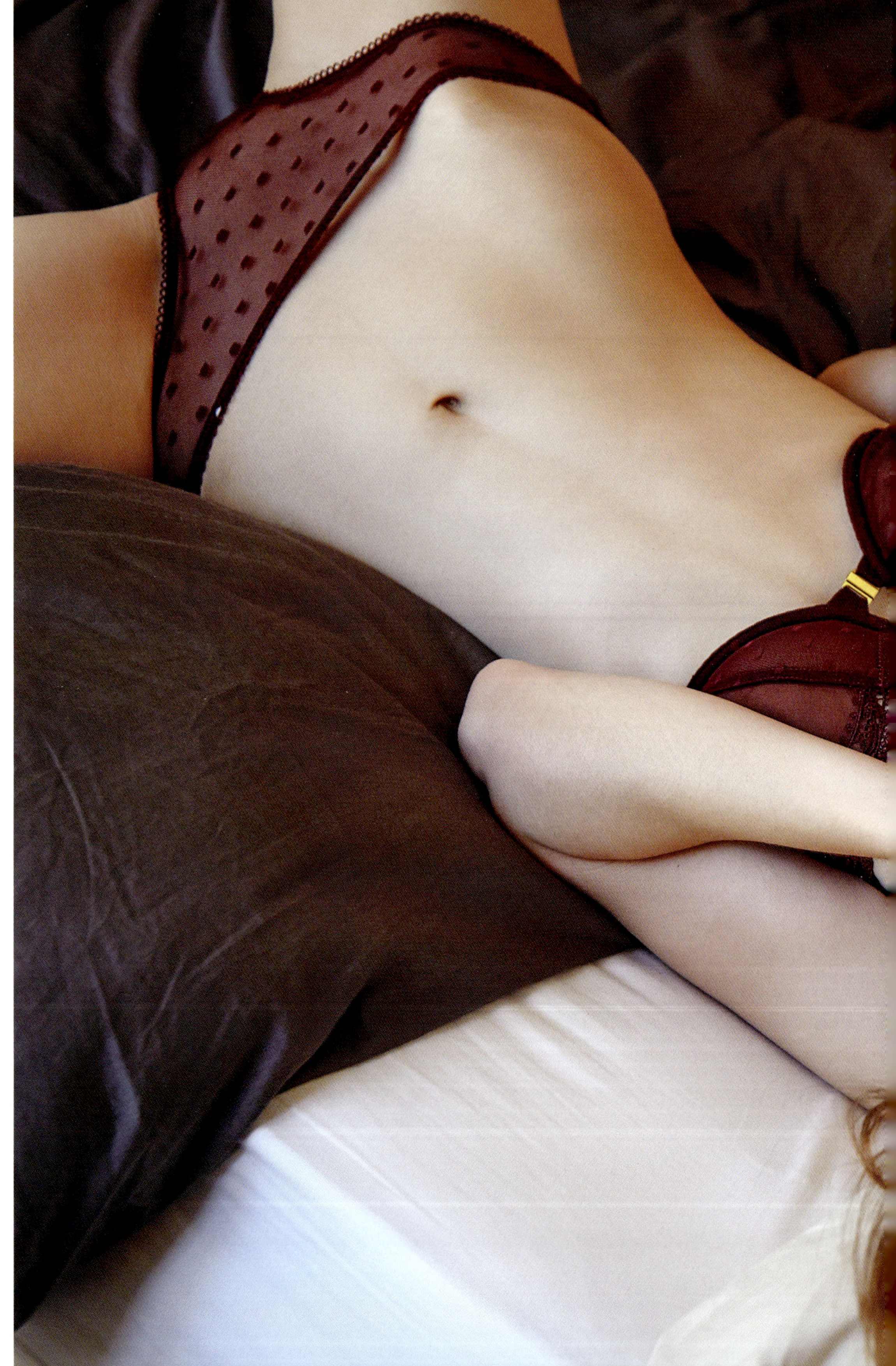

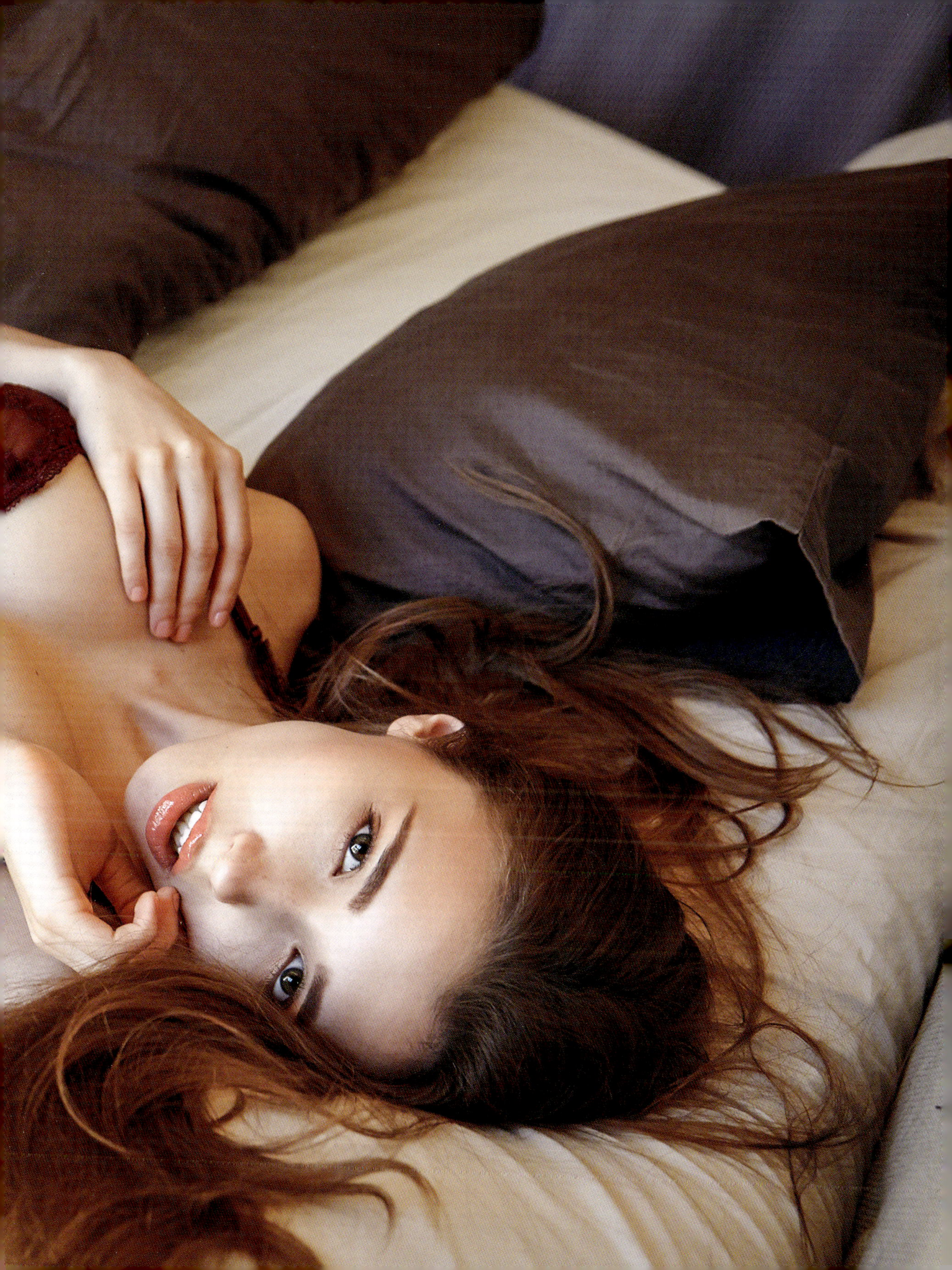

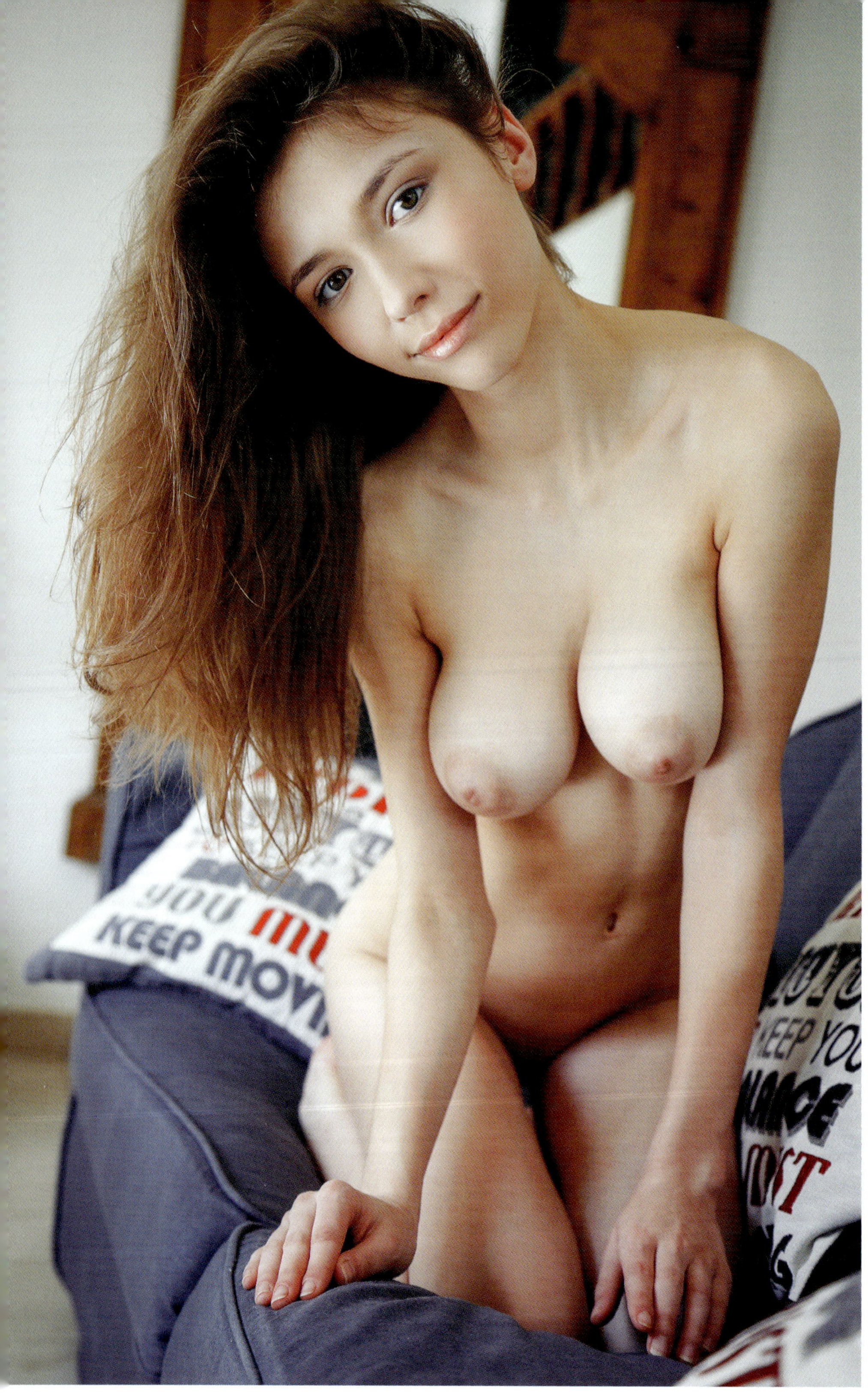
YOU
KEEP
KEEP YOU

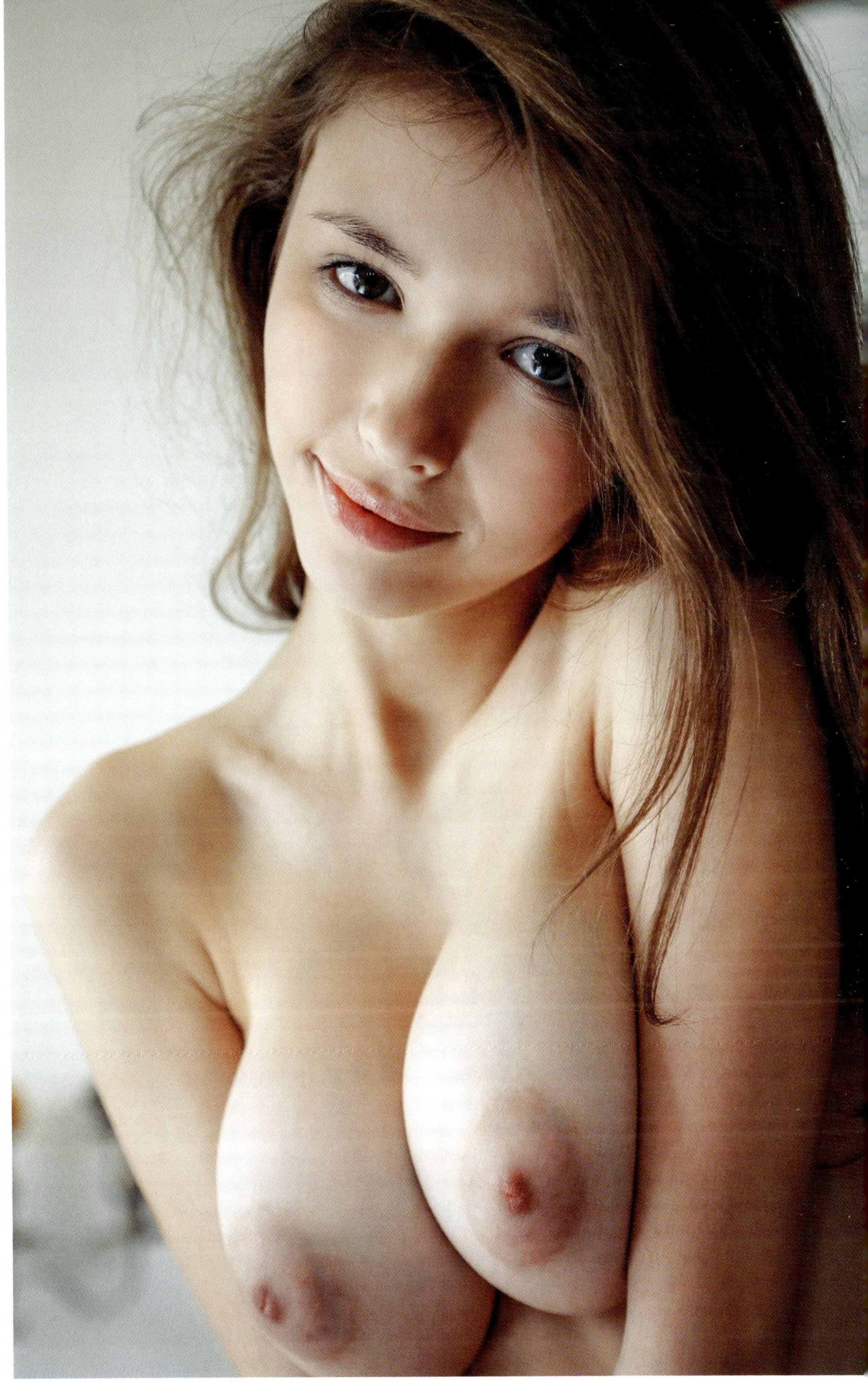

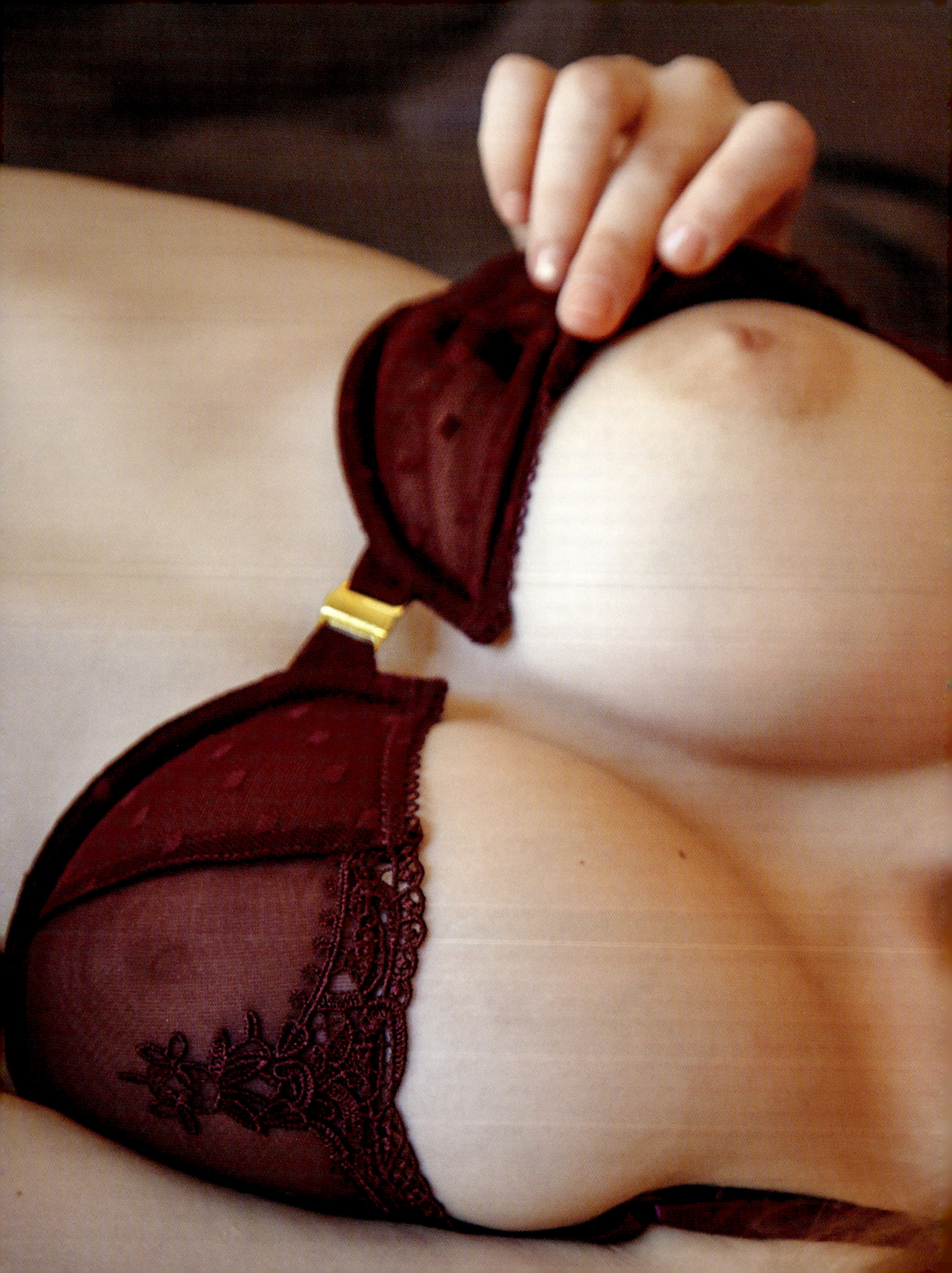

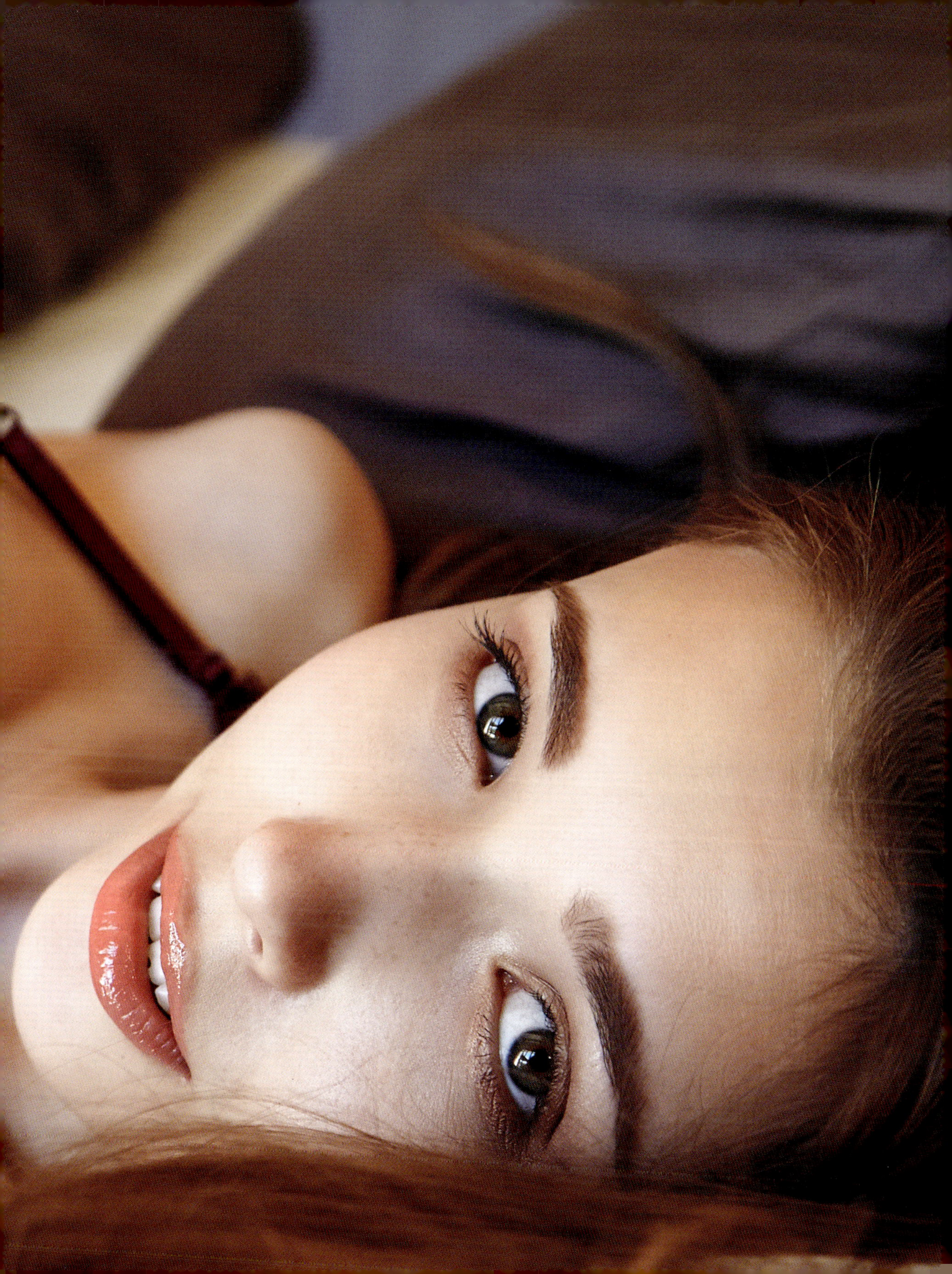

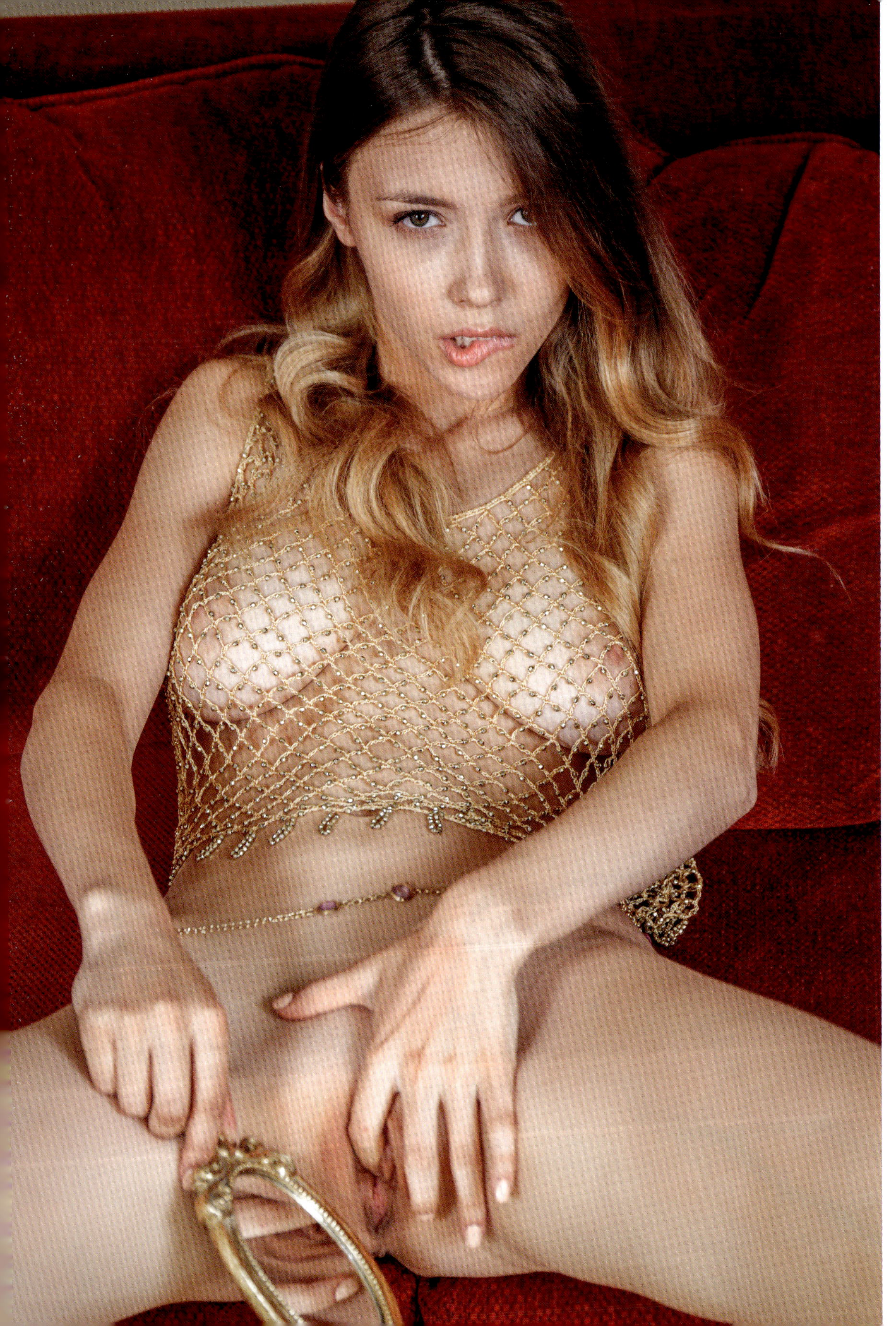

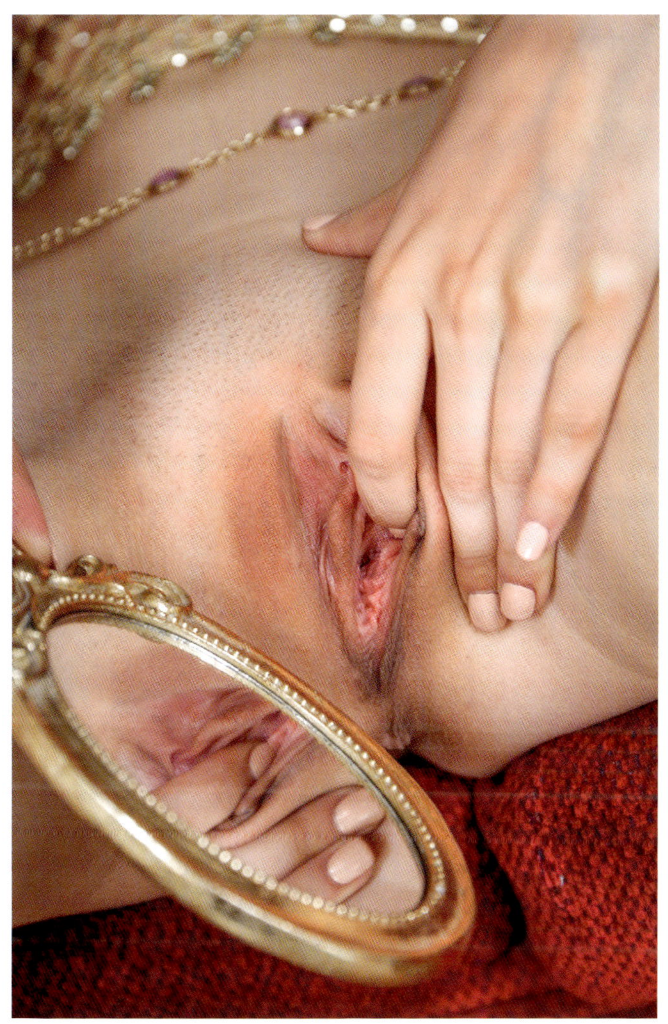

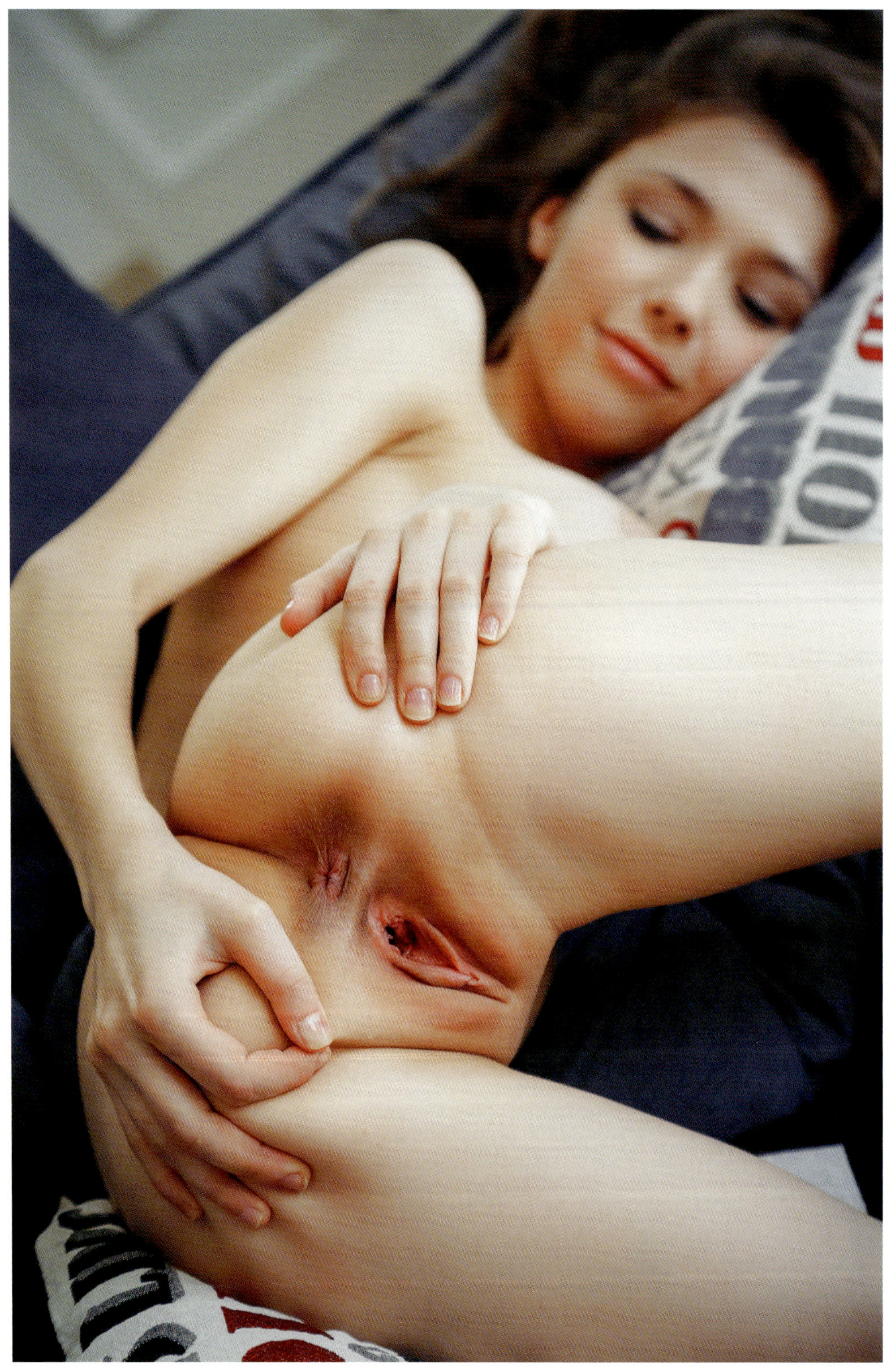

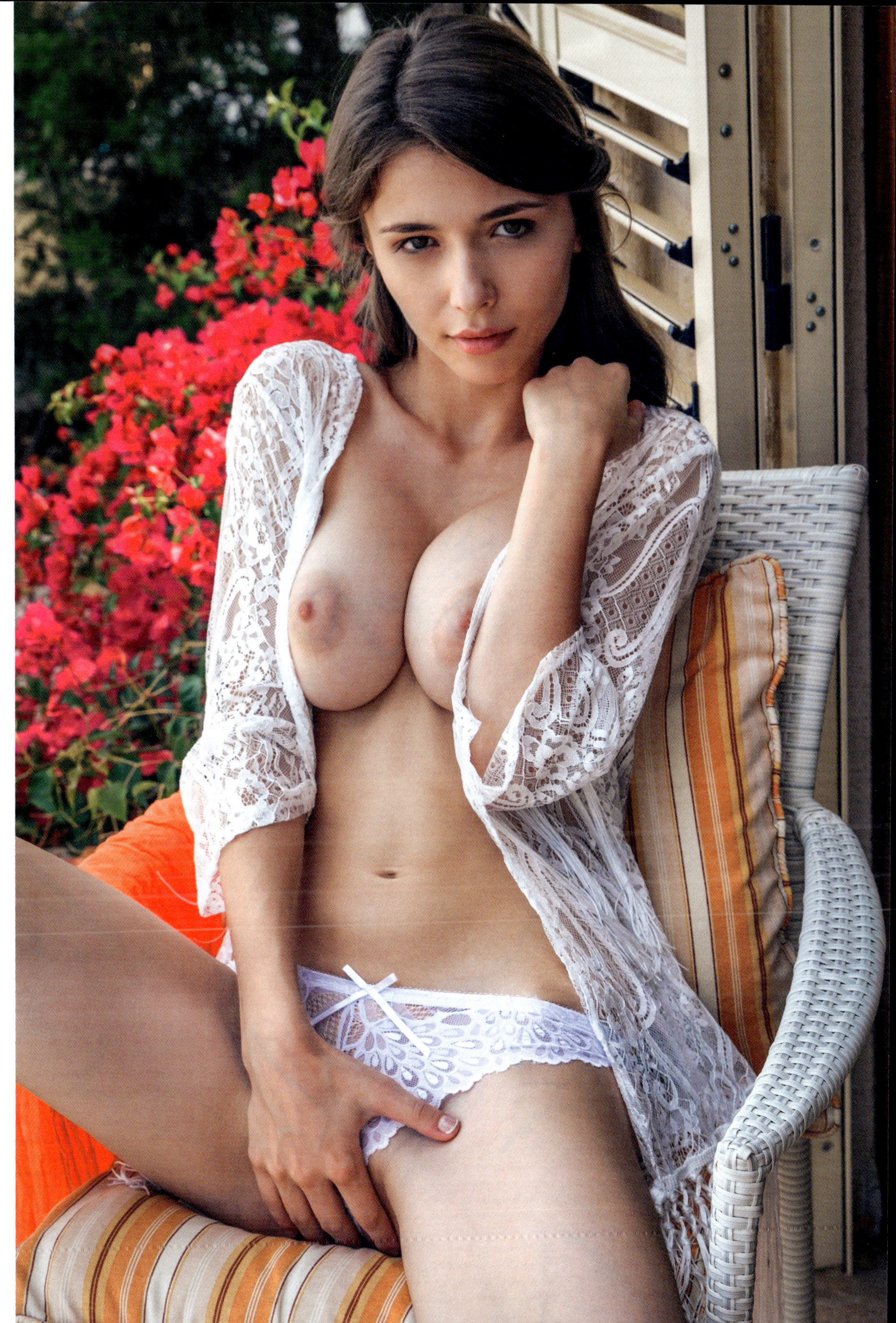

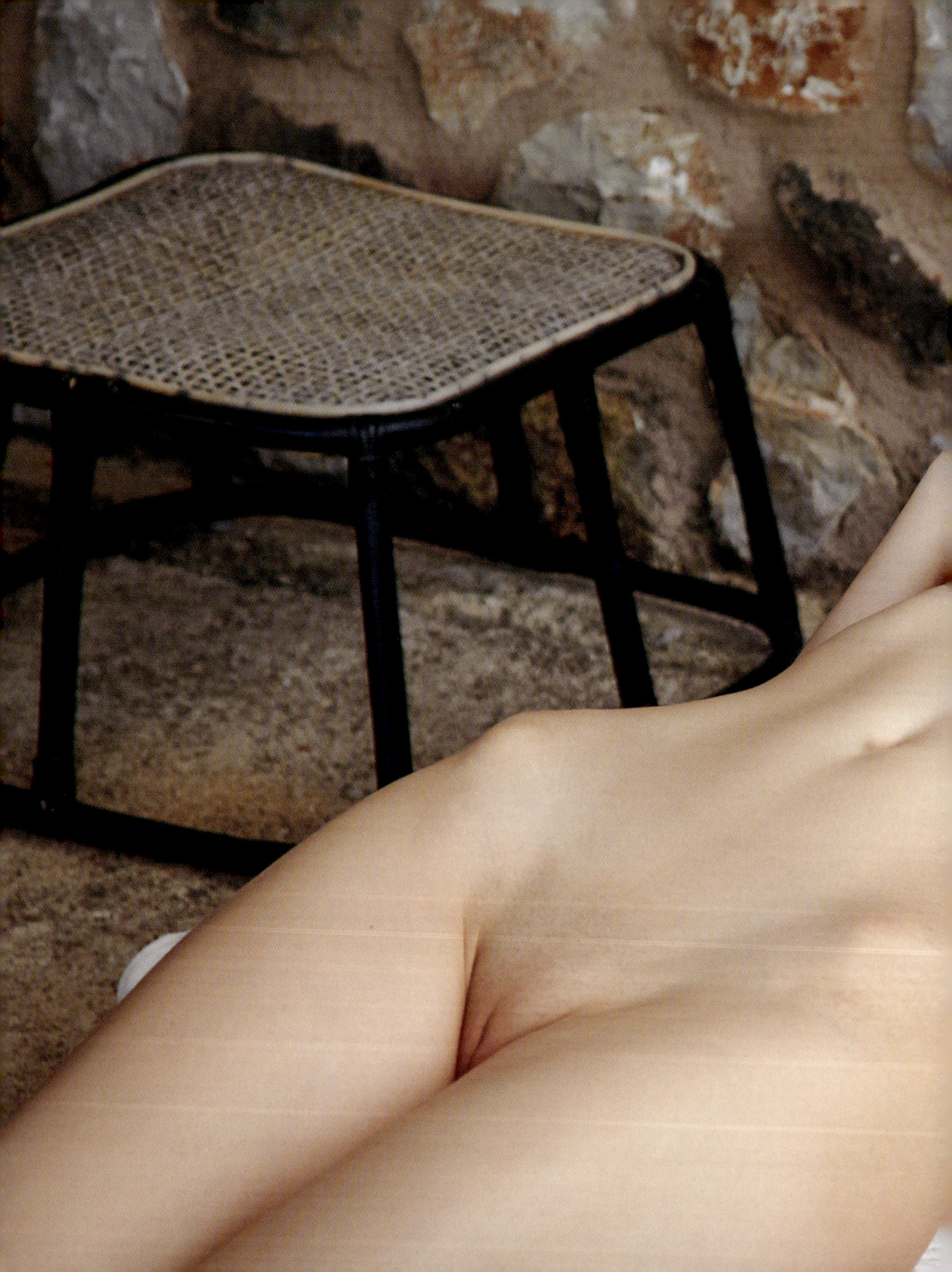

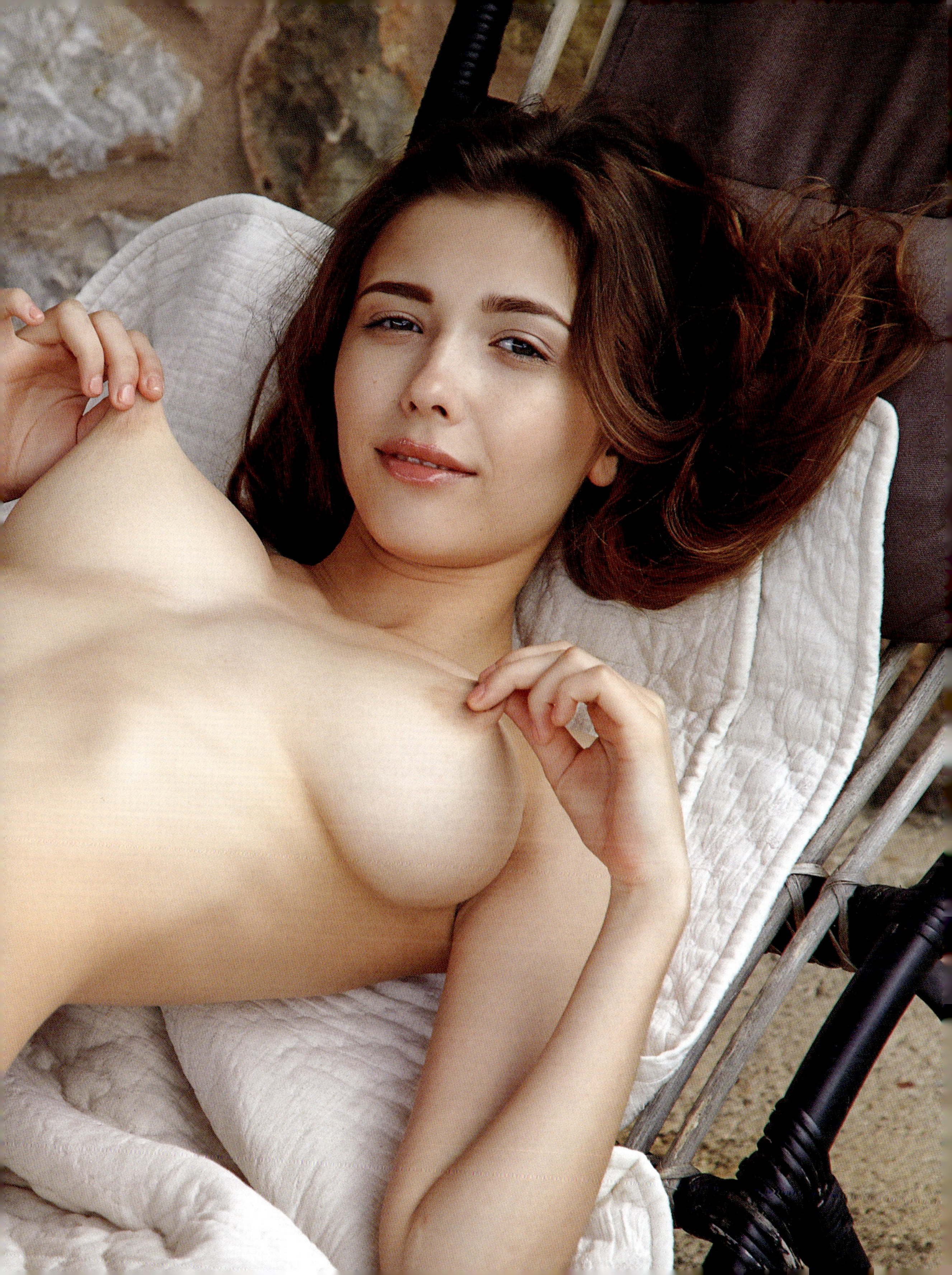

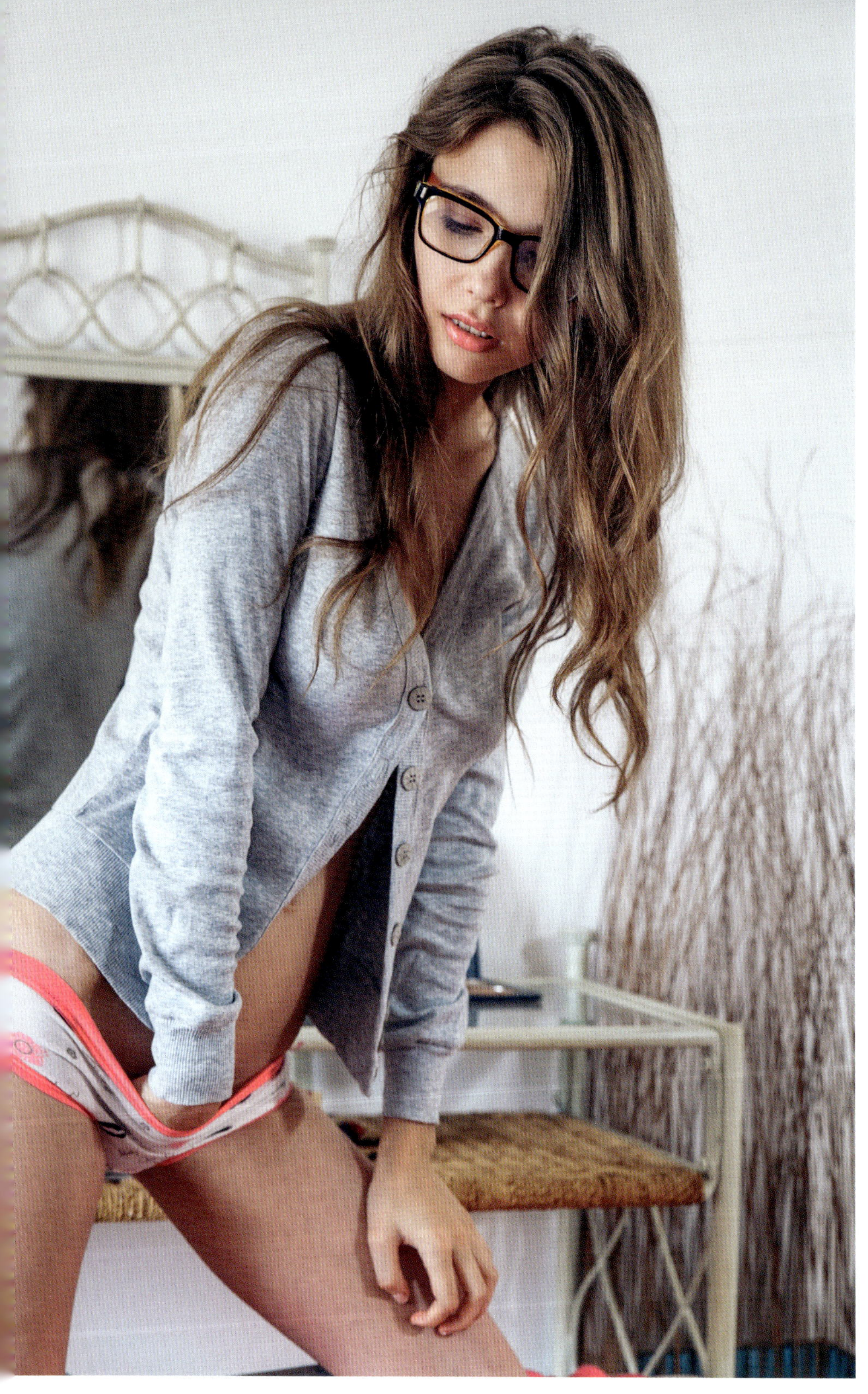

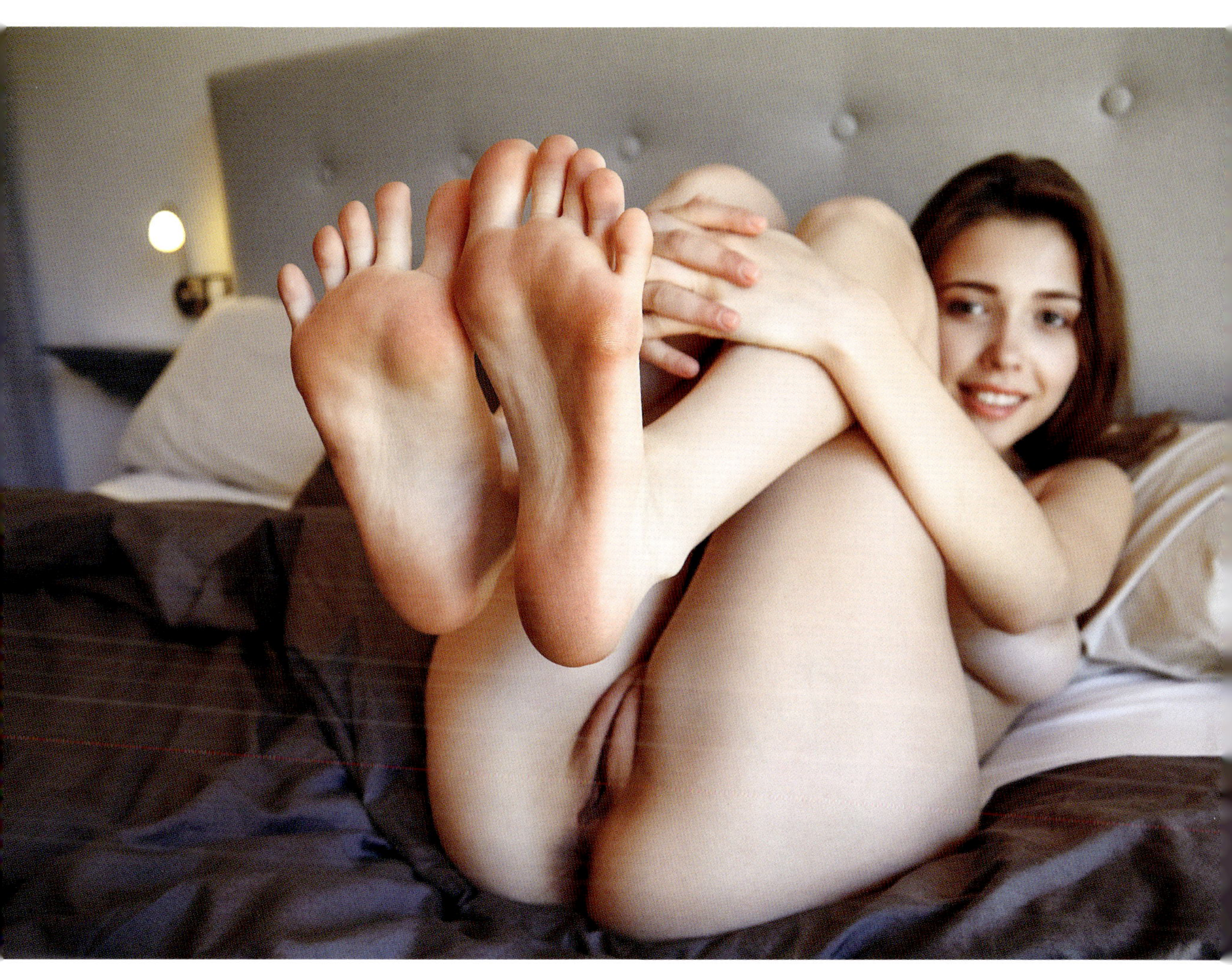

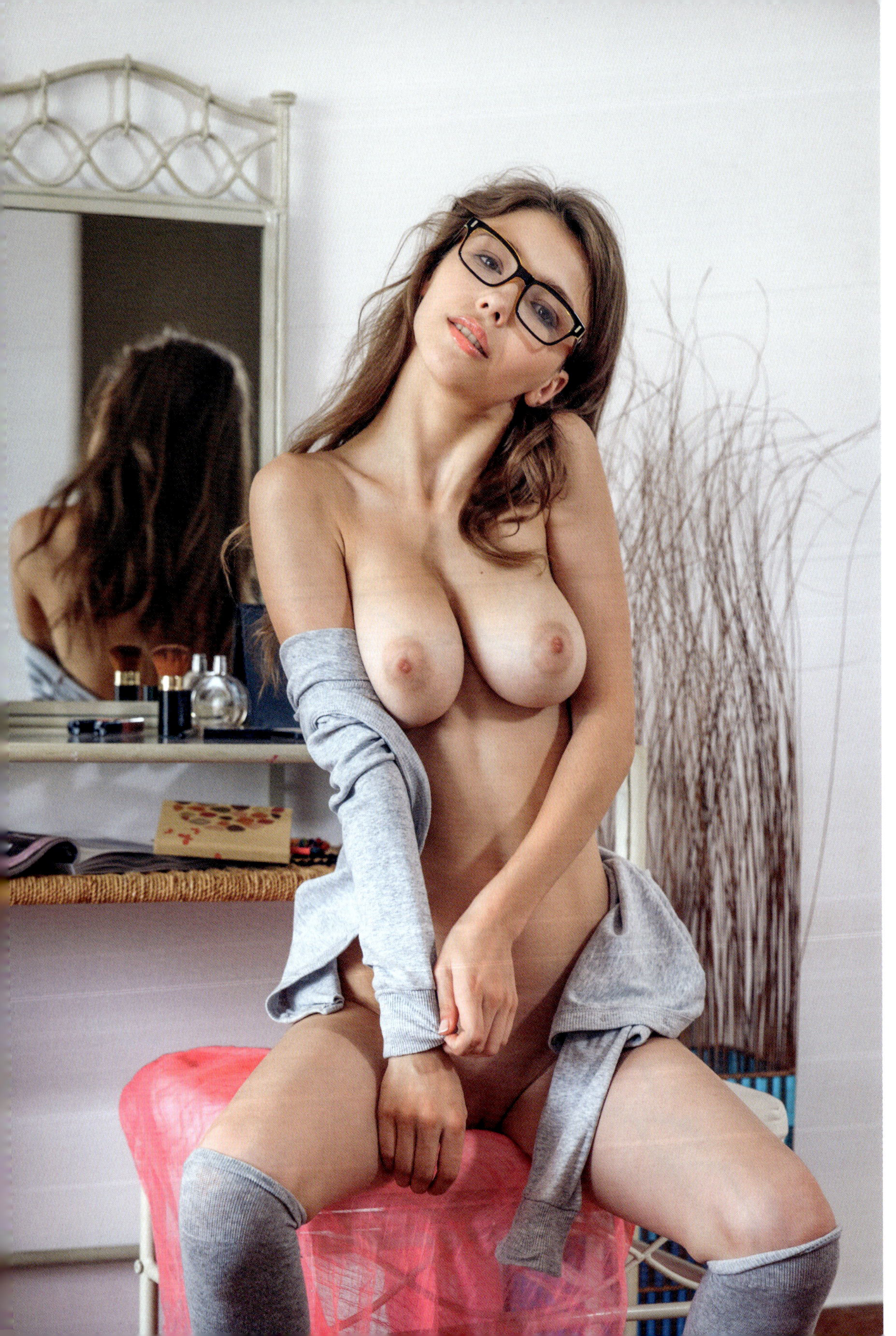

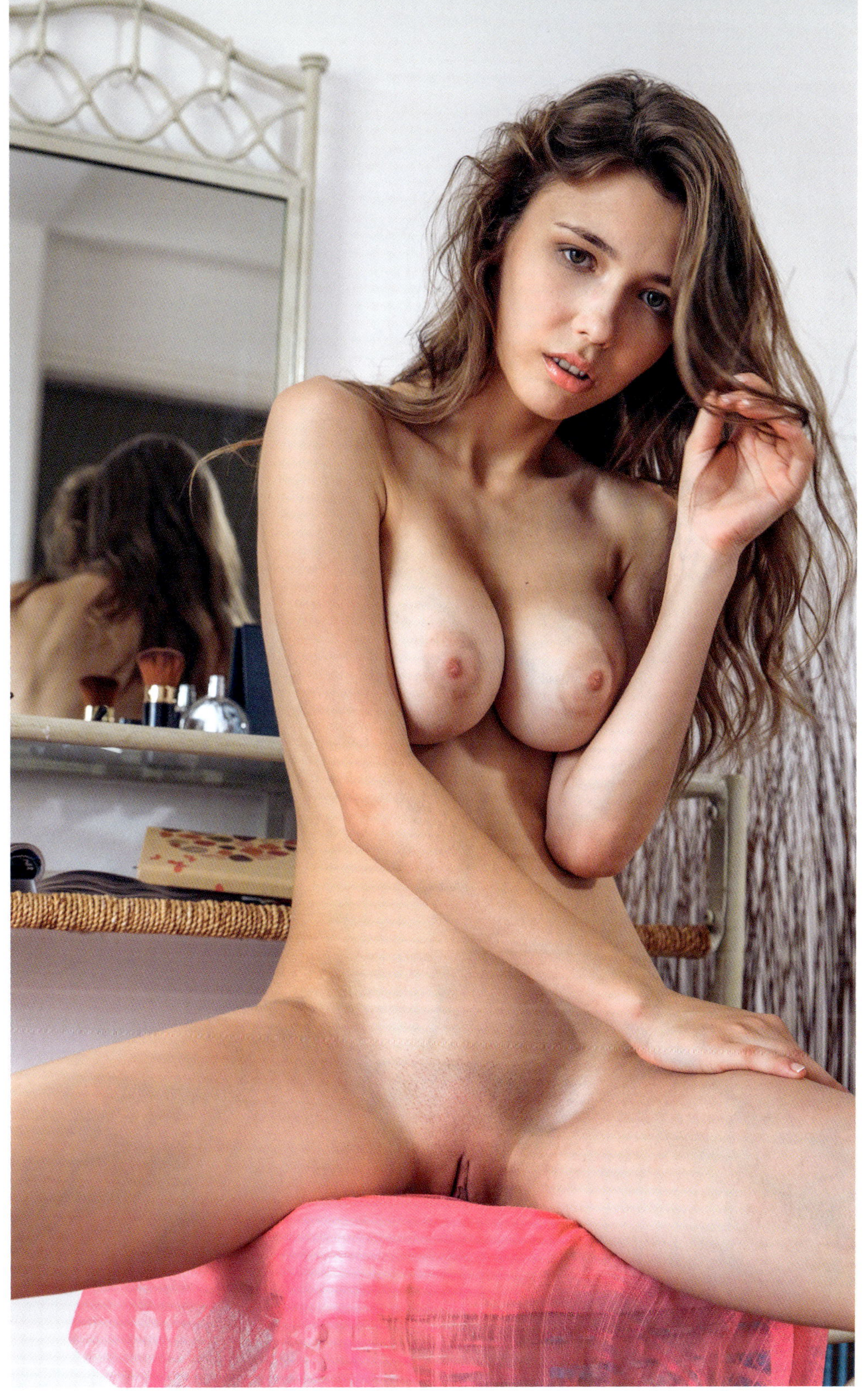

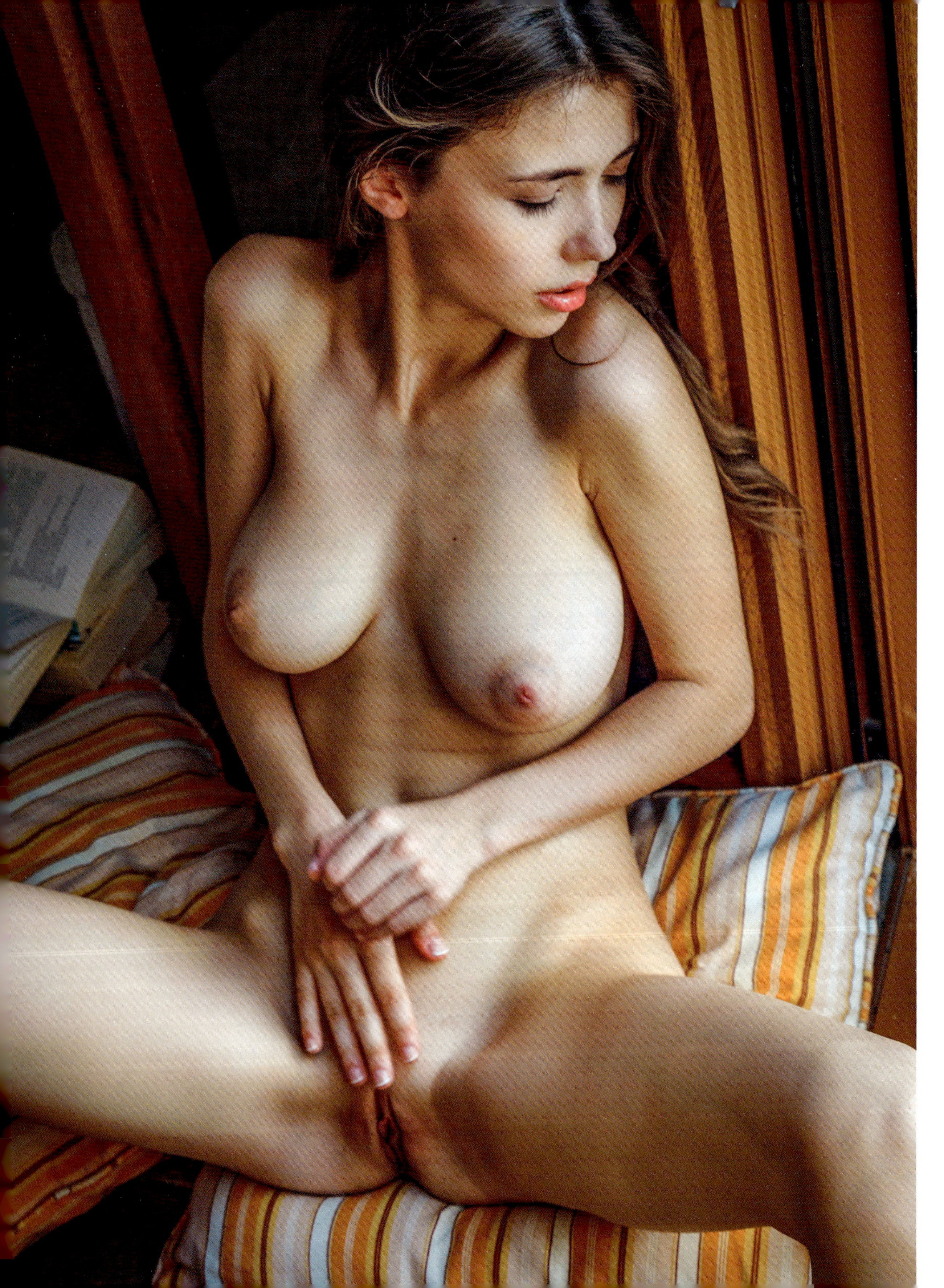

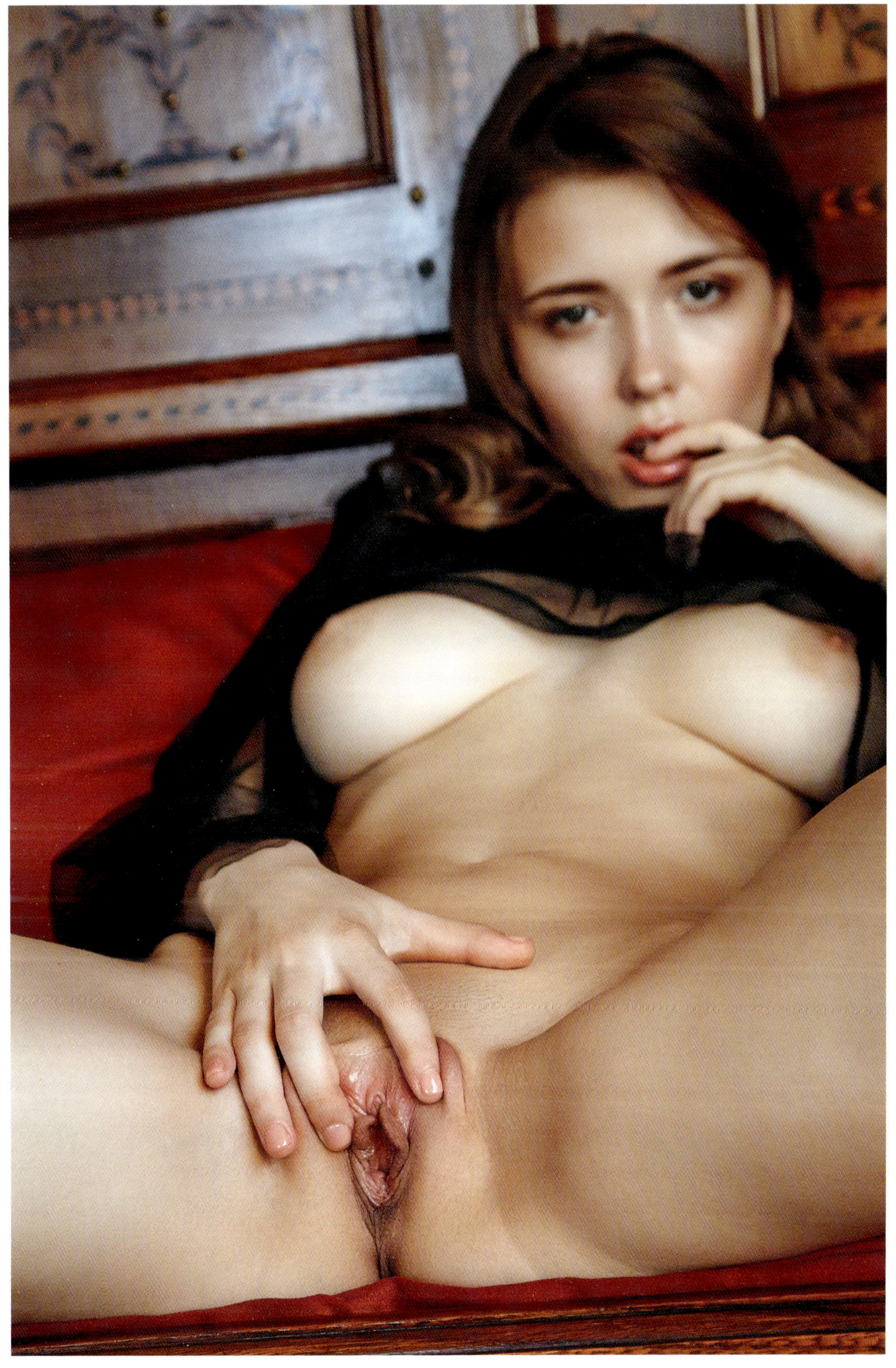

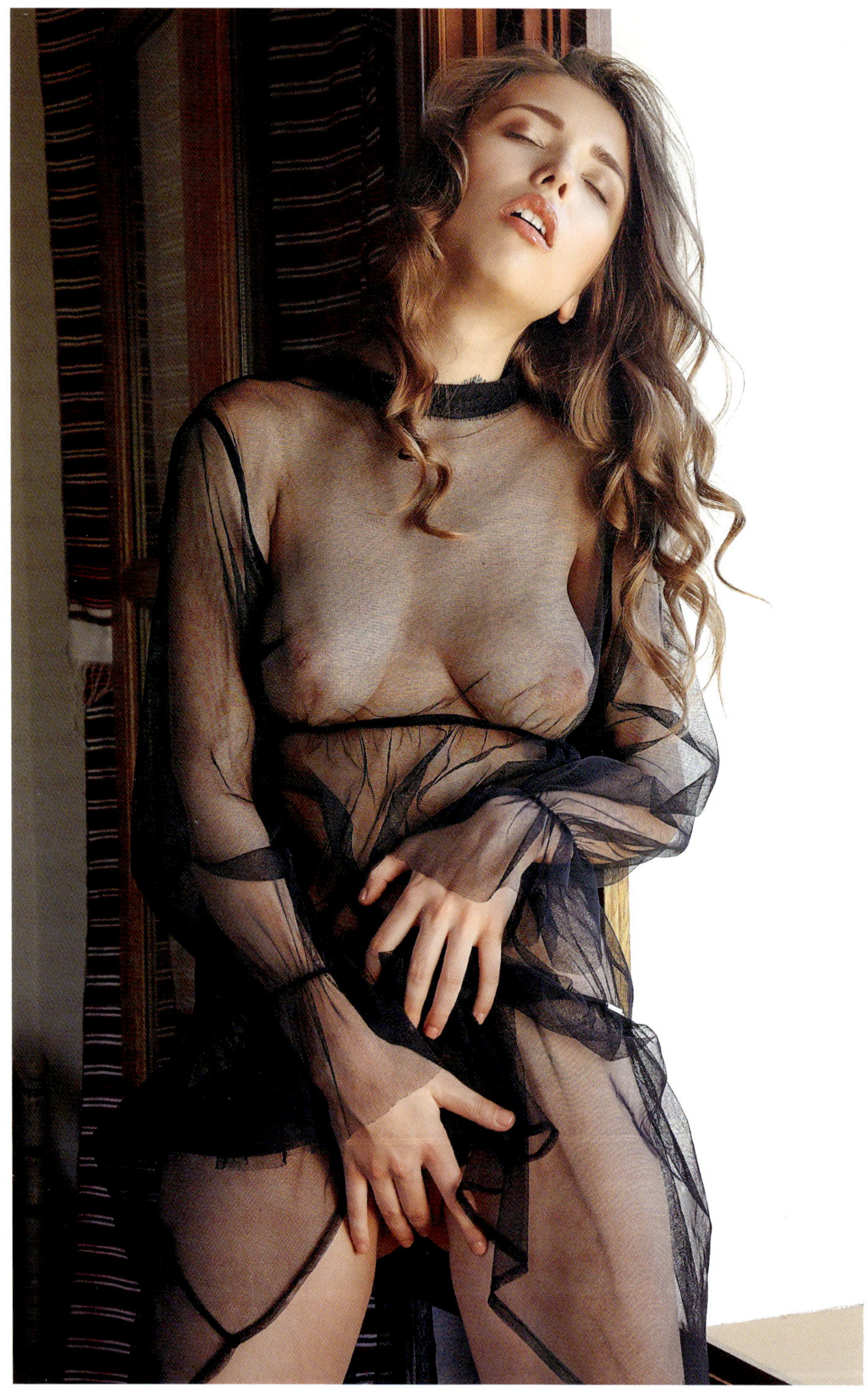

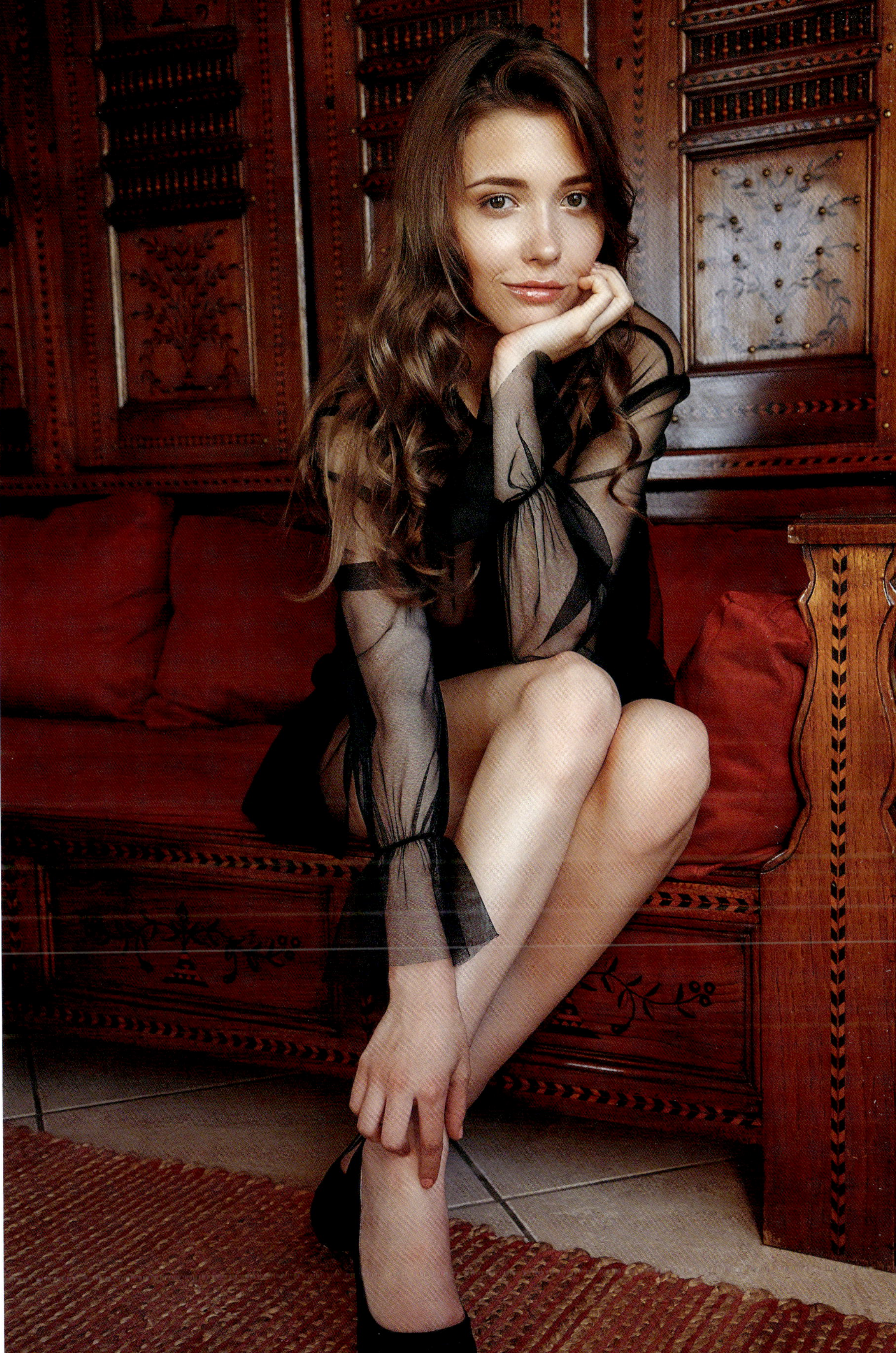

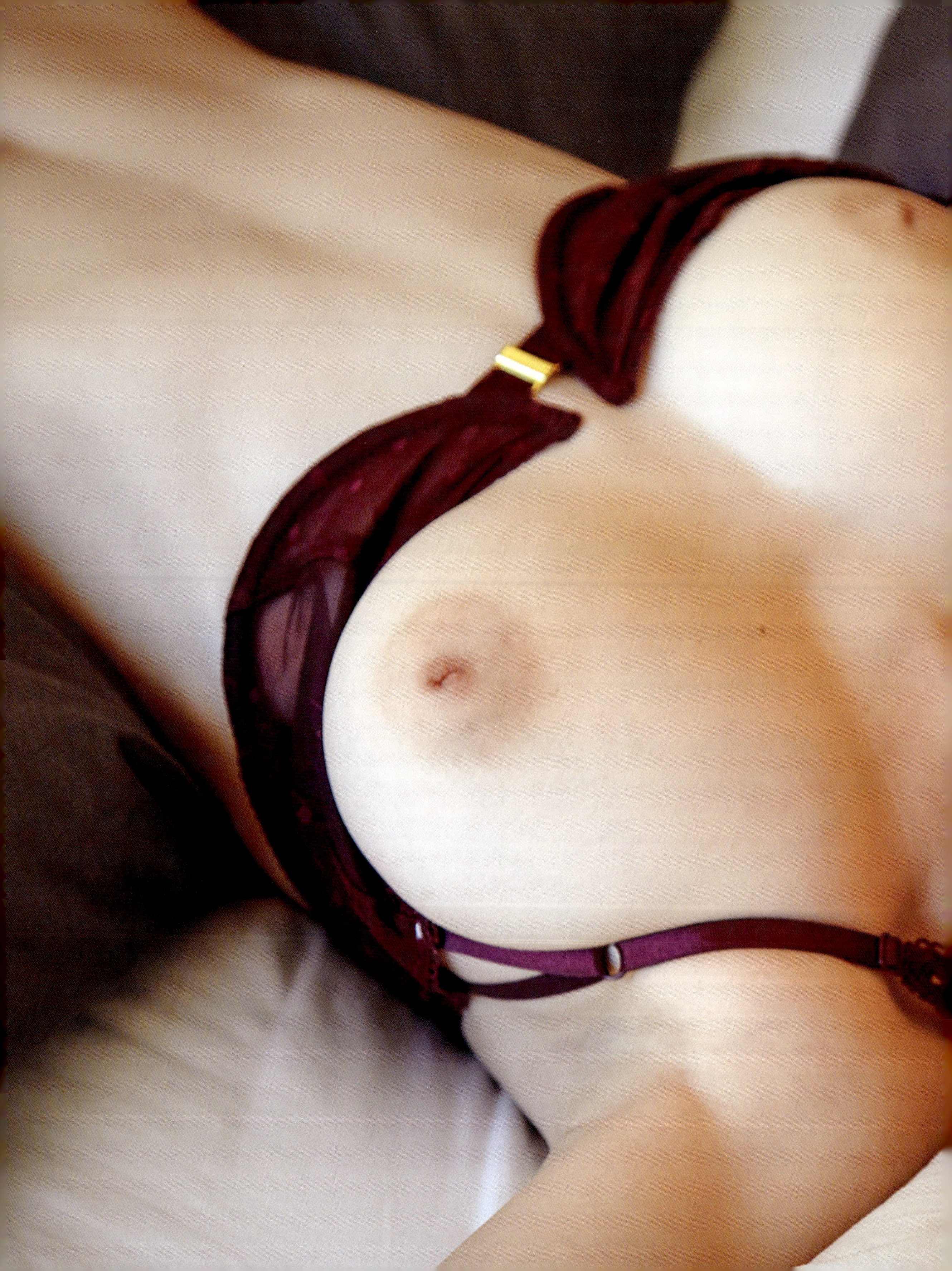

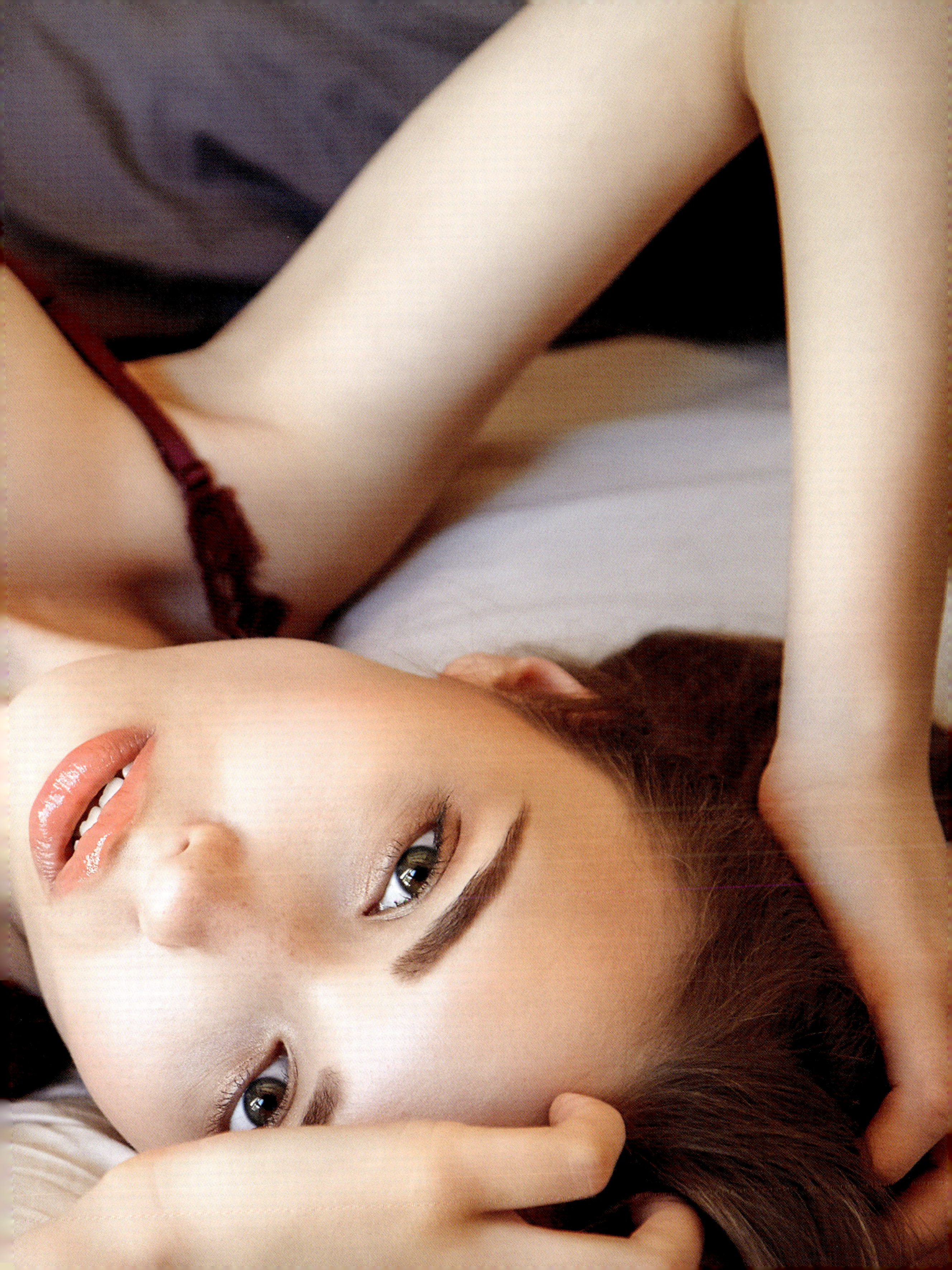

COLLECT THEM ALL: OUR MOST BEAUTIFUL

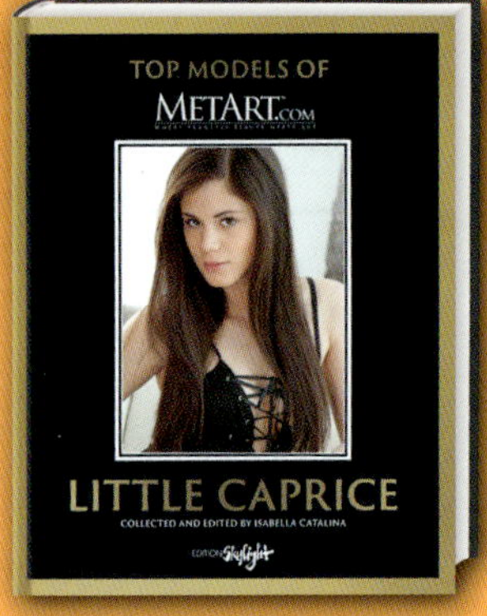

ISBN 978-3-03766-659-3

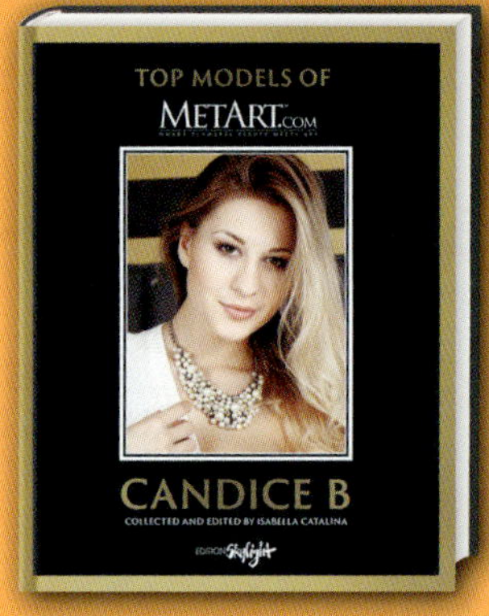

ISBN 978-3-03766-660-9

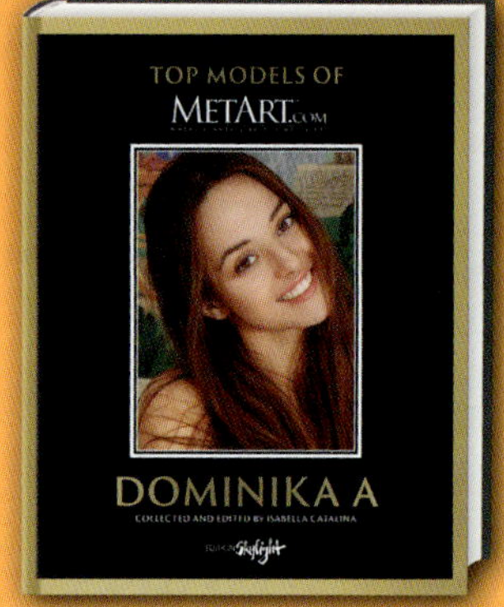

ISBN 978-3-03766-679-1

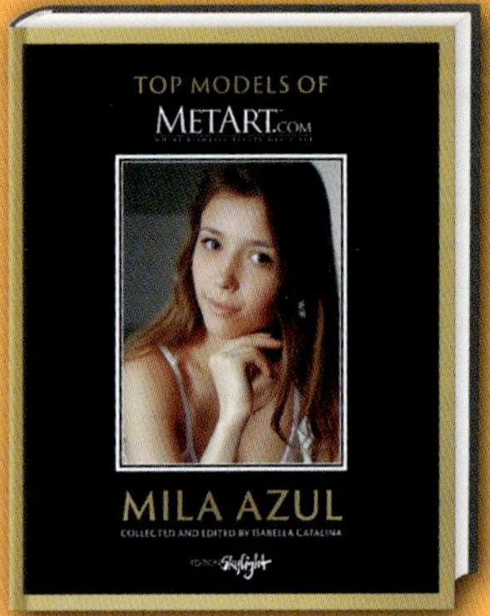

ISBN 978-3-03766-680-7

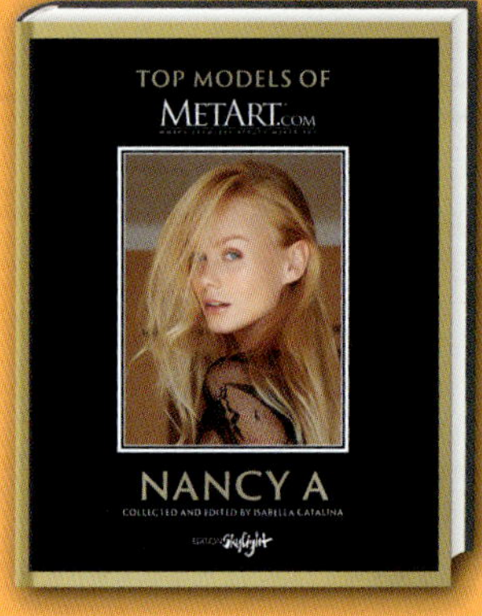

ISBN 978-3-03766-687-6

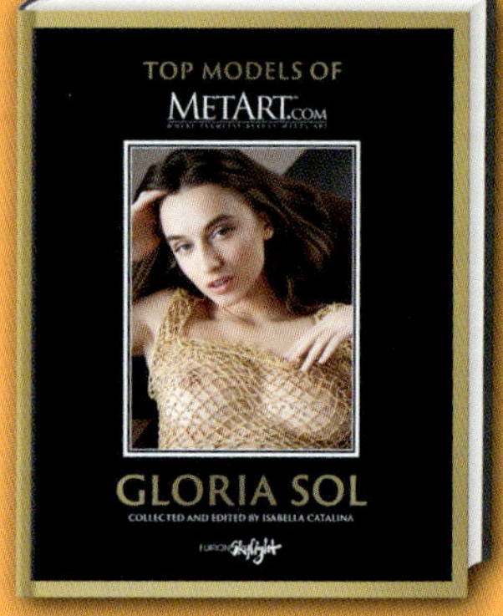

ISBN 978-3-03766-688-3

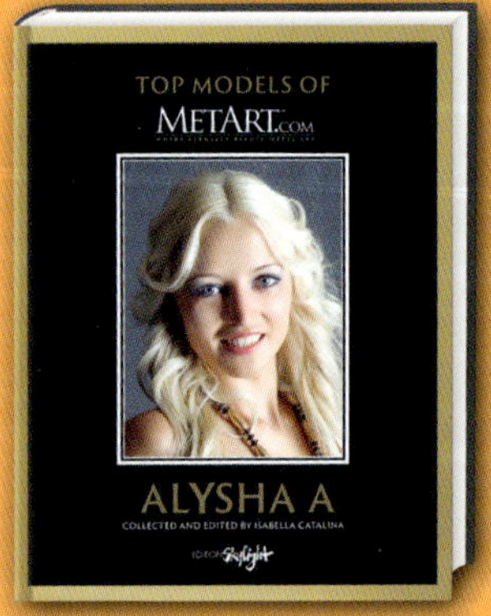

ISBN 978-3-03766-692-0

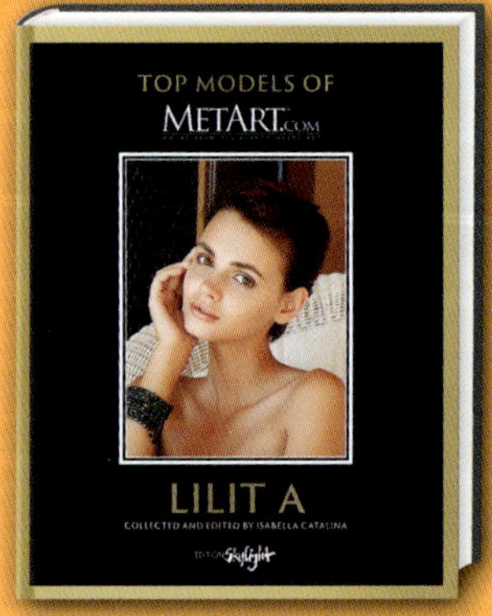

ISBN 978-3-03766-693-7

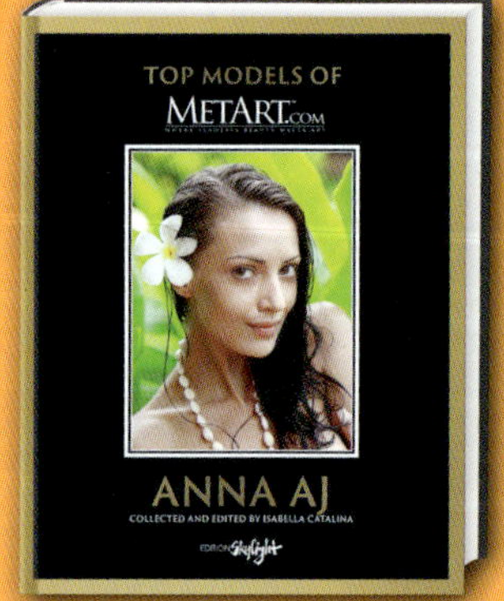

ISBN 978-3-03766-695-1

WWW.EDITION-SKYLIGHT.COM